THE FLYERS

Other books by the author

A   M.S.W.J.R.   ALBUM
A Pictorial History of Swindon's Other Railway, Vol 1, 1872-1899

SWINDON'S   OTHER   RAILWAY
The Midland & South Western Junction Railway 1900-1985

(both books written in conjunction with Denis Bird and David Barrett)

THE FLYERS

The untold story of British and Commonwealth Airmen
in the
Spanish Civil War and other air wars from 1919 to 1940

Brian Bridgeman

Published in 1989 by
BRIAN BRIDGEMAN
69 Sandringham Road,
Swindon, Wilts. SN3 1HT.
in association with
The Self Publishing Association Ltd.,
Upton-upon-Severn, Worcs.

A MEMBER OF

British Library Cataloguing in Publication Data

Bridgeman, Brian
    The Flyers: the untold story of British and commonwealth
    airmen in the Spanish Civil War and other air wars from
    1919 to 1940.
    1. Air operations, history
    I. Title
    358.4'14'09

ISBN 1-85421-054-8

Designed and Typeset by The Self Publishing Association Ltd.
Printed and Bound in Great Britain by Eastern Press, Reading.

These, in the day when heaven was falling,
The hour when earth's foundations fled,
Followed their mercenary calling
And took their wages and are dead.

Their shoulders held the sky suspended;
They stood, and earth's foundations stay;
What God abandoned, these defended,
And saved the sum of things for pay.

A.E. Houseman, *Epitaph on an Army of Mercenaries.*

FOR PAM

Contents

List of Maps

INTRODUCTION

The origins of this book go back to the early seventies when I became intrigued by references to British airmen having served in the Spanish Civil War (1936-39) in various histories of the conflict. Who were these men? Initial research proved extremely difficult as only the barest details were given and only a few names. I soon discovered that their story was not included in accounts written by former members of the International Brigades, as most of these men were disowned by them as going to Spain for money and adventure alone. Gradually, however, the picture became clearer and I came to realise that here was a story that had never been told before. Much of the information already published turned out to be false, when original records were examined and witnesses interviewed, but the true story found was even more amazing than originally suspected. My research, of necessity, then spilled over on to other air wars of the 1919-40 period as I discovered that many of the men who flew in Spain had also been involved in these other conflicts. In order to give a complete record I have also included in this book the story of other flyers who made their appearance in Spain and elsewhere as charter pilots, or for other reasons, during these romantic and exciting days of aviation.

This book, although basically about British and Commonwealth (including South African) airmen, also includes many references to pilots from other countries including the USA. I make no apology for this; it would be incomplete without mention of them as their actions often directly affected the men from Britain.

Thanks are due to the staff at the Ministry of Defence RAF Personnel Records Dept and their colleagues at the Officers' Records Dept for kindly answering all my requests for information within the constraints allowed; Mrs J.M. King ALA, of the RAF College Library at Cranwell; the staff of the RAF Museum, Hendon, and of the Public Record Office at Kew. The Ministry of Defence (Air Historical Branch) also provided much useful background information. Abroad, the USA, Canadian, Australian, New Zealand, South Africa, Finnish and Spanish service authorities also helped whenever it was possible. Finally I must thank all my friends and correspondents throughout the world who have supplied much information and encouragement during this project. Without their help and enthusiasm this book could never have been written: Jim Carmody (a mine of information regarding Spanish Civil War aviation), Denis Bird, Justin Brooke, Douglas Cluett, Gerald Howson, Bob Massey, Chris Shores, Stuart James and Leslie Hunt in the UK; Richard Sanders Allen, Victor Berch, Ed Leiser (San Diego Aero-Space Museum), Allen Herr, Bob Miller, Tom Sarbaugh and Georg von Rauch in the USA; Gerry Beauchamp and Allan Levine in Canada; Eino Ritaranta in Finland; Ole G. Norbø in Norway; Angelo Emiliani and Corrado Ricci in Italy; Patrick Laureau, Rémy Tiger and William Labussière in France; Justo Miranda Fernandez, Emilio Herrera Alonso and Juan Arráez Cerdá in Spain; Mrs Sally Chao, Dave Duxbury, David Yerex and Errol Martyn in New Zealand. Lastly, but by no means least, to the families of all the

British and Commonwealth airmen whom I managed to contact for answering my questions and allowing me sight of much that otherwise would have been unavailable to me, and flyer-of-fortune Hilaire du Berrier, for all his memories of flying in Ethiopia, Spain and China in those halcyon days of aviation. Specific sources are listed in the Bibliography or notes at the end of each chapter.

Brian Bridgeman, Swindon 1989.

CHAPTER 1

Latin-American Caballeros

The end of World War I in 1918 released a new breed of adventurer on to an eager market, that of air mercenary. These were young men trained to fly and fight over the battlefields of Europe who now found it difficult to settle down and obtain employment in the austere conditions prevailing in post-war Britain. One part of the world glad to take advantage of their skills was Central and South America. The many countries in this vast and sprawling continent, where revolutions were a common occurance, soon realised that they had to set up their own air arms in order to maintain control within their borders and also to have any chance in the constant warfare with their neighbours. War surplus aircraft were obtained from Europe and the USA and airmen recruited from abroad to teach their own nationals to fly. These foreigners often took part in air warfare and, on occasion, met other air mercenaries employed by the opposing side in combat in the skies. The revolutionary movements within this unstable continent also employed foreign air mercenaries during the never-ending warfare of the twenties and thirties.

One of the first South American countries to employ airmen from Britain was Chile. Major Frank P. Scott was contracted in November 1920, together with other Britons including Major Pickthorn and Captain Manning, to be part of a training mission. Colonel James Travers (a former Royal Navy officer who had transferred to the Royal Flying Corps) also arrived in Chile in 1921 and trained Chilean navy pilots on Short 184s and Avro 504s. Other British airmen in Chile included former RFC pilots James and Finn. Travers returned to England and was killed at Croydon whilst testing a fighter of his own design in February 1924. Peru also contracted an English instructor, Major Jack Sisson (ex-RAF) who headed the training centre at Maranga. In May 1921 Sisson flew over the Peruvian Andes aboard a Bristol F.2B Fighter. His career in Peru ended when a Congressional investigation found him guilty of negligence – a number of Italian-built aircraft under his charge had been left out in the open and had rotted away. Sisson was stripped of his post and returned to England with his Peruvian wife. Chile also had the services of an American, James C. 'Jimmie' Angel, as a test-pilot. This was to be the start of many years association with Latin America for Angel.

During the twenties Buenos Aires in Argentina was the base of a group of out-of-work European and American combat airmen. These included Dean Ivan Lamb from the USA (born in Pennsylvania, 1886), who had flown as a Sergeant Pilot in the RFC with No. 4 Squadron in France during World War I. He claimed to have shot down a German Gotha bomber over England in July 1917 whilst serving with a Home Defence Squadron. Lamb was one of the first ever air mercenaries, having flown during the Mexican Revolution of 1913. In April 1921 he had flown a Bristol F.2B Fighter into the Central American country of Honduras where he became Director General of Aviation, Commander of Artillery and Machine Guns, but soon left when insufficient money was forthcoming. In Buenos Aires there was also an Englishman named Stewart (born in London, 1896), who had migrated to Argentina in 1910, returning to Britain in 1914 to serve as an infantryman in the Army before graduating from flight training at Hendon into the RFC. Stewart returned to Argentina after the war and flew in Major Kingsley's airline *Cia Rio Platense de Aviación* (River Plate Aviation Company). Also with Major Kingsley's company was another air adventurer, Sydney Holland (see Chapter 5). Stewart and Lamb made their way to Paraguay in 1922 where a civil war had broken out. Selling their skills to the highest bidder, they joined in the conflict, a fatal decision for Stewart for he was killed in July 1922 when the two-seater aircraft he was flying (believed to be an Italian SVA 10 purchased in Argentina) caught fire and crashed. Lamb, however, continued to follow an adventurous career in South America before returning home to the USA. After service in the USAAF in World War II he died in Arizona in 1955. Amongst several other pilots from the USA reputed to have flown in various South American Wars during the 1920s were Harry La Guardia, from Alhambra, California, a cousin of the famous Mayor of New York City, and Herbert 'Bert' Gibson, also from California (see Chapter 13). La Guardia had flown in World War I and later also flew in China in the 1930s before joining the Royal Canadian Air Force in 1939. Commissioned into the RAF in September 1940, he was flying as a glider-pilot instructor in England in 1942 at the age of 43. The USAAF later made use of his knowledge and experience.[1]

The next to enter combat in this volatile area of the world was a Canadian pilot named Edward Huestis. Born in Goderich in 1906, he went to New York City with his parents as an infant, later returning to Toronto in Canada where he studied at Humberside Collegiate and Victoria College, University of Toronto. The academic life did not appeal to him and, before long, Ted Huestis went south to the Oklahoma oil fields. While in Oklahoma he enlisted in the United States Marine Corps and took the officers' training course in Philadelphia, eventually becoming a second lieutenant in the 113rd Pursuit Squadron of the US Marines air service. His first foreign assignment with the Marines was during the Haitian San Domingo insurrection of 1923-25, carrying out land and air patrols. Huestis was next in Nicaragua, during the campaign against the rebels led by General Sandino, when he carried out bombing raids against rebel strongholds. Further service for the Marines followed in China and, once again, in Nicaragua in 1930. Huestis retired from the Marine Corps in the following year only to join, he later claimed, a war between Bolivia and Ecuador as a pilot on the Bolivian side. After this conflict the Canadian turned to more peaceful pursuits, becoming a newspaper reporter in San Francisco, helping his father in his publishing business in Toronto and as an insurance salesman. At the beginning of World War II Huestis enlisted in the RCAF and became an instructor at Toronto. Posted to England in 1942 the now Warrant Officer Ted Huestis remained there until March 1944 before returning to Canada, giving the young recruits the benefits of his vast and varied experience.[2] Also in Nicaragua with Huestis during the Sandino rebellion were two American pilots, William C. Brooks (later Chief of Military Aviation in Honduras from 1936-37) and Lee Mason.

Another conflict involving British airmen was the so-called Leticia Dispute between Columbia and Peru during 1932-33. It involved a small port on the north bank of the Amazon River, at the extreme south-east corner of Colombia, which was claimed by both countries. The air forces of both sides were built up during 1933 and the Colombian Air Force increased from almost nothing to over 80 aircraft within a matter of months. Of necessity these aircraft were mostly flown by foreign (mostly German and American) pilots but Henry Vaughan (Colombian born, English father/Colombian mother) flew Junkers K 43s and Curtiss Falcons. Also listed as a 'pilot-mechanic' was an Englishman named Edward I. Eyles. British and American pilots were also involved in the Brazilian revolution of 1932, delivering Chilean-built Curtiss Falcon aircraft to the Paulista rebels with at least one American pilot, Orthon Hoover, carrying out bombing missions against Government forces (see Chapter 5 regarding British involvement).

The most famous foreign pilot in Central America during the thirties was, without doubt, a New Zealander named Lowell Yerex. Born in 1895, he left the country of his birth in 1911 to attend university at Valparaiso in Indiana, USA, going on to teach in North Dakota before learning to fly and becoming a fighter pilot with the Royal Flying Corps in France during World War I. Yerex was shot down, captured, and held in a prisoner-of-war camp in Germany from September 1918 until after the Armistice. Returning to his family in Valparaiso he took them to San Francisco where he joined up with an American and spent the next five years barnstorming around California and the neighbouring states with an air circus. Tiring of stunt flying, Yerex moved to New Mexico with his wife and young family and opened an agency for Packard cars which failed. He went back to flying as a commercial pilot with a new airline which had started up in Mexico. For a time his fortunes prospered but the Depression in the USA forced the closure of the airline leaving Yerex once again out of a job. He made his way to Honduras where he set up his own company, *Transportes Aéros Centro Americanos (TACA)*, which, within a few short years, would be a name known throughout the American continent.

It was now late 1931 and Yerex adopted as his company insignia the scarlet, yellow and blue macaw which was first seen on a five-seater Stinson Detroiter biplane he named *Espiritu de Honduras*. Flying from Tegucigalpa, Yerex was soon flying passengers and freight from one end to the other of this mainly mountainous country. Rough airstrips were carved out of the hillsides near to the silver and gold mines and in the rain forests. In early 1932, however, a military uprising began against the elected government of General Tiburcio Carías Andino and the New Zealander was asked to airlift arms and ammunition from the neighbouring republic of El Salvador for Carías, as the rebels had seized most of the equipment available in Honduras. In a few days Yerex had ferried all the available arms into Tegucigalpa.

Lowell Yerex then teamed up with an Irish adventurer named Guy R. Moloney, who had fought for the USA in World War I and a former New Orleans police chief, and converted one of the Stinsons (he had obtained several more by now) for bombing and ground strafing – simply by removing a door, so that a bomb could be rolled out, and positioning a Lewis gun to fire through the open doorway. In this make-shift bomber Yerex and Moloney carried out many missions over the next few weeks until the rebels made one last effort to assault the capital. Drastic action was required so Yerex converted two further aircraft for fighting and led his 'squadron' to attack the column of troops. After using up all his ammunition on a strafing run, he made a low level attack to drop his bomb in the face of a fusillade of rifle fire from the ground. One unlucky shot came through the cabin floor and struck Yerex in the right eye. Bleeding profusely he managed to retain control of the aircraft and fly back 25 miles to land safely. Yerex was taken to New Orleans but the doctors could not save the eye; he wore a glass eye for the rest of his life. The aerial assault had brought the revolution to an end, and the grateful President Carías paid *TACA* generously for all the help it had given. He also contracted Yerex to create an air force for Honduras. This was the beginning of a decade which resulted in his company becoming the largest air-freighting company in the world and the largest privately-owned airline. It linked the USA with the whole of Central America and the continent to the south, competing successfully with the might of Pan American Airways, until political deals between the American and British governments resulted in him having to sell out.

This remarkable man died in Buenos Aires in 1968. A biography of Lowell Yerex, written by his nephew David Yerex, was published in New Zealand in 1985.[3]

Lowell Yerex (on left) with stuntman, Freddy Lund, of his flying circus in USA, c.1924. (Courtesy David Yerex)

The next scene for air warfare in the American continent was the vast area of tropical jungle and marsh, known as the Gran Chaco, between Bolivia, Argentina and Paraguay. One portion, the Chaco Boreal, was disputed between the neighbouring states of Bolivia and Paraguay and was the battleground for a bloody war that was fought in 1932-35 and brought to South America one of the most colourful British flyers-of-fortune, Thomas Wewege-Smith.

'Wiggy' (as he was known to his friends) was born on 16 June 1908 in Manchester. His father was a South African who had fought in the Boer War, and Tom spent his early childhood in the Transvaal. When World War I broke out his father joined the armed forces and was killed-in-action in German East Africa in 1917. Tom came to England after his father's death and went to preparatory school, witnessing the air raids on London in 1918. After the war ended his mother remarried another South African and Tom returned there with her, attending King Edward's College in Johannesburg (probably the best known public school in South Africa), where he was known for his prowess in boxing and rugby rather than academic achievements. Soon after leaving college the family came once more to England and Tom became a clerk in the head office of a large firm of shoe dealers – a job he found very boring. In April 1928, at the age of nineteen, he joined No. 601 (County of London) Squadron, Auxiliary Air Force, to train as an air-gunner. In the best traditions of this squadron (see Chapter 3) he arrived in a Daimler when he reported for duty. The Commanding Officer of No. 601 Squadron was the highly individualistic Lord Edward Grosvenor whose magnetic personality and romantic tales of his service in the French Foreign Legion were to have a great influence on young Wewege-Smith.

After an unhappy love affair Tom decided to follow Grosvenor's example and try his luck in the Foreign Legion. In August 1928 he presented himself at the Legion's recruiting office at Dunkirk. The officer-in-charge took one look at the young Englishman in his plus-fours and suggested he should have a good lunch and consider carefully what he was about to do. Tom, however, insisted and signed up for duty. He was given five francs and a third-class rail warrant to Marseilles where he joined up with other recruits before crossing to Oran. After spending six weeks recruit training and road-making in Saida, Tom wished he had taken the advice of the officer at Dunkirk.

Drafted back to Sidi-Bel-Abes he was told to expect an early posting to Morocco. Tom decided to escape and confided in a English medical orderly, who suggested to the French authorities that Tom's eyes were not in good condition (they were perfect). He was sent to Oran for tests. Somehow he managed to persuade the French that he was unfit for service. He was eventually certified 'Reformé Numéro Deux' and returned to Marseilles awaiting discharge. After a couple of weeks Tom returned home to London, via Paris, after nine months in the Legion.

Arriving home on a Saturday night, he made his way to Hendon the following morning to report back for duty with No. 601 Squadron. He only then realised that, technically at least, he was liable to severe penalties for deserting. The adjutant of 601, then Flight Lieutenant Thornton (later Air Vice-Marshall Thornton), was not in the least pleased to see him and was in the middle of giving Tom a good 'dressing down' when Lord 'Ned' Grosvenor entered the orderly room and welcomed him back. Soon Tom and his commanding officer were exchanging yarns about life in the Legion and any thought of punishment for his escapade was forgotten.

Wewege-Smith was soon afterwards promoted to Corporal and continued to fly as an air-gunner with the squadron at weekends. He also worked for his private pilot's licence at Stag Lane aerodrome (Edgware) and the Cinque Ports Club (Lympne). At Stag Lane he met Amy Johnson, whilst she was learning ground engineering for her flight to Australia, Jim Mollison and Jean Batten. In April 1930 Tom took his flying certificate at Stag Lane. He also continued his career in the shoe business becoming manager of a branch in the West End of London.

Tom was discharged from the AAF in April 1932. When another love affair failed in early 1934 his wanderlust came to the fore once more and he decided to try his luck in South America, where the Gran Chaco War had broken out. Knowing nothing of the politics involved, he looked through *Whitaker's Almanack* and came to the conclusion that Bolivia might be wealthier than Paraguay, so decided to make his way there to volunteer, obtaining letters from two Bolivians of high standing in London of personal introduction to the government at La Paz. Tom's first problem was to obtain a passport. The authorities had kept his old one and would not issue a new one as they had suspicions regarding his wish to go to Bolivia. Tom then shaved his upper lip, had a new photograph taken, deleted 'Wewege-' from his name and obtained a new passport under the name of Smith. This time he also made no attempt to obtain a visa for Bolivia. Tom left Liverpool Street Station bound for Harwich on a fine Sunday in June 1934. It was to be two years before he was to see London again.

It took until mid-August to reach Bolivia. Tom sailed from Amsterdam on a Dutch steamer *Alkmaar* bound for Mollendo in Peru, going via the Panama Canal. In late July the ship called at Buenaventura in Colombia, where Tom met several British pilots serving in the Colombian Air Force, which was by this time officered mainly by Americans and Germans. On arrival in Peru he took a train for the Bolivian capital, La Paz, after managing to get his passport endorsed after a week's wait, which used up much of his remaining funds. When he finally arrived in La Paz, after two days journey by train and steamer across Lake Titicaca, Tom, with his usual flair, booked into the best hotel in the capital, the Hotel de Paris. Early the next morning he called at the War Office, with his letters of introduction, only to find that the ministers to whom they were addressed were now out of favour and office.

The next month was spent in an effort to contact the Bolivian Air Force authorities – a difficult matter at first because foreign recruits were unpopular since a German had been found dropping photographs of Bolivian positions over enemy lines. Eventually, however, he was introduced to Colonel Jordan, Chief of the Bolivian Air Force, with the help of Cliff Travers, an American test pilot for Curtiss Aircraft, who was delivering a number of Curtiss Hawks and Falcons to Bolivia (he had lent Tom some cash to keep him going until he could obtain employment), and Tony Ashton of Webster and Ashton, a

British firm dealing extensively with the government of Bolivia. Finally, in mid-September 1934, Tom signed a contract with the Bolivian Air Force, for one year's service, with the immediate rank of full Lieutenant. His pay was 500 *pesos* per month whilst on active service, with a further 250 *pesos* per month credited to him in sterling in La Paz. In his contract was also a clause to say they would bury him (free of charge) and send a month's salary to any person named in his will. Tom threw a party to celebrate his appointment and went out to buy his uniform in field grey with a splendid cavalry cloak (see Photograph on p.23). He only later heard that the reason he was accepted for the Bolivian Air Force was that the War Ministry thought he was one of the pilots who had flown in the Schneider Trophy – in fact he had been in 601 Squadron's team that won the inter-squadron Esher Trophy*.

Tom left for the front in late September accompanied by Major Murphy, the representative of one of the largest armament firms in the USA, who was in Bolivia to sell aircraft, guns and other arms. A long tiring journey ended at their destination, Villa Montes, which was almost at sea-level in the Chaco. Here he experienced for the first time why this region was known as the 'Green Hell'. The town comprised a mixture of adobe (mud-over-bamboo) huts and corrugated iron shacks. It had a population of 20,000, mostly Indians. The temperature was like a hothouse and the whole region had an abundance of poisonous insects, reptiles and virulent fevers. The airfield, one mile outside the town, was the chief aerodrome of the Bolivian Air Force at the time, which comprised about thirty aircraft, a few new Curtiss Hawk IIs, Falcons and Curtiss-Wright Ospreys, three Junkers W 34 transports and one or two dilapidated Vickers Vespa III bombers purchased in 1928. Posted to the front line aerodrome at Carandaiti, Tom was welcomed by the sight of millions of the tiny *marihui* insects which attacked any human invaders of their domain in swarms, leaving the body covered with bites that gave an exquisite itch. These minute black flies, together with the millions of mosquitos, were no more than the vanguard of the host of tiny enemies that buzzed and stung and gave their victims no rest. When the wet season arrived they were joined on the ground by scorpions, whose sting would cause agony, and large, hairy spiders that would run along the ceiling and drop on to the heads of the pilots.

The war was not going well for Bolivia. The Paraguayan Army – now some 60,000 strong – had encircled the Bolivian forces in the Chaco. Most Paraguayan troops were Guarani Indians and knew the ground well, successfully hacking trails through the dense bush to cut off the Bolivian lines of communication. The well nourished and outfitted Bolivian troops, who came mostly from the high Andes, were unable to withstand the perils of the feverish tropical climate, whereas the bare-footed Paraguayans (known as *Pilas* – derived from *Pata Pilada* meaning bare-foot) were quite accustomed to the dangers and treachery of the territory which was their home. Only the efforts of the *Cuerpo de Aviación* (as the Bolivian Air Force was called) prevented the retreat from becoming a rout. Paraguay, in contrast, was by now desperately short of aircraft, with only several Potez 25A-2 light reconnaissance-bomber sesquiplanes and a handful of Fiat CR.20bis fighters.

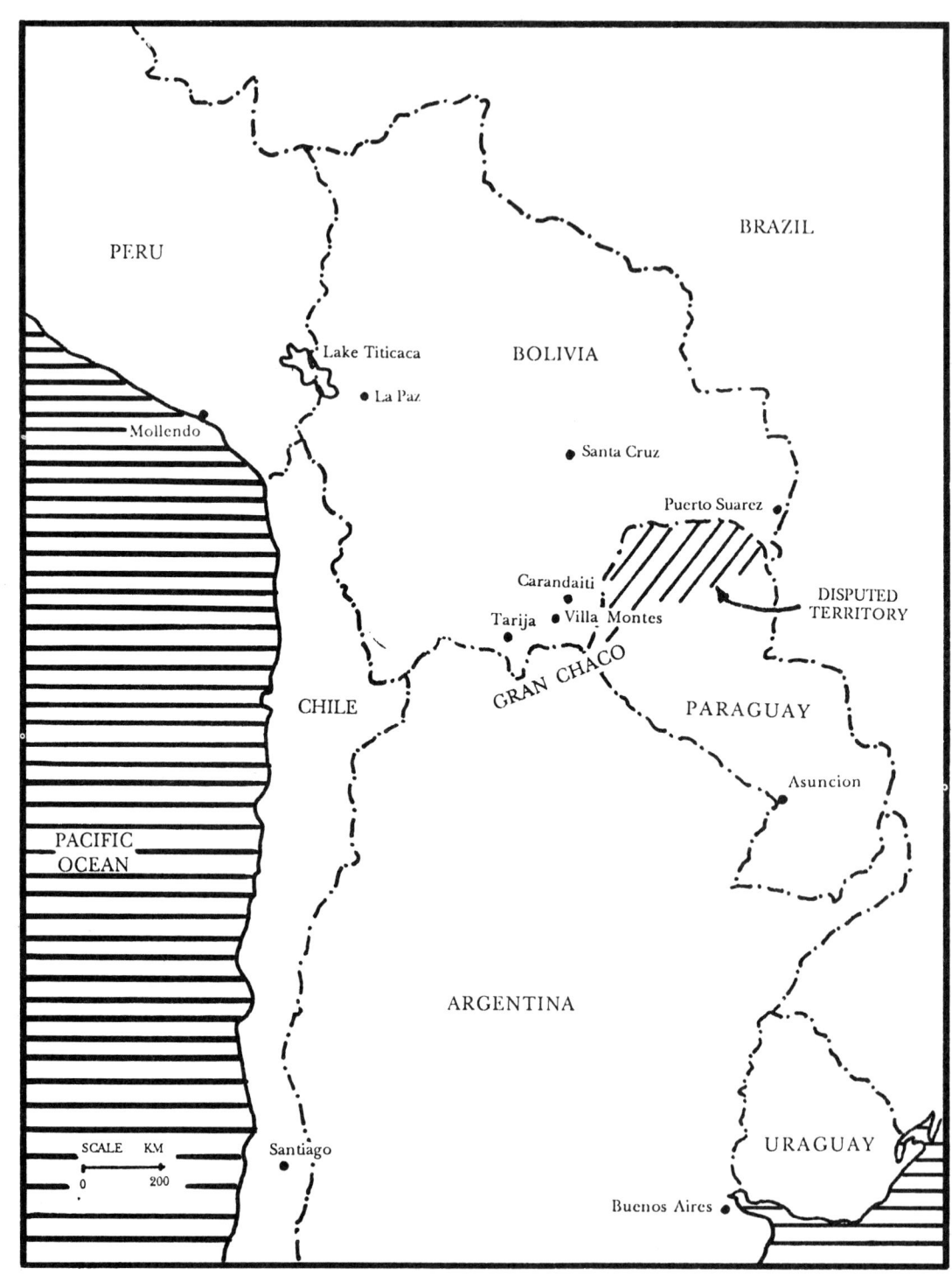

PERU

BRAZIL

BOLIVIA

Lake Titicaca

La Paz

Mollendo

Santa Cruz

Puerto Suarez

Carandaiti

DISPUTED
TERRITORY

Tarija Villa Montes

CHILE

GRAN CHACO

PARAGUAY

PACIFIC
OCEAN

Asuncion

ARGENTINA

SCALE   KM

0   200

Santiago

URAGUAY

Buenos Aires

GRAN CHACO WAR

20

Flying with the Paraguayan Air Force *(Fuerzas Aéreas Nacionales)* were two Uruguayans; one of whom, Luís Tuya, later flew for the Republican Air Force in Spain, and a number of White Russians. A pilot with the Anglo-Saxon sounding name of Walter Gwynn served in the Paraguayan Air Force before being killed in June 1933. Research has shown, however, that he was a Paraguayan national with American/Paraguayan parents. The Bolivian Air Force included in its ranks pilots from Chile and one or two from the USA including Leon Donnelly, from Seneca, New York, who had, however, returned home due to ill health prior to Tom's arrival.

This then was the situation that greeted Wewege-Smith when he arrived at the front. The Squadron at Carandaiti comprised 3 Curtiss Hawk IIs, one Falcon and 3 Ospreys. The airfield was the dried bed of a lake surrounded on all sides by low trees and undergrowth. The pilots slept in tents and the aircraft were left out in the open, there being no hangers. Tom was soon out on patrol in the Falcon and spent the next few days flying over the Chaco acting as observer/rear gunner on raids on Paraguayan troops. One day two Junkers W 34s arrived and these were used on further raids. No proper bombsights existed so Tom would lay full length looking through the observation hatch and yell out when to release bombs (which were just pushed through a hole cut in the floor of the aircraft).

A big offensive was planned by the Bolivian forces in October 1934 and plans were made to bomb the Paraguayan headquarters about 200 miles east of Carandaiti. The rainy season had arrived, and heavy rain fell before plans were complete, turning the airstrip into a quagmire and caving in the roofs of the pilots' grass roofed huts (which had replaced the tents). The temperature dropped from 52°C to 15°C. The next day the rain continued all day and thousands of lizards invaded the camp, and the night was made hideous by the croaking of frogs. Some attempts were made to carry out bombing missions but the state of the strip and the low cloud caused these to be aborted.

Tom was happy to receive a summons to Villa Montes to experiment with the Junkers for heavy bombing. In the corner of the hangar he found some German (Busche) bomb sights and fitted these to the three Junker W 34s. He also stripped the seats from the three transport aircraft, fitted underwing racks for up to six 200lb bombs and 7.65mm Vickers-Berthier machine-guns through holes cut through the cabin floor and roof. This trio of aircraft were hurriedly sent to Cucurenda, a small beaten earth airstrip near the Pilcomayo River, to join the so-called *Punta de Alas* (Pointed Wings) *Escuadrón*. Torrential rain prevented any operations until mid November. The Paraguayan troops had their first experience of a heavy bombing attack when the three Junkers attacked Camachu from a height of 6,000 ft. Previously the Paraguayan troops had experienced bombing from low altitude from light bombers, with nothing heavier than 55lb bombs, so the 200lb bombs dropped by the Junkers, from a height that gave then no chance to shoot back, came as a shock and caused considerable damage and disruption.

Despite all the efforts of the Junkers the *Pilas* continued to advance and the airstrip at Cucurenda was threatened with encirclement, so Tom and his fellow airmen with the *Punta de Alas Escuadrón* were pulled back to Villa Montes, 130 miles to the west, where the Bolivian forces were being regrouped to make one last stand. Tom was sent by road by lorry, which took eight hours, and he passed apparently endless columns of retreating Bolivian soldiers. At Villa Montes Tom was given the job of training anti-aircraft crews as well as continuing to fly in one of the Junkers as co-pilot/bombadier. He had, by now, painted the Flying Sword emblem of No. 601 Squadron on the nose of his aircraft.

Encounters with the Paraguayan Air Force now became more frequent despite only about 20 aircraft being available to the Bolivians and only 7 to Paraguay. On a bombing raid towards Capireida in late December Tom's Junkers was attacked by two Paraguayan Potez 25s. He fired at one of the Potez and saw it spin off into the clouds obviously damaged. The pilot of his Junkers was usually a Bolivian named Suárez, who had been educated in France and had spent several years in England. He was later transferred to transport work behind the lines.

From December 1934 until the end of the war some six months later, the fighting was intense on the Villa Montes front. There was a shortage of spares for aircraft due to the embargo placed by the League of Nations. Due to the shortage of aircraft, many of the aircrews were sent back to the ground forces. They included an American named Dickerson who had flown in Tom's squadron on a few missions. Discussions were held as to whether to bomb the Paraguayan capital, Asunción, but the Bolivians were afraid this would cause the League of Nations to brand them as the aggressors.

Storms brought torrential rain in January 1935 – it was like being in a constant Turkish bath with the heat and damp – very little flying was done and the aircrews spent their time playing cards, shooting dice and drinking. Not surprisingly, many of the men went down with fever and Tom himself became ill with *paludismo* (a local variety of malaria). He continued to fly, however, when possible, dosing himself with huge doses of quinine. In early February he became really ill and was confined to bed for a week or so. Tom rejoined the squadron later in the month and continued to fly on bombing raids until sent to Tarija to pick up spares. Tarija, with its cool climate due to its 6,000 ft altitude, was a welcome relief after months in the Chaco, and Tom was in no hurry to return to Villa Montes. Return he did, however, after a few days and continued to raid Paraguayan troop concentrations now only a few miles from the airfield.

By March 1935 the war had ground to a stalemate with both countries on the verge of economic collapse. Although the Paraguayans had gained most of the disputed territory, this had been at the cost of over 30,000 dead and nearly 4,000 captured.

Tom was sent to Puerto Suárez on the Brazilian frontier in early April to ferry much needed spares to Bolivian forces. His pilot was Captain Rojas, now nominally in charge of the Junkers squadron. This entailed a flight over enemy lines. They flew over 1,200 miles between sunrise and sunset before returning to Santa Cruz in Bolivia where they spent three days unofficial leave.

In late April Tom flew in an Osprey to his old air strip at Cucurenda, now 100 miles behind enemy lines, on an observation trip. Later, wounded Bolivian Indians were flown back to Tarija by Suárez in a Junkers which flew in to Cucurenda.

Thomas Wewege-Smith in Bolivian Air Force uniform, 1937.
(Gran Chaco Adventure)

Wewege-Smith (centre of back row) with Bolivian Air Force
aircrew in front of Curtiss-Wright Falcon aircraft.
(Gran Chaco Adventure)

In early May Colonel Aliaga, a devil-may-care Chilean pilot about 35 years old, took over as commander of the Junkers squadron. The Bolivian High Command decided to send the *Punta de Alas Escuadrón*, now comprising only the three Junkers and three Hawk IIs, to Santa Cruz-Puerto Suárez for long distance raids on ports down the Rio Paraguay. On 25 May, when taking off from Puerto Suárez, Aliaga crashed, completely writing off one of the Junkers. He was badly injured and died subsequently when infection set into his wounds. Tom, who was flying as Aliaga's bombadier, received superficial injuries including a twisted knee and was taken to Villa Montes by Suárez in a Junkers Ju 52/3m transport in early June.

In the meanwhile, preliminary discussions had been going on between the two antagonists in the war, under the auspices of the League of Nations, and an armistice was signed in mid-June. On that day a Breda Ba 44 light transport aircraft bedecked with red crosses, escorted by a very patched and dilapidated Potez 25, landed at Villa Montes carrying a party of Paraguayan officers. Tom and the other Bolivian airmen greeted their former opponents cordially and discussed the battles of the past years.

A few days later Tom returned to La Paz where he was to spend the next months hosted by Major Murphy and Tony Ashton. Here he received several awards from the Bolivians for his service in the Gran Chaco conflict – the President himself, Tejado Sorzano, presenting Tom with the Order of the Condor of the Andes and appointing him as a Cabalero of the Order of Military Merit. He also received all the back pay due to him plus a bonus of £100 sterling. The next few months went pleasantly by, with a round of parties and receptions continuing for weeks on end. The ladies too did their best to turn his susceptible head and Tom kept putting off his return to Britain. Finally, however, in early 1936 he took the ship back home leaving his friends behind. Two of them, the Englishman Tony Ashton, together with his partner J.W. Webster, were later, in January 1937, jailed by the Bolivians charged with the allegation that they had sold worthless equipment to the armed forces during the war. They were not freed until the following August when the charges were dropped having not being proved.

Tom returned to England with no special plans for the future but paid a visit to his old squadron at Hendon. With his usual sense of dramatic he emerged from a taxi, a gorgeous sight with eagle-crowned helmet, his cloak slung carelessly from his shoulders, wearing a sword and tall boots. It was a pity that Lord Grosvenor was not there to greet him – the ex-Legionaire had died some years previously.

Tom wrote a book about his Bolivian experiences entitled *Gran Chaco Adventure* that was published in 1937. Extracts from this were also reprinted in aviation magazines the following year, when the book was re-issued under the title *War Planes & Women*. By 1939 he was apparently employed as a Sales Manager.

Back in South America the war finally ended when the Treaty of Buenos Aires was signed by Bolivia and Paraguay in 1938, with Paraguay being awarded three-quarters of the disputed area and Bolivia being given an outlet to the sea via the Paraguay River. Another airman from Britain also claimed later to have fought for Bolivia in the Gran Chaco War. This was an Irishman (born in Liverpool) named Terence MacGovern, who wrote a book about his experiences in the war that was published in 1939.[4] In this he stated that he had served as an observer/air-gunner before his aircraft was forced down in Paraguayan territory. He managed to escape but his health was broken by his experiences. No mention of MacGovern is made by Wewege-Smith, however, and so few details are given by MacGovern of the aircraft involved that one is led to doubt if he actually flew in the Bolivian Air Force, although he may have served with their ground forces. MacGovern also mentions having served with several American airman in Bolivia including one with the unlikely name of Patrick O'Keneally from Chicago.

Thomas Wewege-Smith was granted a commission in the Royal Air Force in July 1940. In October 1941 he was stationed at Luqa airfield on the island of Malta as a wireless operator/air-gunner with No. 107 Squadron. On 9 October 1941 he was flying in a Bristol Blenheim IV bomber (Z7638), piloted by Wing Commander 'Bunny' Hart, that attacked a large passenger ship at low level. After dropping his bombs the pilot turned away but collided with another Blenheim and both went into the sea. The crews of both aircraft were all lost. The body of Flying Officer Wewege-Smith, the archtype soldier-of-fortune, was later recovered and buried in Catania War Cemetery, Sicily. His attitude to war was expressed in an article he wrote for *The Aeroplane* magazine in 1938 '. . . For my part, I like war, I like its thrills, its comradeship, its uncertainties. On two different occasions I have been an ill-paid mercenary, gaining but a tithe of what I could in my well-paid job at home, because I am drawn to wars as thousands have before me, just for the love of it. But for all that, I am at heart a pacifist . . . The war of the future is no longer confined to the battle zone, no longer can it be isolated to within a few miles of a given line. And with this fact slowly being discovered by all I can see the ultimate arrival of a real and lasting peace. . .'[5] Prophetic words - let us hope for the sake of all mankind that he was right.

CHAPTER 1 – SOURCES/NOTES

Much information regarding aviation in South America was provided by Richard Sanders Allen, Bob Miller, Georg von Rauch and Adrian English.

1. Information regarding La Guardia from Captain John Cross, Librarian, Museum of Army Flying, Middle Wallop.

2. Information from Allan Levine. See also Royal Canadian Air Force (Directorate of Information) *Release 1233*.

3. *Yerex of TACA : A Kiwi Conquistador*, by David Yerex; Carterton, New Zealand, 1985. Foreign Office F0371 File (1940) 24207, now at Public Record Office.

4. *It Paid to be Tough : The Life of a Modern Mercenary & Vagabond*, by Terence MacGovern (as told to E. C. Trelawney-Ansell); London 1939/Courtesy Allan Levine.

5. *The Aeroplane*, 28 December 1938.

FOOTNOTE

* The Esher Trophy, a bronze statuette of Mercury, was presented by Lord Esher for a competition between the Auxiliary Squadrons for bomb-aiming, gunnery, photographic reconnaissance, wireless and general all-round efficiency. The Esher Trophy is on display at the RAF Museum at Hendon from time-to-time.

CHAPTER 2

To Start a Revolution: British Pilots with the Nationalists

During the afternoon of 9 July 1936 the thirty-year old Captain Cecil Bebb of Olley Air Service Limited was called into the office of his managing director, Captain Gordon Olley, at Croydon Airport and introduced to an elegant Spaniard, Señor Luis Bolin, a journalist who was correspondent for the Madrid newspaper, *ABC*, in London. Captain Olley explained to the young, red-haired pilot that Bolin required an aircraft to ferry a "Riff" leader (one of the guerrillas operating in the Riff mountains in North Africa) to Morocco "to help start a revolution". The whole operation was to be secret. To cover the real reason for the trip, which was to be from the Canary Islands to Spanish Morocco, Bebb would be flying the Spaniard and three English friends to the Canaries from Croydon. Because of the nature of the charter flight Bolin undertook to insure Bebb's life for £2,000 and the aircraft against total loss.

Captain Cecil Bebb in the 1930's.
(Courtesy Captain Bebb / Sutton Libraries & Art Services)

Two days later, early in the morning of 11 July, the passengers for the journey gathered together at Croydon: Bolin, a retired Army major named Hugh Pollard and two excited young girls – Hugh's daughter Diana (aged 19) and her friend Dorothy Watson, a couple of years older. Shortly afterwards the de Havilland D.H.89 Dragon Rapide of Olley Air Service (G–ACYR) left the ground bound for its first destination, Bordeaux in France. Also acompanying the party was a radio operator hired from Marconi and a flight engineer named George (?) Bryers.

When the aircraft arrived at Bordeaux in a torrential rainstorm it was met by several more Spaniards. One of these, the Marqués de Merito, accompanied the party on the next stage of their journey when they took off for Lisbon in Portugal after lunch. Bryers, the flight engineer, was left behind to make room for the extra passenger; he had to make his own way by another aircraft to Casablanca where he was to join up with them again. Bad weather over the western Pyrenees forced Bebb to turn back. He had to land at Biarritz to re-fuel. Here he worked out a new route and the flight was resumed, Lisbon finally being reached in the morning of 12 July after an over-night stop at Oporto. Leaving Bebb and the radio operator to look after the aircraft the passengers went into the city. The Spaniards then made contact with the exiled General Sanjurjo, who was one of the chief conspirators in a plot to overthrow the left-wing elected government in Spain by a coup set to begin on 18 July. All this, however, was unknown to Bebb as the travellers left Lisbon on the next stage of their flight to Casablanca in Morocco.

That night, whilst the travellers were sleeping in the Hotel Carlton in Casablanca, an event took place that was to advance the plans of the right-wing conspirators in Spain. Calvo Sotelo, the leader of the opposition to the Republican Government in the Cortes (the Spanish parliament), was murdered in Madrid. The news reached Casablanca the next morning and at once Major Pollard told Captain Bebb to prepare to leave for the Canary Islands as soon as possible. The pilot, however, required a whole day to make the Dragon Rapide ready for the long flight and to overhaul the engines, so they did not leave until the morning of 15 July. The group now comprised Pollard, the two girls (plus large quantities of French dresses they had purchased in Casablanca) and the flight engineer, Bryers, who had joined up again with them. The radio operator was paid off and returned to England by sea whilst the two Spaniards remained behind to allay suspicions in the Canaries. Major Pollard was given the job of contacting the conspirators there and arranging for the "Riff" leader to be flown by Bebb to Spanish Morocco.

After a stop at Cape Juby, a Spanish outpost on the edge of the Sahara Desert, to refuel, the Dragon Rapide reached the airport of Gando, on Grand Canary, during the afternoon. Leaving Bebb and the engineer behind at Gando, Pollard and the two girls made their way by steamer to Santa Cruz, Tenerife. Bebb, in the meanwhile, was left to wait on events. The following day he was taken by soldiers from his hotel room and interrogated by a group of high ranking officers about why he was in the Canary Islands. Captain Bebb replied only that he was the pilot for a group of British tourists visiting the islands and was waiting to take them home. The next day he was again contacted by these officers and, during the evening at the villa of a General Orgaz near Las Palmas, he discovered that they had been previously trying out his loyalty and were themselves involved. Major Pollard was at the meeting and Bebb found out from him later that his mysterious passenger had arrived on Grand Canary that day and that he would be required to fly him to Spanish Morocco the next day. Once again the pilot wondered who this passenger could be and why the Army was so involved in an attempt to start an Arab rising in Morocco. He was also told of the passwords to be used to recognise his passenger.

De Havilland D.H.89 Dragon Rapide (G-ACYR) of Olley Air Service Limited.
(Quadrant/Flight)

Woken at 3 am on 18 July Bebb made his way to the airfield after first saying his goodbyes to Pollard and the two girls who were now returning to England by sea. At Gando he was kept waiting until the afternoon when the mysterious passenger finally appeared and was introduced to Bebb as General Franco, then in virtual exile as Military Governor of the Canary Islands. He had been posted there by the Spanish Government, who were worried about his loyalty and wanted him safely out of the way. Franco had helped to plan the military rebellion about to take place.

Franco quickly boarded the aircraft, and Bebb took off on the first stage of the flight to Agadir on the African coast. During the flight Franco changed out of his uniform into civilian clothes. At Agadir he remained on board whilst Bebb sent a cable (the text had been dictated by Pollard) to Casablanca to tell Bolin that Franco was on his way. The Dragon Rapide finally reached the airport at Casablanca at 9.15 that evening where it was met by Bolin. They spent the night at a secluded hotel near the coast but, by first light, Bebb was back at the airfield with the flight engineer and was told to set course for Tetuán in Spanish Morocco. It was 5 am when the aircraft left the ground with Franco, Bolin and some other officers on board. Once in the air Franco changed into his uniform again. The Dragon Rapide landed at Tetuán two hours later to be greeted by a cheering crowd of soldiers of the Spanish Foreign Legion – Franco was to take command of the Legion in the rebellion that was just starting.

It was decided that Bebb should fly Bolin to Lisbon to see General Sanjurjo so, after taking his farewells of General Franco and receiving his thanks, he took off again in the Dragon Rapide for Portugal. Here Bolin met Sanjurjo and told him of Franco's safe arrival at Tetuán. Bebb was then asked if he could fly General Sanjurjo to a small airstrip at Pamplona in Spain, but he refused because of the short length available to land there and the roughness of the ground. It was decided that the general would fly in a smaller aeroplane, a de Havilland D.H.80 Puss Moth (EC-VAA), which would be flown by a Spanish pilot named Juan Antonio Ansaldo. Bolin would fly in the Dragon Rapide to Biarritz en route to Italy where he was to endeavour to persuade the Italian Government to supply aircraft and troops to help the rebels. Unknown to Bolin, however, when he left was the news that Sanjurjo had been killed earlier that day (20 July) when his aircraft had crashed on take-off from Cintra, thus removing from the scene the only rival to Franco as leader of the rebels.

The journey to Biarritz was a bumpy one. Eventually the airfield at Parma was reached. On the following day Captain Bebb flew Bolin to Marseilles where they said their farewells – Bolin leaving for Rome by another aircraft whilst Bebb returned to Biarritz. By now his flight engineer, Bryers, had been replaced by another sent over from England named Petre (son of a Rear-Admiral in the Royal Navy and later with BOAC). Bebb's adventures were not yet over, however, for he next flew further Spaniards to Marseilles where they boarded an aeroplane for Berlin – negotiations were going on with the Nazi Government in Germany for assistance to the rebels. Over the next week or so Bebb remained in Biarritz, occasionally ferrying Spanish Nationalist (as they were now calling themselves) agents between the south of France and Biarritz. He was also asked to fly Juan March, a millionaire backer for the revolt, to Majorca but when the Dragon Rapide landed at Perpignan the French authorities detained it and later told Bebb that they had to return to Biarritz. A few days later Bebb was asked to fly to Burgos, the rebel headquarters in the north of Spain, but before he could leave he was taken before the local Commissar of Police who told him that his aircraft was impounded and that he could not proceed anywhere without permission. After two days under open arrest Bebb was ordered to fly back to England without any further landings in France. So, five weeks after leaving Croydon, the Dragon Rapide landed again at Croydon Airport.

Two years later, with the Spanish Civil War coming towards its close, Bebb was awarded by General Franco with the Grand Cross of the Imperial Order of Red Arrows and other Spanish decorations. The aircraft that carried General Franco to Tetuán, D.H.89 Dragon Rapide (G–ACYR) was later presented to him after World War II and is now preserved in the Museo del Aire near Madrid.[1]

On 21 July, the same day that Captain Bebb flew Bolin to Marseilles, another Dragon Rapide, piloted by the celebrated 41 year old Robert Henry McIntosh (known to one and all as "All Weather Mac"), took off from Gatwick Airport en route to Le Bourget, Paris. Two days previously Captain McIntosh had been told that British Airways had been asked to reserve a stand-by aircraft for a special charter. The next day he received instructions to fly to Paris to collect a party of journalists and to fly them wherever and whenever they required for an indefinite period.

When the dark-blue D.H.89, carrying only McIntosh and a flight engineer named Riley, arrived at Le Bourget it was met by two correspondents of *Paris Soir*. One of them was Louis Delaprée, who was mortally wounded later in December 1936 when the French Embassy aircraft he was flying in was shot down in Spain. The other was H.R. Knickerbocker of the International News Service of America. McIntosh then flew to Biarritz where Sefton Delmer of the *Daily Express* was collected. Delmer's newspaper had chartered the aircraft for a news-gathering expedition to Spain at £150 a day. After lunch this party flew on towards Burgos, where the rebel General Mola was in charge of the Nationalist Northern army.

McIntosh, having no permit to enter Spanish territory, and the war being only a few days old, avoided flying near to the town itself and made for the aerodrome at Gamonal, four miles to the east. He landed well away from the hangars and other buildings and switched off the engines. Before long the aircraft was surrounded by armed troops and the journalists and aircrew were taken off to be interrogated.

Captain Robert McIntosh whilst with Imperial Airways, c.1928.
(Sutton Libraries & Art Services)

Knickerbocker soon convinced the aerodrome commandant that they should be allowed to stay, pointing out that the publicity engendered would be good for the Nationalist cause. Whilst the journalists went to Mola's headquarters, McIntosh and Riley went off to find a hotel in Burgos. When the correspondents arrived at their hotel late that evening they told McIntosh that it would be his job to fly to Biarritz each morning to telephone their different stories to the respective Paris offices of their newspapers, as all telephone lines were blocked from Burgos. McIntosh flew this flight for a couple of weeks. He also quite often flew to other rebel-held towns such as Vitorio and San Sebastian, always flying low so that the British registration letters could be seen clearly.

One evening McIntosh was summoned to Mola's headquarters. Fearing arrest (he had flown out some uncensored news material) McIntosh was taken to General Mola who asked him if he knew of any large aircraft for sale. The Englishman told him of four Fokker F.XIIs belonging to British Airways at the new aerodrome of Gatwick. Mola expressed interest, and the following day McIntosh telephoned the British Airways manager in Paris from Biarritz to set up the deal.

Mola also asked McIntosh if the Nationalists could hire his Dragon Rapide for 24 hours and if he would be prepared to fly a General Ponte and another officer to Lisbon. McIntosh agreed to go. When they arrived at Lisbon a heavily-bandaged man was carried on board the aircraft on a stretcher which was placed between the seats. McIntosh flew back to Burgos where General Ponte left the aircraft, the pilot being told to take the injured man on to Biarritz. When the Dragon Rapide landed at Biarritz it was met by the injured man's wife. Unknown to McIntosh, the man was Juan Antonio Ansaldo, the pilot of the Puss Moth in which General Sanjurjo had been killed some days previously. Major Ansaldo had escaped with minor injuries and would later command a reconnaissance squadron of aircraft flying out of Burgos. Captain McIntosh eventually returned to England in mid-August[2] leaving the journalists in Burgos. By now more British pilots, however, had arrived in Spain.

On the day after McIntosh left Gatwick for Le Bourget, Roland Falk (see also Chapter 4) of Air Dispatch Ltd left Croydon at 4.30 am flying an Airspeed Envoy (G-ADAZ) on his normal early morning newspaper run to Paris. At Le Bourget he picked up Karl von Wiegand and two other journalists and flew, via Biarritz, to Barajas aerodrome at Madrid. Here von Wiegand, who had chartered the aircraft on behalf of Hearst newspapers, and Falk stayed at the Palace Hotel and witnessed the early days of the Spanish Civil War from the Loyalist (Republican) side. During the next two days Falk was approached by many people of Nationalist sympathies who were prepared to pay highly to be taken out of the country. However, he left Madrid on 24 July, together with his wireless operator, Murphy, and engineer, Hawkes, with four passengers carried at the request of von Wiegand, two Americans and two Mexicans. It was later reported that the Airspeed Envoy had been chased for some distance by a rebel aircraft before being eventually left alone. Over the Pyrenees an exhaust valve failed in one of the engines and the radio became inoperative. Repairs were carried out at Biarritz and Falk returned to London on 27 July to resume his normal duties.[3]

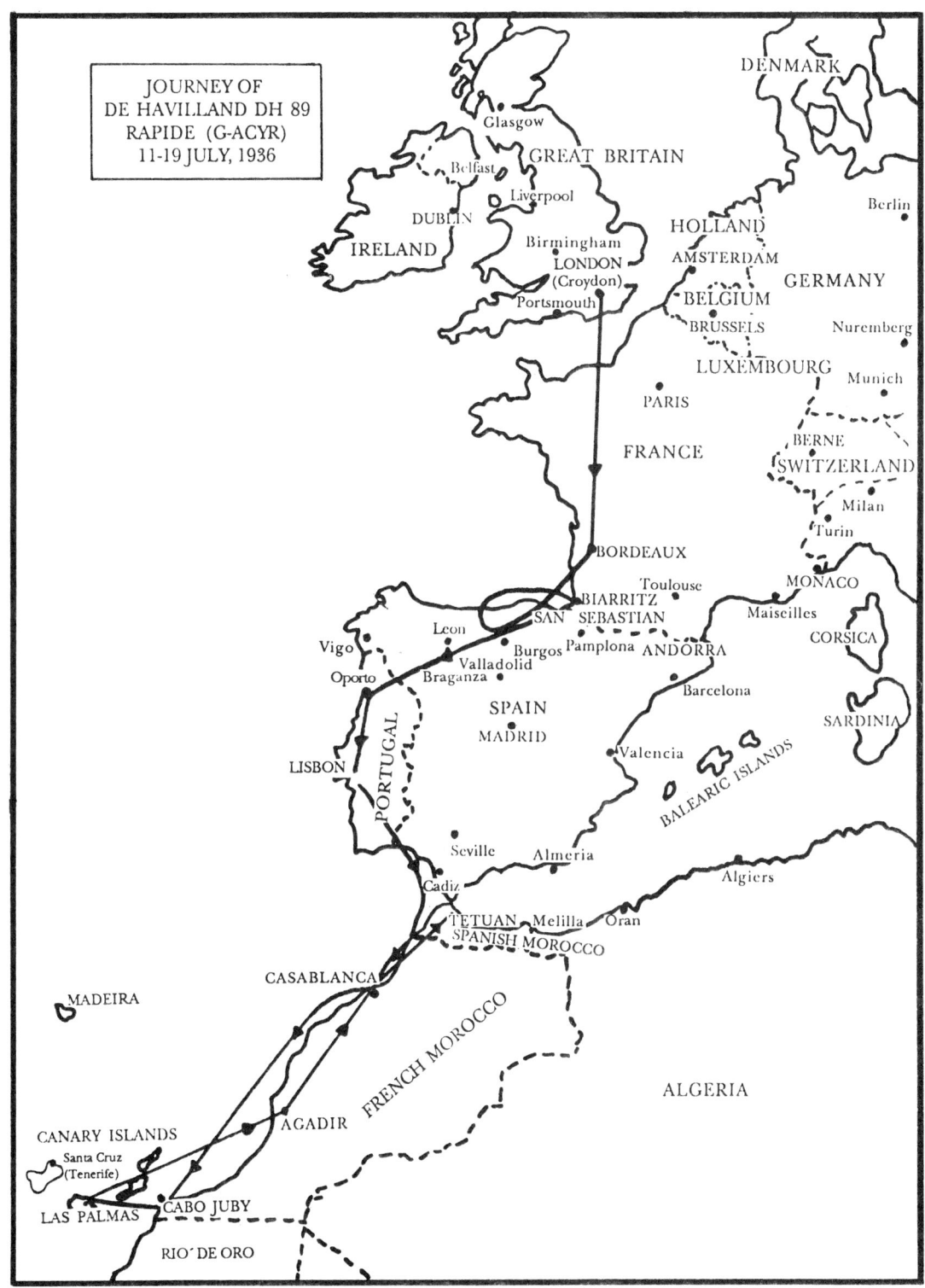

JOURNEY OF
DE HAVILLAND DH 89
RAPIDE (G-ACYR)
11-19 JULY, 1936

DENMARK

GREAT BRITAIN

Glasgow

Belfast

Liverpool

Berlin

IRELAND

DUBLIN

Birmingham

LONDON
(Croydon)

Portsmouth

HOLLAND

AMSTERDAM

BELGIUM

BRUSSELS

GERMANY

Nuremberg

LUXEMBOURG

Munich

PARIS

FRANCE

BERNE

SWITZERLAND

Milan

Turin

BORDEAUX

Toulouse

BIARRITZ

SAN SEBASTIAN

MONACO

Maiseilles

Vigo

Leon

Burgos

Pamplona

ANDORRA

CORSICA

Oporto

Valladolid

Braganza

Barcelona

SPAIN

SARDINIA

MADRID

PORTUGAL

LISBON

Valencia

BALEARIC ISLANDS

Seville

Almeria

Cadiz

Algiers

TETUAN

Melilla

Oran

SPANISH MOROCCO

CASABLANCA

MADEIRA

FRENCH MOROCCO

ALGERIA

CANARY ISLANDS

AGADIR

Santa Cruz
(Tenerife)

CABO JUBY

LAS PALMAS

RIO DE ORO

33

A few days after McIntosh and his party had arrived at Burgos another British aircraft arrived at the airfield there. The pilot was a well-known sportsman aviator, and part-time journalist, the Marquess of Donegall. He had been given an introduction to General Mola as he wished to be allowed to fly over the battle front, or to take his place with the rebels' ground troops. General Mola refused his request. Nevertheless, the following day Donegall was asked to fly Captain Pedro Autori, who was the head of the Northern air forces at this time, over the Guadarrama front as suitable aircraft were in short supply at Burgos. With his co-pilot Rupert Bellville, Donegall duly flew the Nationalist officer over the battle raging in the Sonosierra, about thirty miles to the north of Madrid. The aircraft returned safely to the airfield at Burgos and Bellville and Donegall returned to Bordeaux, France, around 25 July and Donegall thence to London.[4]

Marquess of Donegall (centre) toasts newly-wed Amy Johnson and Jim Mollison, London, 1932.
(Irving Rosenburg Collection / Courtesy Richard S. Allen)

On 30 July 1936 another famous British pilot arrived at Burgos. This was Tom Campbell Black, co-winner of the MacRobertson Air Race in a de Havilland D.H.88 Comet in 1934. Campbell Black and Juan de la Cierva, the inventor of the autogiro whose C.30A machines were being produced in England, were intermediaries in plans to sell British civil aircraft to the Nationalists. Juan de la Cierva had already been instrumental in the hiring of the Olley Air Service Dragon Rapide with Luis Bolin. Campell Black had collected the Marqués de Rivas de Linares the previous day at Le Bourget airport in Paris,

34

the Marqués having chartered his aircraft to take him to Burgos and then to Lisbon. After an overnight stop at Bordeaux his silver and grey de Havilland D.H.80A Puss Moth (G-ABYW) landed at Burgos to be instantly surrounded by a circle of armed soldiers. Unknown to Campbell Black his aircraft had been the target for rifle fire from the ground whilst circling round in search of a landing place. The hostile demeanour of the troops changed completely to an enthusiastic welcome as soon as the Marqués was seen to appear out of the cockpit.

Campbell Black made plans for the flight to Lisbon the following day and discussed the arrangements already well under way for the delivery of several aircraft to Spain. During the long trip to Lisbon over the war ravaged land Campbell Black only saw one other aircraft. Luckily for them it was a rebel fighter aircraft which veered off after closely inspecting the Puss Moth. When they landed at Lisbon the Marqués left, with several other Spaniards, on another aeroplane for a visit to Seville and Morocco. Campbell Black left his Puss Moth at the aerodrome for an overhaul and went into the city of Lisbon to await the return of his passenger.

When the Marqués returned a couple of days later from his secret mission to Morocco he told Campbell Black that three or four of his friends also wished to return to Burgos. This, of course, gave Campbell Black a problem because the Puss Moth would not be able to carry the extra passengers so he persuaded another British pilot then in Lisbon, Captain Steel who ran a charter service in Portugal, to carry them to Burgos. Due to a stiff head wind the aircraft ran short of fuel and had to put down at Valladolid. Unfortunately the town had just been bombed by Republican aircraft and Captain Steel had to make his landing run in the face of concentrated rifle fire from the ground. As soon as the aeroplane came to a halt on the runway the passengers jumped out and showed their credentials which had the desired effect. The Marqués then went off to the military headquarters to requisition petrol so that they could continue the journey to Burgos leaving Steel and Campbell Black at a restaurant in the town.

Shortly afterwards the two Englishmen were roughly bundled into a car and driven off to the local Fascist militia headquarters where they were interrogated in Spanish which neither of them knew well enough to understand what was being asked. After some time they were hustled out again and into the car. Only the intervention of the Marqués, who had heard of their arrest and had chased after them in his car, prevented Steel and Campbell Black joining the long list of those summarily executed during the early days of the Spanish Civil War.

That evening, back at Burgos, Mola apologised profusely to Campbell Black and Steel for what had happened at Valladolid. The first British aircraft obtained by Juan de la Cierva had now arrived at Burgos, a de Havilland D.H. 89 Dragon Rapide (G-ADCL). This had been flown non-stop to Burgos on 1 August by Lord Malcolm Douglas-Hamilton with Richard L'Estrange Malone of Airwork Ltd as his navigator. Further aircraft arrived during the next few days. Campell Black made arrangements for the return of the ferry crews back to England and left himself for the frontier by car on 4 August 1936. His Puss Moth was still in Lisbon. (It was sold subsequently to the Nationalists in

February 1937). Steel had, in the meantime, returned to Portugal. Campbell Black sold the story of his adventures in Spain to a Sunday newspaper after his return to England later in the week. This duly appeared the following weekend. No mention however, was made of the aircraft exported from England to the Nationalists.[5]

In the second week of August, Campbell Black was back in Burgos negotiating sale of aero-motors from Britain and returning ferry pilots back to Britain. On 19 September 1936 Tom Campbell Black was killed at Liverpool Municipal Airport at Speke when his Percival Mew Gull (G-AEKL) collided with a Hawker Hart of No 611 Squadron AAF on the ground — a sad end to a famous airman.

Another famous British racing pilot also arrived at Burgos on 3 August 1936. Owen Cathcart-Jones had been co-pilot of the de Havilland Comet that had taken third place in the MacRobertson Air Race behind Campbell Black in 1934. Cathcart-Jones had flown to Cannes, France, on 31 July, in an American Stinson aeroplane. On the following day at a cocktail party he had met Victor Urrutia Usaula, a Spanish millionaire and electric power magnate. Urrutia was sympathetic to the Spanish rebels and wished to buy an aircraft for various diplomatic missions in Spain and around Europe on their behalf. Cathcart-Jones suggested that a new American long-range aeroplane, a Beechcraft B.17R (NC15816), that had recently arrived in Europe might be available at the right price.

The Beechcraft was owned by James Haizlip, a well-known American businessman and pilot who had been formerly Assistant Manager of Shell Petroleum Corporation in the USA. Haizlip had brought the Beechcraft with him to Europe on a sales tour, the machine being shipped, partly dismantled, in the airship *Hindenburg*. The Englishman contacted Haizlip, then at Ostend in Belgium, and told him that he had a buyer if he could fly to Agens, in south west France, to meet Urrutia. Haizlip, who had already heard that the Spanish Nationalists were interested in obtaining aircraft, duly flew to Agens next day where he met Cathcart-Jones and Urrutia. Whilst Cathcart-Jones was familiarising himself with the Beechcraft in the air, he gave Haizlip Urrutia's cheque for £3,000 in payment for the aeroplane. In the meanwhile the Spaniard managed to persuade the French authorities that he was on a pleasure trip with Cathcart-Jones (France supported the Republican Government in Spain). Eventually Cathcart-Jones, who was only wearing sandals, sweater and shorts, and Urrutia took possession of the Beechcraft and took off from the airfield bound for Spain whilst Haizlip flew on to Cannes with the Stinson.

Cathcart-Jones set course for Burgos over the Pyrenees. He flew at 14,000 feet over the mountains but by now it was getting dark and they were low on fuel. They decided to land at Pamplona where there was a rough airstrip. Unfortunately the Beechcraft was painted in yellow and mauve colours, the colours of the Spanish Republic, so when the aircraft came into land it was greeted with machine gun fire from the ground — luckily this was inaccurate once again. This, however, seems to have been the normal welcome for all aircraft at this time. The aircraft was refuelled and the following morning took off for Burgos. There, although word had been sent along that they were coming, the Beechcraft was again fired on over the airfield, despite the extra precaution that Cathcart-Jones had taken off having black identification stripes painted on the undercarriage.

Thomas Cambell Black and his Percival Mew Gull aircraft, shortly before his death in September 1936.
(S & G Press Agency Ltd)

Owen Cathcart-Jones (right) and his co-pilot, Ken Waller at Mildenhall for the MacRobertson Air Race to Australia, 1934.
(Courtesy Anthony Cathcart-Jones)

Beechcraft B.17R (NC15816). (The Aviation Bookshop)

Later that day the Englishman went into the town and met General Mola at his headquarters. Cathcart-Jones, still in his shorts and sandals, felt out of place amongst the immaculately dressed officers. General Mola, however, was delighted to obtain the Beechcraft because it meant that he could send dispatches to Italy and Germany non-stop without having to land in France. He, therefore, instructed Cathcart-Jones to fly Urrutia to any destination he indicated. A few hours later they were on their way to Rome.

Cathcart-Jones spent three days at Rome whilst Urrutia was negotiating with the Italian authorities. He made sure he bought himself a pair of long trousers to replace his shorts. Urrutia then told the Englishman that he wished to be flown to Prague to see the exiled Spanish monarch, King Alfonso; by now the party had been joined by the Marqués de Luca de Tena, millionaire proprietor of the newspaper *ABC*. Plans were changed as the former King of Spain was at Marienbad in Czechoslovakia so Cathcart-Jones, after a stop in Venice, set course for Czechoslovakia over the Alps. It was now getting late so he landed at a small airfield at Pilsen and the two Spaniards went to see the King leaving Cathcart-Jones to look after the aircraft. At the break of dawn on the following day (8 August) he flew off to Marienbad but as soon as he arrived at the aerodrome he was told that the Beechcraft was being detained.

Cathcart-Jones drove out to visit the King and then decided to get away as soon as possible. Returning to the airfield he obtained permission to climb into the cockpit on the

38

pretext that the motor needed tuning and was away before the police realised his intentions. Bad weather forced him to land at Innsbruck in Austria. The authorities there immediately took possession of the aeroplane whilst Cathcart-Jones went off to see the British Consul. Advised to get out of Austria as soon as possible he took a train back to the Italian-French border, then hired a taxi to take him to Cannes. With Haizlip he then returned to England after two exciting weeks. The Beechcraft was eventually released but never found its way back to Spain, being owned by the *Ala Littoria* airline of Rome in 1938.[6]

During all these comings and goings the journalists brought by McIntosh had remained in Burgos. In late August Knickerbocker flew to Seville by way of Lisbon, flying in a de Havilland D.H.85 Leopard Moth piloted by William Ross, said by him later to be "young, ice hockey star and aerobatic ace." Ross also flew him from Seville to Gilbraltar and back. At Gilbraltar they landed on the polo ground, " the first plane to land on the rock in two years".[7]

Sefton Delmer also referred to Ross, whose identity remains uncertain (a Canadian?), later in his autobiography, as arriving over Burgos airfield in his Leopard Moth during an air raid on 1 September 1936. Ross, who was carrying films from the southern front, circled lower and lower, the target of all the batteries, but landed unscathed and without even knowing the danger he had been in.

Two 'tourists' from Britain arrived at Burgos airfield on 5 August 1936. These were Gordon Selfridge Jr, department store executive, and his brother-in-law Vicomte Jacques de Sibour. Both men were well known pilots, and de Sibour had carried out several long distance flights around the world. They arrived at Burgos in Selfridge's own aeroplane accompanied by two ladies. They had flown directly to Burgos and managed to persuade the Nationalists to allow them to accompany a party of journalists bound for the front where they observed a Republican attack being repulsed. Five hours after arriving they were on their way back home. A week later the Vicomte de Sibour arrived at Tangier piloting a de Havilland D.H.90 (G-AECX) bringing some American ladies out of Spain to safety.[8]

DRAMATIS PERSONAE

BEBB, CECIL WILLIAM HENRY.

Born in London, 27 September 1905. Son of a dentist. Entered the RAF in 1921 as a 16-year-old apprentice. By 1926 was a Sergeant Pilot. Passed CFS Instructors' Course 1929. Left RAF in 1931 and became pilot to Southern Aircraft Ltd, 1931-32. Toured South Africa with Alan Cobham Aviation Ltd, 1933. 'B' Licence holder No 3560. With Olley Air Service Ltd, 1936-39. Personal pilot to Air Marshall Sir Arthur Barratt, AOC-in-C, British Air Forces in France 1939. Chief Test Pilot, Cunliffe-Owen Aircraft Ltd, 1939-43. Chief Test Pilot, A.W. Hawkesley Ltd, 1943-44. Appointed Chief Test Pilot, Dunlop Aviation Research Dept, 1944. Chief Pilot, Olley Air Service Ltd, 1946-53. Operations Manager, Transair Ltd, 1953-60. Operations Manager, British United Airways 1960s.

BLACK, THOMAS CAMPBELL.

Born 22 August 1899. Educated at Brighton College. Served in RNAS and RAF from 1917 to 1920. Pioneer of air transport in East Africa – made thirteen flights between Kenya and England. Won, with C.W.A. Scott, the England-Australia race for the MacRobertson Cup 1934. Record flights between London and Cairo in 1935. Killed in accident at Speke 19 September 1936. Held 'B' Licence No 1211. His wife was the famous comedienne, Florence Desmond.

CATHCART-JONES, OWEN.

Born in London, 5 June 1900. Served in Royal Navy from 1922-1930. Learnt to fly in 1924. Pilot in aircraft carriers *HMS Hermes, Eagle, Argus* and *Courageous* 1925-30. First fighter pilot to make deck landing at night. Left the Royal Navy in 1930 with rank of Lieutenant. Became personal pilot to Lt/Cmdr Glen Kidson, RN, with whom he made record flights around Europe and from London to Capetown in 1930 and 1931. Later went into free-lance flying before flying D.H.Comet, with Ken Waller, into third place in MacRobertson Race in 1934. Established record return flight England-Australia and back. Wrote book, *Aviation Memoirs* (London 1934). Later went to the USA where he became a friend of Hollywood actor, Errol Flynn, and a well-known polo player. Was awarded the de Havilland Trophy Medal in 1984. He died at Santa Barbara, California, in November 1985.

DONEGALL, EDWARD ARTHUR DONALD ST. GEORGE HAMILTON CHICHESTER. MARQUESS OF. . .

Born 7 October 1903. Educated at Eton and Christ Church, Oxford. Had a flamboyant career as a journalist, war correspondent, jazz club proprietor and radio commentator. Had a lifelong interest in aviation and was a well-known private pilot. War correspondent in Spain and during World War II. Disc jockey with BBC in 1949. As journalist best known for "Almost in Confidence" column in *Sunday Dispatch* for many years. Died 24 May 1975.

FALK, ROLAND JOHN. OBE, AFC & Bar

Born in Hampstead, 26 February 1915. Educated at Stowe. Obtained 'A' Licence in 1932 at age of 17. 'B' Licence 1934 (No 4717). Flew for press in Ethiopia and in Spain 1935-36. On London-Paris newspaper service 1936-37. Director, British-American Air Services 1938-39. RAF 1939-1946. Chief Test Pilot at Farnborough 1943, then Experimental Test Pilot with Vickers-Armstrongs Ltd. Joined A.V.Roe & Co as Chief Test Pilot 1950. First flight of Vulcan B.Mk1 1952. Subsequently transferred to Hawker Siddeley Aviation Ltd.

HAMILTON, LORD MALCOLM AVENDALE DOUGLAS- OBE, DFC

Born in Strathaven 12 November 1909. Third son of 13th Duke of Hamilton. Educated at Eton and RAF College, Cranwell. Served in the RAF 1927-1932. In civil aviation 1932-39 and also AAF(No 603 Squadron). RAF 1939-46. MP for Inverness Division of Ross &

Cromarty 1950-54. Died 21 July 1964 when his aircraft was lost on flight from Monrovia, Liberia, to Douala, Cameroon.

MCINTOSH, ROBERT HENRY.   (later Wing Commander) DFC, AFC

Born in Waterloo 23 September 1894. Served in Royal Engineers 1914-16 and then with RFC/RAF 1916-1919. With Handley Page Transport and Imperial Airways 1919-28. Spartan Airways and British Airways 1934-37. Airwork Ltd 1937-39. Served in RAF 1939-45, commanding No 280 Coastal Command Squadron. Held 'B' Licence (No 314). Rejoined Airwork Ltd after World War II. Won *Daily Express* Air Race Trophy 1952. Second in Kings Cup Air Race 1958 and 1961. Commanding Officer of No 622 Squadron, RAuxAF. Sales representative for British United Airways in 1960s. Flew over 23,000 hours. Died in the early '80s.

MALONE, RICHARD L'ESTRANGE.

European sales manager of Airwork Ltd. Died 24 August 1946 in air crash in Egypt.

SELFRIDGE, HARRY GORDON JNR.

Born in Chicago, USA, 2 April 1900. Educated at Winchester and Trinity College, Cambridge.

SIBOUR, VICOMTE JACQUES DE.

Born in Cannes, France, 6 April 1896. Served in French Air Force 1916-19. Completed round the world tour 1928-29. Paris-Moscow-Peking-Nanking and back 1931. Round Africa flight 1932. Paris-Hong Kong 1934.

CHAPTER 2 – SOURCES/NOTES

1. Sources consulted include books by Luis Bolin, Peter Jackson and Douglas Cluett etc. Also various newspaper and magazine accounts including Capt Bebb's articles in the *News Chronicle* of 7 November 1936 and the *Aeroplane Monthly* of August 1986. Additional information has also been supplied by Capt Bebb, Muriel Hughes (Capt Olley's secretary) and other former Olley Air Service employees. See also Foreign Office FO371 File (1936) 20525, now at Public Record Office.

2. Information from books by Wing Cdr McIntosh, Sefton Delmer and Juan Antonio Ansaldo. Also interview with Wing Cdr McIntosh by Gerald Howson in January 1978. See also FO371 File (1936) 20524.

3. *The Aeroplane*, 5 August 1936, and letter from Mr Falk, May 1977.

4. *Daily Mail*, 27 July 1936. Article by Marquess of Donegall.

5. Information from various newspaper reports in July/August 1936 and Campbell Black's article in the *News of the World*, 9 August 1936. See also FO371 Files (1936) 20527 and 20533.

6. Information from Mr Anthony Cathcart-Jones and various newspaper reports of August/September 1936 including articles by Owen Cathcart-Jones in the *Daily Express*, 11 August 1936 and the *Sunday Graphic & Sunday News*, 13/20 September 1936. The *Index to the Foreign Office Archives* at the Public Record Office also lists several documents concerning his activities at this time.

7. *The Siege of the Alcazar: A Warlog of the Spanish Revolution*, by H. R. Knickerbocker; London 1937.

8. Information from the *Foreign Relations of the United States; Diplomatic Papers 1936, Vol II*; Washington DC, 1954, and various newspaper articles.

CHAPTER 3

A Taste of the Thirties : British Pilots in Nationalist Spain.

Rupert Bellville was born at Lubenham near Market Harborough, Leicestershire, on 28 December 1904. His father, Captain Frank Ashton Bellville, who held a country estate at Papillon Hall, Market Harborough, sent Rupert to be educated in the manner expected of a boy of his class, first to prep school and then to Eton College. By his late teens Rupert was six foot two inches tall, broad-shouldered, strong and, with his fair complexion and blond hair, already irresistible to the fair sex. Packed off by his family to friends in the south-west wine-producing provinces of Spain he learnt to speak Spanish fluently by his early twenties and was accepted into the intimate circles of the dons of the sherry business. During these formative years Rupert acquired a lifelong devotion to Spain and love of bullfighting.

Back home the young man became a member of the renowned White's Club of St James's in London where, in the mid-twenties, he was recruited by Lord Edward Grosvenor for his recently formed No 601 (County of London) Squadron, Auxiliary Air Force. Rupert obtained his commission in August 1926 and joined many other wealthy young men infected by the love of flying at Northolt each weekend on the de Havilland D.H.9A biplane bombers operated by the squadron. Rupert proved to be an exceptional, although ungovernable, pilot with a personality so famed that a letter sent from abroad addressed just to "Rupert Bellville, RAF" found him safely. In August 1932 Flying Officer Rupert Bellville relinquished his commission in the AAF on completion of service.

Rupert now became personal pilot to the Honourable Mrs Edwin Montagu and flew with her to the Far East in August 1932. By March of 1936 he was reported to have flown over 1,500 hours of civil flying, in Europe, Syria, Iraq, Palestine, Iran, India, Siam and China. This information was put forth by his lawyer when he pleaded guilty in Croydon Police Court for lighting cigarettes on four occasions during an Imperial Airways flight from Paris to London. Rupert, true to his nature, considered the ban on smoking should not apply to him being an infringment of his personal freedom.[1]

When the Spanish Civil War broke out in July 1936 there could be no doubt where Rupert's sympathies would lay. He attended the funeral of Calvo Sotelo, the Monarchist politician whose murder by Republican police was the signal for the outbreak of the Civil War. He flew to Burgos with the Marquess of Donegall in late July in Bellville's D.H.85 Leopard Moth (G-ACLN) which was registered to Mrs Montagu. When Donegall returned to England Rupert Bellville flew to Barcelona in Republican territory in order to obtain information for newspaper articles. Here he was to remain for several weeks as permission to leave was constantly withdrawn.

De Havilland D.H.60G Gipsy Moth (G-AAJO) at Don Muang airfield, Siam, autumn 1932. In front (left to right); Siamese Air Force officer, Hon Mrs Montagu, Rupert Bellville. (W. J. Clennell/Courtesy Aeroplane Monthly)

De Havilland D.H.85 Leopard Moth (G-ACLN). (A. J. Jackson Collection)

During this period Rupert saw the arrival of the first military aid sent to the Spanish Republic - Dewoitine fighter aircraft and Potez bombers from France. In mid-August Rupert finally received permission to leave Barcelona. He flew over the war front to Saragossa, which was held by the rebel forces. Rupert finally reached Perpignan in France, and safety, on 16 August. The following morning the story of his experiences in Barcelona appeared in the London *Daily Telegraph*.

Before the end of the year Rupert was again in Spain. He spent three weeks with the Falangist militias at Jerez in the south-west of Spain. There he joined up with many of the friends he had made in the twenties and took part in operations in Andalusia, including the execution of Republican prisoners. The officer-in-charge of the firing squad, however, made it known to Rupert that he would turn a 'blind eye' if he fired over the heads of the condemned men - a concession that the tall Englishman was only too glad to obtain. A photograph of Rupert in a 'mono' (the one-piece outfit worn by the militias) with the Falangist insignia on his breast appeared in the Italian newspaper *Il Corriere Della Sera* in December 1936. Rupert returned to Spain at Easter 1937 when he spent a few days on holiday in Seville. In August 1937 he collected the Leopard Moth at Lympne and flew down to Spain for, ostensibly, another holiday at San Sebastian with a friend Ricardo González Gordon, a prosperous Spanish wine merchant. In reality he had been asked to obtain technical information for the Air Ministry in London. Rupert stopped off at Biarritz where he met Virginia Cowles, an American journalist, who was waiting there for permission to enter Nationalist Spain. Rupert told her to forget about waiting for a visa to arrive and to fly with him to San Sebastian in the morning being confident that, as the Nationalist authorities knew him well, they would be granted entry. They flew to San Sebastian the next day but were at once placed under house arrest at a hotel. Their aircraft was impounded. After twenty-four hours Miss Cowles was allowed to return to France and the Leopard Moth returned to the embarassed Bellville, who by now had been vouched for by González. Rupert remained in San Sebastian with González and they spent the next few days lying in the sun and in the colourful company of several bullfighters in local bars.

The fall of Santander to the Nationalists was announced in San Sebastian on 25 August 1937 (prematurely as it turned out) with much bell-ringing and shouting in the streets. Rupert and González conceived the bright idea of greeting the victorious troops. They set off in the Leopard Moth immediately that summer evening with three cases of González best sherry on the spare seat in the aircraft. On landing at Santander, however, they belatedly discovered that the city and airport were still in the hands of the Republican troops and they were taken into custody by the Basque militia. González made out that he was an Englishman "Richard Gilbey" and was held prisoner for ten hours until freed with the actual entry of the Nationalists into Santander.

Meanwhile Rupert, with little choice in the matter, was asked to fly two Republican officers to Llanes. The aircraft was fired at by Heinkel He 51s of the German *Legion Condor* en route but managed to reach Llanes safely. Rupert was taken on to Gijon and put in jail, accused of being a spy for Franco and relieved of his money, his gold lighter and cigarette case. Here he remained for several weeks whilst negotiations continued for his release between the Spanish Republicans and the British Foreign Office. Finally Rupert's release was granted in exchange for British promises to the Governor of Gijon that efforts would be made to secure the release of an important Republican prisoner held by the Nationalists.

A British destroyer, *HMS Foresight,* was sent to collect Rupert on 10 September but his Leopard Moth was confiscated by the Spanish Republic and later reported to have been destroyed in an air raid. Rupert sold the story of his adventures to the London *Evening Standard*[2] and, returning to Biarritz, again met Virginia Cowles. They went to the casino there together where he lost the four hundred pounds he had received from the *Evening Standard* in exactly ten minutes. Later the Foreign Office in London wryly suggested to the Air Ministry that greater care should be exercised in selecting people to obtain technical information in future.[3]

In October 1938 Rupert married Jeanette Fuqua, daughter of the US Military Attache in Spain. Whilst honeymooning on a world cruise he again made the headlines at home over non-payment of a painting bill to a London contractor whom he asked to paint all the gates on his country estate, Papillon Hall (which he had inherited at the death of his father in 1937), in General Franco's colours.

Elegant Biarritz during the late thirties was the summer home of many upper-class playboys. Splendid parties were held nightly in the great villas. In the Casino money was thrown around like scraps at a paper-chase. The war in Spain was generally ignored unless one of the group, like Rupert Bellville, became involved.

Another member of this exclusive 'club' also found himself involved in the Spanish conflict in the autumn of 1938. Count Theodore Zichy, who held dual Hungarian and British citizenship, was born at Eastbourne on 13 June 1908. His father was an Hungarian aristocrat and his mother was British. In the late twenties he became well-known as a motor rally driver and won the Hungarian Automobile Championship in 1928. He learnt to fly in 1937, bought a second-hand Puss Moth and toured the Continent clocking up hours, following the round of hectic parties and social activities. In the late summer of 1938 Zichy was invited to go on a public relations visit to Nationalist Spain. Leaving his Puss Moth (G-AAXY) behind at Biarritz he drove his Ford V8 convertible into Spain where he spent several weeks being shown around.

Zichy travelled far and wide in Nationalist Spain (including meeting the imprisoned American pilot, Whitey Dahl – see Chapter 10) before arriving at the north-west suburbs of Madrid, where through binoculars he watched the University City defended by the Republic since the autumn of 1936 – two long years before. At a nearby airfield he met the Nationalist 'ace' fighter pilot, Joaquín García Morato, whom he had seen previously in Saragossa. After an enormous lunch and large quantities of wine, he expressed admiration for the Fiat CR.32 fighter aircraft lined up in front of the hangar. According to Zichy, Morato then invited him to accompany him on a flight over the lines in one of the Fiats. The flight initially proved uneventful but then two Republican fighters were seen approaching. Count Zichy, as ordered, immediately peeled off and dived away to land safely at the airbase leaving Morato and another pilot to deal with the Republican aircraft. Eventually Morato returned with yet another victory to add to his growing total. Making his way back to Burgos, Count Zichy collected Peter Kemp, an Englishman who served with the Nationalist ground forces, who had been badly wounded. Kemp was going home on leave so Count Zichy gave him a lift to Biarritz and then flew him in "Jacksie" to London, glad to leave war-torn Spain behind.[4]

Count Zichy at Brooklands Aerodrome, 1937. (Courtesy Count Zichy)

Very little information can be found regarding the presence of other British flyers in Nationalist Spain. Reports of Englishmen at Seville, in October 1936, exist but it it has been possible to identify only one of these men – Peter Humbertum, born in London on 14 December 1910. Said to be an aeronautical engineer and from an English titled family, he joined the Spanish Foreign Legion in October 1936. Having proved his ability as a pilot, Humbertum was posted initially to a Breguet Br.19 squadron. In early November he joined Grupo 1-G-12, with Romeo Ro.37 aircraft, under the command of Fernández Pérez, based at Talavera de la Reina, and took part in the air battles around Madrid. On 1

December 1936, Humbertum was posted to a fighter squadron, 1-E-2, equipped with Heinkel He 51s, under the command of Manrique Montero, which was based at Torrijos. He flew with this unit until April 1937 during the battles for Madrid and Jarama. In April 1937 he joined Grupo 1-G-70, at Cadiz, which flew Dornier-Wal seaplanes, and later the same month 2-G-62, equipped with Cant Z-501 flying boats. Humbertum remained with this unit for over a year, building up 180 hours flying time. After being grounded for several months due to ill health, he was posted to a German *Legion Condor* squadron AS/88, which flew Heinkel He 59 seaplanes, as an interpreter in October 1938. Humbertum was discharged from the Nationalist Air Force on 2 April 1939 with the rank of *Teniente* (Lieutenant). The above information comes from Spanish sources but no data is available at present from UK records regarding this man.[5]

A Canadian pilot was also reported to have been in Lisbon at the beginning of October 1936 on his way to join the Nationalists at Burgos. The Foreign Office Files at the Public Record Office reveal the name, Warde Harry Phelan. Born in Toronto on 17 July 1911, he arrived in Salamanca during October 1936 to offer his service to the Nationalist cause, having with him a letter of introduction from Tom Campbell Black. He was not accepted as he could not speak Spanish and was later arrested as a spy by the suspicious Nationalist authorities because they thought that he would probably join the Republican Air Force on release. Phelan had held a commission in the RAF for the brief period of two weeks at the beginning of 1936. He reported that he had flown from Cáceres to Salamanca in a Junkers aircraft piloted by a Canadian (perhaps Ross?). Phelan remained in prison for several weeks whilst the British Foreign Office tried to obtain his freedom. He was finally released in early 1937 and returned to Canada.[6]

An Irishman, William Dickson Winterbottom, born in Dublin on 7 May 1911, was reported to have acted as a pilot for General Franco during the early months of the Spanish Civil War. At the commencement of the war he was a translator in the Military Commandant's office at Algeciras before later joining the Spanish Foreign Legion and carrying out several special flying missions in and out of Spain. He later claimed to have flown as co-pilot in Franco's personal Douglas DC-2 aircraft. When the Non-Intervention Law was enforced on Britain, General Franco sent Winterbottom on a special mission to England. Winterbottom returned to Dublin in March 1937 and later became a newspaper correspondent in South America, including Ecuador and Chile.[7] He was not the only Irishman to try to fly for Franco in Spain as two others, Jack Colley and Hugh McDaniel, went to Burgos in February 1937 to volunteer for the Nationalist Air Force. They arrived at Gilbraltar at the end of the month saying they could not agree to the terms offered but had then been detained and told that any attempt at escaping would result in them being shot. Despite this threat the two Irishmen still managed to find their way to safety.[8]

In Berlin during 1937 a book was published written by an Englishman with the Germanic sounding name of Conrad Everard.[9] In this he described how he had flown in the Nationalist Air Force in Spain from the autumn of 1936 when he had flown air drops of provisions for the Alcázar of Toledo, later taking part in bombing raids on Cartagena and Malaga. No information regarding Everard has been found from sources in the UK.

Back in England during the summer of 1937 a young pilot, Malcolm Frederick Craig Strathdee (born in Thornton Heath on 24 March 1915), who had been learning to fly at Brooklands Aviation at Sywell in Northamptonshire, obtained a Short Service Commission in the RAF and was sent to No. 7 Flying Training School at Peterborough. His commission was terminated in January 1938. In the following April he enlisted in the Army. After service in the Royal Armoured Corps he was one of the first to volunteer for training as a glider pilot in late 1940. Strathdee was a combative character and a fine pilot who created much confusion by wearing RAF wings on his khaki uniform. While at Haddenham (Thame) in the early spring of 1941 Strathdee was renowned for his stories, known to all as "Strathdeeds". One of these was that while he had been serving in the RAF in 1937 he had been stationed at Gibraltar for a while flying Gloster Gladiator fighters. Being bored with peacetime flying and with the Spanish Civil War happening a few miles away he one day flew his Gladiator over to the Spanish Nationalists and placed his services at their disposal. During the next few weeks he had flown one of the Messerschmitt Bf 109 fighter aircraft operated by the *Legion Condor* before returning home to be court-martialled and dismissed from service.

Strathdee was, without doubt, an excellent pilot and was the first to glide solo in March 1941. This bushy-moustached staff-sergeant was killed in action over Norway in Operation Freshman in November 1942 — an abortive and disastrous attempt to destroy by glider troops the heavy water plant at Rjukan. Strathdee's claims to have fought in Spain have been publicized in various books in recent years but, unfortunately, a close relative has recently revealed he never went there.[10]

After the outbreak of World War II both Rupert Bellville and Count Zichy joined the Air Transport Auxiliary which had been formed from civilian pilots to deliver aircraft from the factories to service units. Rupert Bellville served in the ATA from February to November 1940 and during June, together with two other pilots, delivered Fairey Battle light bombers to Chateau d'Un in France with the German ground forces closing in around the airfield. The three men managed to get out just in time in some Hurricane fighters written off as unserviceable. They spent the night at Dinard. The following morning Rupert took one of the battered Hurricanes up on an 'offensive patrol' as aircraft were in such short supply. Luckily no enemy aircraft were seen and he returned with the others to White Waltham in England in the evening.[11] Zichy also flew many Hurricanes from factory to service units during the next few months whilst the Battle of Britain raged overhead. He had previously resolved to go to Finland in March 1940 to fly against the Russians but missed the ship after a night's carousing with friends.[12]

Rupert found post-war Britain not to his liking and spent much time on the Continent in Paris, Spain and New York. Now divorced he acquired a string of girl friends and spent much time in the company of the famous American author, Ernest Hemingway, whom he had first met on their way to Spain in 1937. Rupert loved to gamble and some of his happiest hours were spent playing backgammon or bridge. He acquired an 'A' flying licence again in 1946. On this he put his occupation as 'bullfighter'. He continued his love-affair with Spain and spent many months there, often with Hemingway and his wife, during the fifties. Rupert Bellville died peacefully in London on 23 July 1962, a man whose tragedy it was to be born in the wrong age.

Count Zichy still lives in London and continues to write colourful accounts of his youthful adventures during those long gone days of the thirties.

CHAPTER 3 – SOURCES/NOTES

1. *The Aeroplane*, 25 March 1936.

2. *Evening Standard*, 14/15/16 September 1937.

3. FO371 File (1937) 21376. Documents listed as being in file 21404 are missing.

4. This journey, however, is not mentioned in Peter Kemp's account of his adventures in Spain (see Bibliography).

5. Information regarding Humbertum from Emilio Herrera Alonso (via Juan Arráez Cerdá). See also his book *Entre el añil y el cobalto : Los Hidroaviones en la Guerra de España*; Madrid 1988.

6. FO371 Files (1936/1937) 20554.

7. *The Aeroplane*, 28 June 1939.

8. *Daily Worker*, 2 February 1937. Documents concerning Colley and McDaniel listed in *Index to Foreign Office Archives* (1937) are missing from files.

9. See Bibliography.

10. Information from Captain John Cross, Museum of Army Flying, and Peter Yeates, H. E. Harvey, J. S. Sproule, J. R. Hebden, J. A. Caslaw.

11. Information from Miss Lettice Curtis and from her book, *The Forgotten Pilots: A Story of the Air Transport Auxiliary 1939-45;* Henley-on-Thames 1971.

12. Information from Count Zichy and from his various articles and autobiography.

CHAPTER 4

The Artistic Adventurer

Hugh William Arthur Oloff de Wet was born on 1 April 1912, at St. Lawrence, on the island of Jersey in the Channel Isles. He came from a well-known South African family and was reputed to be a descendant of Rembrandt's pupil, Jacobus de Wet. His father was Thomas Oloff de Wet, the son of a Boer general, who was an officer in the Royal Navy. From his Irish mother, Elizabeth Bradstreet, Hugh derived a certain fey quality and sensitivity. However, this was balanced by the stubborness of the Cape Dutch inherited from his father.

Captain Thomas de Wet was the Principal Naval Transport Officer during the evacuation of Constantinople in 1923 and was later stationed in Egypt, where the young boy learned a smattering of Arabic. Hugh commenced his education in Brussels and was sent to Monkton Combe School, near Bath, in September 1924 at the age of 12. He graduated to the senior school there in 1926. His career at public school would seem to have been undistinguished although he rowed bow in his house crew and ran for the school athletic team.

Destined by his upbringing and family for a military career he joined the Royal Military Academy at Sandhurst in January 1930. By now Hugh's volatile personality and rebellious spirit were beginning to show themselves. Of his training at Sandhurst he was later to say "I learnt to abhor discipline. They solemnly warned me that to command one must learn to obey. But I – I have never had the slightest desire to command anyone..." Hugh also started to show a liking for strong liquor. It is reported that on one occasion, whilst at Sandhurst, he hit the fingers of his right hand with a hammer so that he would not have to sit an examination. In June 1932 Hugh resigned his cadetship.

All this, of course, did not go down well with his family, and relations became more and more strained between father and son. However one more attempt for a formal military career lay ahead and Hugh was granted a Short Service Commission in the Royal Air Force in March 1933. By April of that year he was an Acting Pilot Officer at No.3 Flying Training School, Spittlegate, which was situated on high ground just outside the town of Grantham in Lincolnshire. His day started with physical training and drill followed by lectures in the theory of flight, airmanship, navigation, rigging etc. During his year at the school Hugh was taught to fly on, initially, the Avro Tutor, de Havilland Tiger Moth and later graduated on to the Armstrong Whitworth Atlas and A. W. Siskin 111DC. In March 1934 his training was completed and he was posted to No.10 (Night Bomber) Squadron at Boscombe Down, near Amesbury in Wiltshire. This squadron was equipped with the large biplane bomber aircraft, the Vickers Virginia X. By mid April, however, Hugh was back at the Royal Air Force Depot at Uxbridge, designated "non effective, sick" after being involved in a motor accident. He was to remain at Uxbridge until his probationary commission was terminated in early August 1934. By his own later account he gave up the service as the many medical boards he had to attend had been unpleasant. Hugh's attitude to authority had not endeared him to the RAF hierarchy.

Hugh's career in these years is often difficult to establish as one of his first rules of life was never to tell his parents anything of where he went or what he did.[1] He later told Hilaire du Berrier that his father once gave him some money and told him to go off and make something of himself. Hugh took the money and went to Ireland and lived with a tribe of gipsies until it was all gone. He returned home, his clothes somewhat shabbier than when he had left and his cravat – the one he had been wearing when he had left home – in extremely bad shape. His replies to all queries were polite and in a low voice, with superb dignity, but giving nothing definite away as to where he had been or what he had been doing. The following year he went to the races with his two sisters, Molly and Lily, They were astonished when a group of gipsies showed joy at seeing Hugh and began conversing in a language which his sisters had never heard before.

By now, even to his father, it was obvious that there was no place in the workaday world for his rebellious son. He could not afford to make his son an out-and-out remittance man so decided that the best course of action was to send Hugh off to wherever there was a war coming and hope that he would make a place for himself with his military training. The opportunity was soon to present itself in East Africa.

During the period of European colonization of Africa towards the end of the 19th Century, Italy, amongst other countries, had tried to establish a colony that would provide a source of cheap raw materials and a place for her own population who wanted to emigrate. A tenuous foothold was finally secured in Southern Somalia and Eritrea. However, in the Mid-Thirties as Italy's trade declined and both poverty and unemployment increased, Mussolini realized that popular discontent was likely to be a threat to Fascist rule in Italy. It appeared to the Duce that a foreign adventure might gratify his people, provide fresh employment and expansion possibilities and add to his own and Italy's prestige, then suffering with the advent of Nazi Germany. He decided to embark on a conquest of Abyssinia (now Ethiopia) using as a pretext imagined transgressions by the Ethiopians against Italian sovereignty in East Africa. Italian and Ethiopian patrols clashed in a frontier "incident" in December 1934 in disputed territory between the boundaries of Italian Somaliland and the primitive kingdom of Ethiopia ruled over by Emperor Haile Selassie.

By the early summer of 1935 Mussolini had nearly a quarter of a million men concentrated in Italy's East African colonies adjoining Ethiopia. Haile Sellasie made it known that he was desperate for any help he could get in the conflict that was surely approaching. Captain de Wet bought his son a ticket for Ethiopia and shipped him off there. Hugh was happy to go as he was hoping to get enough money to marry a French girl he called "puppy eyes" with whom he had fallen in love.

The journey to Addis Ababa was a long and arduous one in 1935 – at this time there was no air service. A long sea voyage through the Mediterranean, Suez Canal and torrid Red

Sea ended at the fly-stricken port of Djibouti in French Somaliland, which was the terminus for the railway to Addis Ababa, some five hundred and fifty miles to the south-west. Hugh found that he was one of several hundred people waiting to catch the train. Eventually he managed to get himself aboard with the few belongings he had brought along with him – including two books, a huge volume of *Carmen* and the *RAF Manual*. The train chuffed slowly across the dust-swept lowland Somali wastes, climbing ever nearer towards the Ethiopian plateau dimly visible through the heat haze. After crossing the frontier of Ethiopia Hugh had his first glimpse of the Emperor's bare-footed soldiers on their way to guard Ethiopia's southern border.

The train crossed the bridge over the Awash Gorge and climbed towards the forbidding mountains ahead. After a long and exhausting journey it finally rattled into the impressive new station at Addis Ababa.

The Ethiopian capital is situated between two high peaks nine thousand feet above sea level. In the late summer of 1935 the city housed some eighty thousand Ethiopians together with another thousand foreigners. The ramshackle collection of buildings of every conceivable African and European type faced onto narrow winding streets, only a few of which were paved. During the day the noise was indescribable with the continuous din of car horns as the vehicles tried to make their way through the crowds of peasants bringing in goods to sell or barter on mules or camels. A regular sight at this time were fierce looking warriors of provincial chieftains arriving to pay their respects to the Emperor – men armed only with spears, long bladed knives and antique rifles. After nightfall the streets were taken over by hyenas, jackals and mongrel dogs who made the hours of darkness hideous with their cries and barks.

Hugh Oloff de Wet in Ethiopia, 1935.
(Linton Wells - Popular Flying)

The temperature soared to 40°C at midday but often fell to below freezing during the night. This, with the daily experience of combatting fleas, lice and bedbugs soon made Hugh wish he was back in England.

Hugh took a room in the Hotel d'Europe, which was run by a German, and went immediately to offer his services as a pilot to the Ethiopian air minister, Thadessa Mechecha. But soon he found this would not be as simple as he imagined due to the lack of aeroplanes available. At this time Ethiopia only possessed some eleven aircraft, only a few of which were in good condition, and none had guns fitted. There were four French Potez 25A-2 (bought in 1928-30), two Fokker F.VIIa monoplanes, one Fokker F.VIIb/3m trimotor, one de Havilland D.H.60M Gipsy Moth, one French Farman 192 monoplane, one Italian Breda 15 monoplane and the Emperor's private aircraft, a Junkers W 33c cabin monoplane, which was usually flown by Ludwig Weber, a German engineer and pilot.[2]

The Director of Aviation was Paul Corriger, a French pilot. There were several Ethiopian pilots including Mishka Babitcheff, the son of a White Russian father and Ethiopian mother. Also in Ethiopia when Hugh arrived was the flamboyant, self-styled "Black Eagle of Harlem", Hubert Fauntleroy Julian. This 38 year old Negro pilot from Trinidad had been in Ethiopia previously, in 1930, when he had crashed the Gipsy Moth whilst performing unauthorised aerobatics just before the Emperor's coronation. That had resulted in his expulsion from the country. Julian had returned to Ethiopia in the spring of 1935 hoping to resume his career in the Imperial Air Force but had been relegated to training infantry recruits. One day in August he was involved in a fight with another black American pilot, John C. Robinson from Chicago, who styled himself the "Brown Condor".

Haile Selassie was greatly embarrassed by this brawl between two foreign volunteers for his cause which was, of course, given much publicity by the foreign press. He banished Julian from the capital by appointing him military governor of the town of Ambo, some three days ride to the north. Robinson, a good pilot, who had already been taken on to fly for the air force, was grounded for a time.

Another guest at the Hotel d'Europe was a 28 year old, debonair, slim and dark American from North Dakota, who bore the unlikely name of Hilaire du Berrier. This would-be adventurer and former barnstorming pilot was to introduce Hugh to the world of the "soldier of fortune". Hugh later described these men "whose only trade is battle , and the only capital they have to invest is their lives". Du Berrier had arrived in Paris in 1931 where he became one of a group of World War I veterans and swashbuckling foreign adventurers who spent their time re-living old battles and always on the lookout for any wars or revolutions around the world where their "expertise" could be of use – at a price. This group was led by the famous American soldier-of-fortune, Charles Sweeny, who had followed an unparalleled career in Latin America, in the Foreign Legion in World War I, in Poland against communist Russia and in North Africa in the twenties.

Another pilot in the group was Vincent Minor Schmidt, from Pennsylvania, USA, who had been an artilleryman in World War 1, fought in a Mexican revolution and piloted for big-game hunts in Africa in the twenties and flown for a Chinese warlord in 1931-32.

Hilaire du Berrier's mother had died in 1935 and left him a small inheritance which he decided to use to finance a trip to Ethiopia. Before leaving Paris he had met Haile Selassie's envoy and offered to form a squadron using soldiers-of-fortune as pilots. He was told to report to the air minister in Addis Ababa, and was informed that additional aircraft were in the process of being obtained. Like Hugh, he reported to Thadessa

Mechecha after his arrival in the Ethiopian capital and waited for the promised aeroplanes to arrive.

Hugh and du Berrier soon became close friends. Hugh would listen open mouthed to the stories by the American of the exploits of Charles Sweeny and his Paris Coterie. He soon had the chance to meet another of these men, for Vincent Schmidt arrived in Addis Ababa to join them.

Before long Hugh's finances began to run out. His father had bought him the ticket to Ethiopia, but had sent out no further money. Besides, Hugh could not get any definite answer to his continual queries of government officials as to when he would be given something to do. They were always promising Hugh a job of some kind but it was always "*ishy naga*", an expression in the Amharic language meaning, "yes, tomorrow". Hugh soon found that "*naga*" never comes. Eventually he was evicted from the hotel because he could not pay his bill. Luckily he was able to locate a vacant house, which had belonged to a Greek who had been expelled, and du Berrier rented it for himself, Hugh and an American journalist, Benny Arnold, to live in. Hugh's sister, Molly, finally sent him a cheque but Hugh had to wait several weeks whilst it was sent for collection. When it was cashed he spent some of the money on a large, black dog.

This group of would-be adventurers came to the notice of several of the newspaper correspondents present in Addis Ababa during the early autumn of 1935, all hungry for news of any kind and frustrated by the strict censorship applied by the Ethiopians. Evelyn Waugh, the famous novelist, was there as foreign correspondent for the *Daily Mail* and he later referred to Hugh in his book *Waugh in Abyssinia* as ". . . an ex-officer of the RAF who started to live in some style with a pair of horses, a bull terrier and a cavalry moustache – he wanted a job too." An accurate description except for the horses.[3]

War finally came on 3 October 1935 when Italian forces invaded Ethiopia from Eritrea and Somalia. Hugh, du Berrier and Schmidt joined the crowds in front of Haile Selassie's Grand Guebi Palace to hear the declaration of war. Every Ethiopian, male or female, young or old, was told to report directly for military service bringing along any weapons they possessed, be it rifle, spear, sword or knife. Old men and young boys were to be sent out to act as snipers using ancient rifles, the women were used as carriers and cooks. The League of Nations, after much fruitless discussion, imposed some "sanctions" on Italy which, in reality, had little or no effect. What actually did result was that the nations of Europe and America, anxious to avoid a military confrontation with Italy, refused to ship any further aircraft to Ethiopia or spares for those already there.

The outbreak of hostilities caused further journalists to rush to Africa. A young British pilot, Roland Falk (later to become famous after World War II as a test-pilot) flew several pressmen from Heston to Addis Ababa in a de Havilland D.H.85 Leopard Moth (G-ACSH) in early October and remained there until the end of the year flying journalists and film crews around Ethiopia. Hugh also met the three pilots of Brian Allen Aviation Ltd (an air-taxi company from England), C.F. French, Newman and Brian Allen, who all undertook the hazardous flight from the UK in small civil aircraft, a Percival P.10 Gull Four (G-ACHM), a Percival P.3 Gull Six (G-ADEP) and a D.H.85 Leopard Moth (G-

ADCO). These aircraft were used to carry photographers to the war fronts and the resulting pictures or film to Cairo and Khartoum.[4] Captain Charles Lloyd, who owned some cotton plantations in the neighbourhood of Roseires in the Blue Nile valley near the Ethiopian frontier, also made frequent flights in a General Aircraft ST-25 Monospar Jubilee (G-ADTE) between Addis Ababa and Port Sudan with high altitude photographs of the war zones. On 26 December 1935, however, the aircraft crashed into a tree whilst attempting to leave rough ground at Addis Alum, some 10 miles from the capital. Lloyd fractured his skull. His wife Ursula, also a skilled pilot, broke both her legs in the crash.[5]

Photograph taken by Colonel Vincent Schmidt in Addis Ababa, December 1935. Left to right (back row); Hugh Oloff de Wet, Benny Arnold, Ethiopian, Hilaire du Berrier. (Courtesy Hilaire du Berrier)

For the frustrated foreign volunteers confined to Addis Ababa news of what was actually happening at the front became increasingly difficult to obtain. The press photographers were getting nearer to the action than they were. The men became irritable, occasionally physically ill and bored to distraction. A French pilot, René Drouillet, arrived in Addis Ababa about this time with an American Beechcraft B.17L aircraft, which he had flown over from France. This was sold shortly afterwards to the Ethiopians for 12,000 dollars, an immense sum at the time, despite the intervention of de Wet, according to his own later account. Another foreign pilot arrived in his own aircraft, a small Heinkel HD 21, from Djibouti in early December. This was a handsome, fair-haired Swedish nobleman and brother-in-law to Marshall Goering, Count Carl Gustav von Rosen. He was subsequently allotted one of the Fokker aircraft for Red Cross use. Julian, however, disappeared from the scene during November. He had come under suspicion after a story had been published in the Italian press that an American in the service of Haile Selassie was in the pay of Italy to assassinate the Emperor. The charge was not true but Julian, discouraged, wrote a personal farewell note to the Emperor, collected his bags and departed from Ethiopia for good.[6]

Hugh tried to fill his time with making drawings (of professional quality according to du Berrier) and writing articles, two of which eventually appeared in 1936 after his return to the UK. The boredom of his existence, however, caused him to take to drinking heavily again when (according to du Berrier) the rigidly dignified, polite "pukka English gentleman" would become a different person, rude and violent. Hilaire du Berrier recalls that, on one evening in Addis Ababa when he tried to talk Hugh out of taking another drink, de Wet waved a revolver in his face and threatened to shoot him. Finally one evening in March 1936, Hugh was drinking at a tawdry bar run by a White Russian. He fell into an argument with a Belgian cavalry officer in the service of the Emperor over a half-Greek half-Ethiopian girl in the bar to whom, he considered, the Belgian was being disrespectful. Hugh challenged the Belgian to a duel and the cavalry officer chose sabres as the weapons to be used.

Count von Rosen under the wing of his Red Cross Fokker aircraft in Ethiopia, 1936. (From Ole G. Nordbø archives)

Sir Sidney Barton, the British Ambassador in Ethiopia, was informed about the forthcoming duel and had de Wet arrested the night before it was to take place. He probably saved Hugh's life. Hugh was immediately placed under close, armed guard and put on the train for Djibouti. So this was the end of the Ethiopian War as far as de Wet was concerned.

Hugh took ship back home to England and arrived there with little or no money to his name to show for his sojourn in Africa. He went to live with his sisters at their flat in London and straightway made arrangements to see Captain W.E. Johns, the author of the *Biggles* stories, who was then also the editor of the aviation magazine *Popular Flying*. This journal had previously published a photograph of him taken whilst he was in Ethiopia and de Wet hoped to interest Johns in some articles about his experiences there. Eventually two highly imaginative articles appeared in the issues for May and June 1936 – for these he drew on his imagination to a large extent and others' experiences of flying in Ethiopia as he himself never actually piloted any aircraft whilst in Africa.

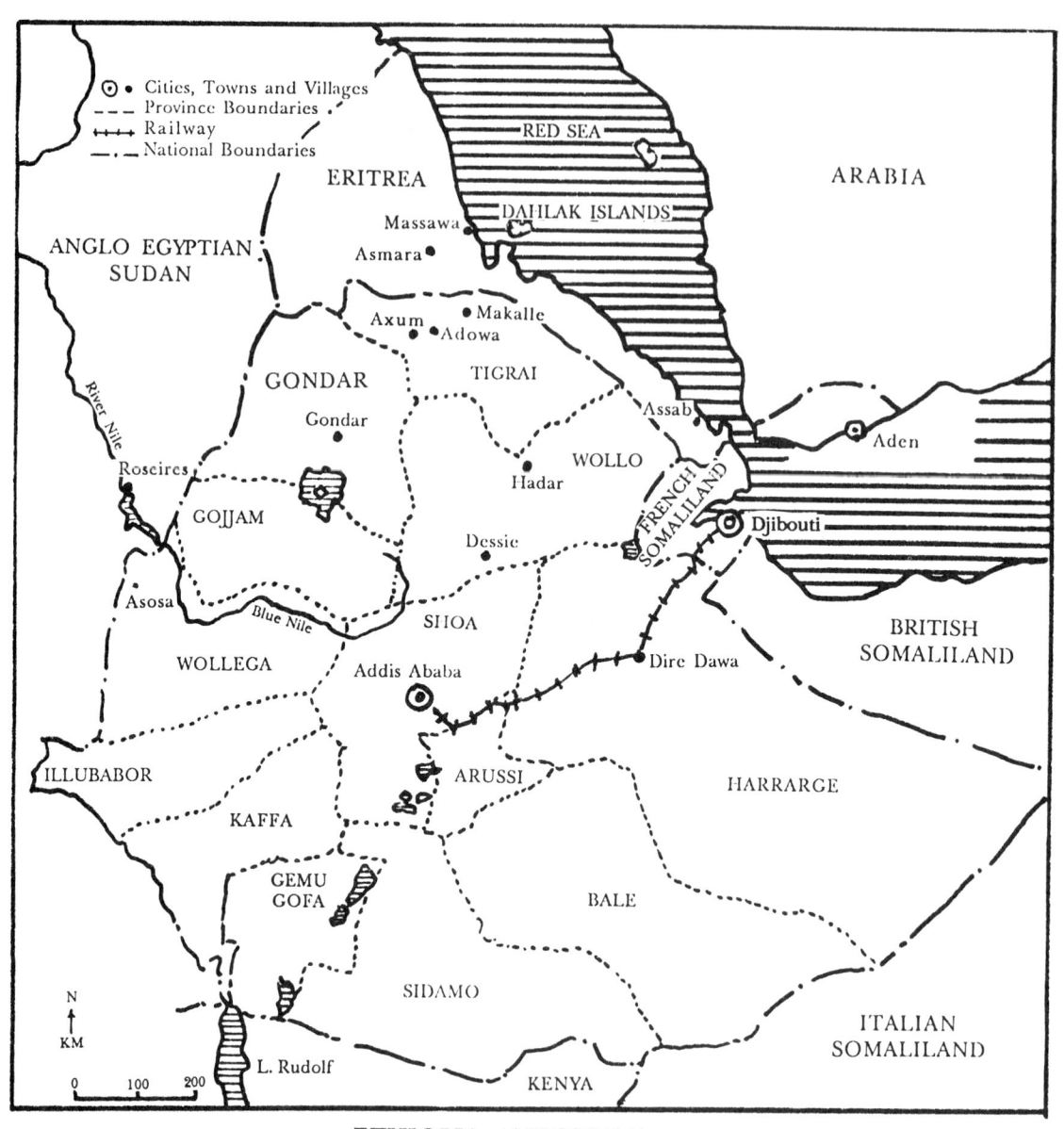

Cities, Towns and Villages
Province Boundaries
Railway
National Boundaries

RED SEA

DAHLAK ISLANDS

ERITREA

ARABIA

ANGLO EGYPTIAN
SUDAN

Massawa

Asmara

Axum • Makalle
• Adowa

GONDAR

TIGRAI

Gondar

WOLLO

Assab

Aden

Roseires

Hadar

GOJJAM

Dessie

FRENCH SOMALILAND

Djibouti

Asosa

Blue Nile

SHOA

BRITISH
SOMALILAND

WOLLEGA

Addis Ababa

Dire Dawa

ILLUBABOR

ARUSSI

HARRARGE

KAFFA

GEMU
GOFA

BALE

N
↑
KM

SIDAMO

ITALIAN
SOMALILAND

0   100   200

L. Rudolf

KENYA

ETHIOPIA (ABYSSINIA)
1935

60

Meanwhile in Ethiopia the war went on. The result was a forgone conclusion as the Italians gradually smashed all Haile Selassie's armies using all the modern weaponry at their disposal including machine guns, tanks and aircraft. The Emperor's troops were bombed extensively with high explosive bombs and mustard gas delivered by the Italian Air Force. The Duce's own two sons Vittorio and Bruno Mussolini flew in one of the bomber squadrons there. Red Cross ambulance units and centres of population were not spared in a foretaste of what was to come in World War II. The few aircraft the Ethiopians could still muster were confined to communications, reconnaissance and ambulance work. The chief pilot then was Babicheff, after the departure of Corriger, who had been recalled to France at the end of 1935. By April 1936, however, most of the aircraft had been destroyed on the ground by Italian bombing raids and strafing by fighter aircraft.

The remaining soldiers-of-fortune still in Ethiopia hastened to leave while they could. Robinson was sent on a fund raising tour to the USA (he returned in 1944 to set up a pilot training centre before dying in Addis Ababa as a result of a crash in 1954).[7] Vincent Schmidt fell out with Babicheff, who denounced him as a German/Italian spy, and was expelled; he paid a visit to de Wet in London shortly afterwards before returning to Paris. Drouillet also left but Weber, von Rosen (who had carried out much valuable and dangerous flying for the Red Cross ambulance units) and Hilaire du Berrier remained until the end. This came on 5 May 1936 when the Italian forces took Addis Ababa. The Emperor had fled for Palestine en route to England at the beginning of the month.

Weber flew out to the Sudan in the Junkers W 33c just before the Italians' arrival in the capital but, from June to August 1936, von Rosen continued to operate one of the ambulance aircraft in the unoccupied western provinces, supporting guerilla units, accompanied by one Captain Maurice Brophil, RN, from Ireland. Another British ex-RAF pilot, Charles Hayter from Whitchurch in Hampshire, also left Ethiopia before the Italians took over. This 35 year old pilot had brought over a de Havilland D.H.84 Dragon (G-ACKD) from England in January for Red Cross use and had stayed on to fly the aircraft, surviving the crash which destroyed it in late February. He was to make the headlines again at the end of the year when he was fined for smuggling cigars and brandy into Britain from France. Hayter rejoined the RAF during World War II and flew for a few months despite the fact that he was now in his forties.[8]

Charles Hayter next to his D.H.84 Dragon (G-ACKD) at Akaki, Ethiopia, February 1936. Note Lion of Judah painted on nose of aircraft. (From Ole G. Nordbø archives)

Whilst Hugh lived as best he could in London off the money he had obtained from his articles, his friend Hilaire du Berrier continued to follow his adventurous career back in Africa. He had acted as an agent for the Central News Agency of London after their man had left Addis Ababa and continued to send telegrams out of the beleagured capital until the end. Captured by the Italian forces entering Addis Ababa, du Berrier managed to escape to Djibouti after a few days where he remained for a month hoping to obtain a position with the Iman of Yemen. The job fell through so he took ship to visit friends in Rumania. There, on the terrace of a hotel in Cluj one day in mid-July 1936, the waiter handed him a newspaper that told of a revolt of a group of army generals in Spain that was to bring Hugh and himself together once again.

Hilaire du Berrier, being a strong monarchist and a friend of the Spanish prince Don Juan de Bourbon, decided at once to offer his services to the Nationalist forces in Spain, under General Franco, who had rebelled against the elected left-wing government. He wrote to his friend de Wet in London to tell him of his intentions, packed his bags and made his way to Tangier. There he contacted Don Caesar Alba, Franco's envoy, who said that he was unable to do anything to help and hinted that this was because du Berrier had been against the Italians in Ethiopia. Fascist Italy now had much influence with the rebel Spanish generals because, together with Nazi Germany, it had commenced to supply much material and manpower support for the Nationalist cause.

Du Berrier next tried his luck in France but Franco's representative in Paris would not see him for fear of causing problems with the strongly pro-Spanish Republican government in France. He decided to make one last attempt to get into the war on Franco's side in London, where he arrived in mid September to be met at the station by Hugh, resplendent in green pork pie hat and plaid suit, carrying a cane with a metal tip on the bottom – he never wore an overcoat, on the theory that the way to avoid colds was to harden himself against the cold. Hugh had spent the summer following his career as a would-be artist and writer, although he had never found time to reply to any of du Berrier's letters.

Du Berrier intended to stay in London just long enough to contact Franco's representative there, or failing that, to try and arrange to cover the Spanish War for the Central News Agency. Hugh, who by this time had little or no money left to live on, was eager to join his globe-trotting American friend in any new project or adventure that he dreamed up.

The two reunited friends chanced to meet one day, in the Gloucester House Hotel, Captain Dobinson whom they knew from Ethiopia. Dobinson had been transport officer for the British Red Cross ambulance unit. Du Berrier and de Wet edged up to the reception counter beside him and du Berrier said, in Amharic (Ethiopian); *"Tenastiling, Geyta. Dehenna, dehennanu?"* (Greetings to you, Master. Are you feeling well?) Without a sign of surprise, Dobinson slipped into unctuous Amharic, as though he had seen them the day before, much to the surprise of the people around. He told them that he had been in the part of Spain controlled by the rebels with a Red Cross team. Hearing of their desire to join forces with Franco he scribbled something on a piece of paper and gave it to du Berrier saying . . . "Here is the name and address of a man to contact, but don't tell him who gave you the information." The name on the paper was *The Marquis de Portago, Dorchester Hotel*. Unfortunately it was all in vain as the Marquis refused to see either du Berrier or de Wet despite countless telephone calls over the period of a couple of weeks.

Disheartened, the two men gave up the effort. Hugh persuaded du Berrier to stay on in England for a while. The two out-of-luck would-be aviators rented a damp houseboat on the River Lea near Broxbourne Aerodrome, Nazeing, Essex. Du Berrier wanted to obtain a British private pilot's licence so he joined the Herts and Essex Aero Club based at the airfield and started to build up the necessary flying hours. He also hoped to purchase his own small private aircraft. He later obtained his licence but not the aircraft.

One morning in early October Hugh borrowed ten shillings (50p) from his friend and went down to London where he paid a visit to the Spanish Embassy and offered his services as a pilot to the Spanish Republican Government. He returned again to the Embassy the following day and met Vincent Doherty, a South African by birth and a former RAF pilot, who had been wounded whilst flying in Spain and who was now in England to recruit further pilots (see Chapter 7). Hugh was accepted by Doherty, pending a check out of his flying ability, and informed that he would receive £20 for every pilot he could recruit himself. Unknown to Hugh his visits to the Spanish Embassy had been duly noted by the Special Branch who reported to the Foreign Office on the 8 October 1936 that "... It is understood that the Spanish Embassy in London is trying to secure the services of a pilot named Mr. H. Olaff of the Broxbourne Flying Club, Essex ..."[9]

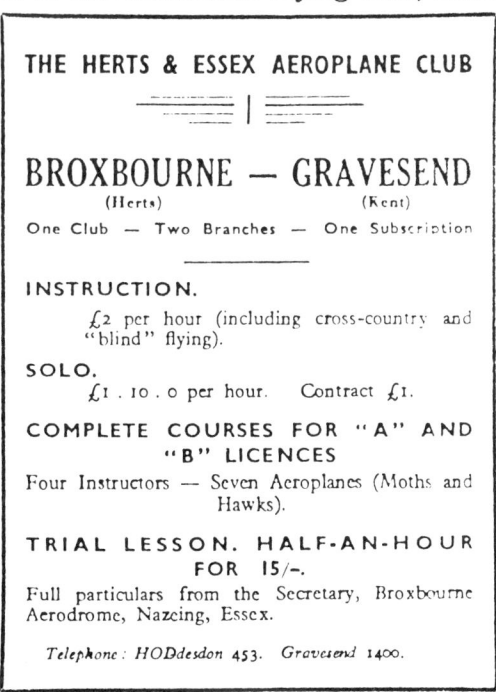

Advertisement for flying lessons at the Herts & Essex Aeroplane Club, 1936.

These visits to the Embassy had been made by de Wet without the knowledge of Hilaire du Berrier, who was most surprised the following morning when Hugh told him that, since Franco did not want to have his services because of the Italians, he was going to Spain to fly for the Republicans – communists or not – just to fight the Italians. Hugh asked du Berrier if he would like to join him (not mentioning the bonus he had been offered by Doherty) and said they would be able to gather material for future publication on the communist influence in Republican Spain and, especially, the Russian aircraft and personnel. Hilaire du Berrier did not take much persuading – the attraction of the combination of adventure, danger and intrigue was enough in itself without the promise of the lucrative contract on offer – a salary of £180 per month plus a bonus of £300 for each enemy aircraft destroyed, £800 for any permanent injury received and £2,000 in case of death. All hotel bills would also be paid by the Spanish authorities whilst they were in Spain.

MINISTERIO DE MARINA Y AIRE
SUBSECRETARIA DEL AIRE

CONTRATO

Entre el Gobierno de la Republica Española representado por el Sr. Subsecretario del Aire y Don H. Du Berrier, de nacionalidad inglesa, se ha estipulado el presente contrato con arreglo a las siguientes condiciones:

PRIMERA - D. H. Du Berrier estará a la disposición del Gobierno español para toda clase de trabajos aeronauticos relacionados con cu profesión en territorio español.

SEGUNDA - El plazo de duración de este contrato será el de un més, que empieza a contarse a partir del dia cuatro de noviembre del ano actual, y que será renovable por meses completos de conformidad de ambas partes.

TERCERA - se abonará a D.H. Du Berrier CIENTO OCHENTA libras mensuales, que se situarán en Inglaterra en el Banco que designe, por mediación de la Embajada española.

Tambien se abonarán a D.H. Du Berrier los gastos de manutención, y de viaje de regreso a su país. Estos pagos se harán en Madrid.

CUARTA - Se establece una prima de TRESCIENTAS libras que percibirá D.H. Du Berrier por cada aparato enemigo destruido, previa comprobación.

QUINTA - D.H. Du Berrier queda aseguradi en caso de imposibilidad física en la cantidad de OCHOCIENTAS libras y en caso de muerte en la cantidad de DOS MIL libras. Estas cantidades serán satisfechas en la misma forma que los haberes mensuales.

SEXTA - D.H. Du Berrier disfrutará de un día libre completo en cada semana.

SEPTIMA - D.H. Du Berrier reconoce como Jefe para sus relaciones con el mando español asi como para las incidencias a que diere lugar este contrato al Sr. Subsecretario del Aire.

Y conforme con estas estitpulaciones, los firmamos, por duplicade, en Madrid a cuatro de noviembre de mil novecientos treinta y seis.

EL SUBSECRETARIO   *EL PILOTO*

Hilaire du Berrier's contract with the Spanish Republic as a pilot. Note that he was considered British because he had been recruited in London with de Wet. (Courtesy Hilaire du Berrier)

Hilaire du Berrier decided to enlist and accompanied Hugh to London where he too was introduced to Doherty – no mention was made that his friend had received £20 for recruiting him. On 17 October they were introduced by Doherty to two other pilots he had recruited, George Fachiri and Robert Bannister Pickett. George Fachiri, of average height, born in Liverpool on 5 September 1902, was the eldest son of a well-to-do family – his grandparents had come over to England from Greece in the mid nineteenth century. Fachiri had been educated at the famous public school at Uppingham (he was often to be seen wearing the old school tie) and initially went into the cotton trade after leaving school. In 1927 he took a Short Service Commission in the RAF and spent three years in the Middle East learning to fly at No. 4 Flying Training School, Abu-Sueir, and then being posted to No. 45 (Bomber) Squadron at Helwan where he flew de Havilland D.H.9A and Fairey IIIF aircraft. After leaving the service at the end of 1930 he ran a branch of his family's business in Bombay for a while before returning to England where he tried his hand working in the building trade. Short of funds and having, like so many of the educated liberal members of his generation, a great dislike for the Fascist ideology, he offered his services to the Republican cause as a pilot despite his lack of flying hours since leaving the RAF.

Robert Bannister Pickett was a different type of man altogether. Born in London on 11 July 1915, he came from a good middle-class family and obtained a private pilot's licence at the early age of 17. Tall, strong and an excellent pilot he was still in many ways an adolescent – tending to be very eccentric at times, surly, tactless and belligerent. Like Hugh, his father had found him quite a handful and was not able to settle him into a respectable career. Pickett had applied for a Short Service Commission in the RAF in the spring of 1936 but had only stayed in the service for three weeks.[10]

Doherty drove the four men out to Heston aerodrome where their flying ability was to be assessed. He indicated an Avro Cadet (G-ACHO) and told them that he wanted several aerobatic manouevres performed by each of them in turn including a loop – they were to be accompanied by a pilot named Davies in the front cockpit. Suddenly showing a certain nervousness Fachiri took de Wet aside and asked him if he could explain what was required. Hugh, surprised at such a question, asked Fachiri if he knew how to perform the manouevres. Fachiri replied that he did but would like to be reminded how to carry them out. Hugh quickly outlined the actual movements of the aircraft controls required.

A minute of silence followed the explanation. Fachiri then asked Hugh to repeat all he had said, only this time much more slowly. Amused by the request but at the same time concerned about Fachiri, Hugh took a piece of paper from his pocket and wrote out all of what he had said. Fachiri took the paper and spent the next half hour walking up and down learning by heart what de Wet had written down, waiting for his turn to fly. Much to Hugh's amazement and relief, the nervous Fachiri performed the aerobatics brilliantly.

The flying tests being successful for all four pilots they were given several lectures over the next few days by Doherty on how to attack the Italian and German aircraft they would be fighting in Spain. They were also told that they would be picking up some Dewoitine fighter aircraft in France and flying these over the border into Spain.

Rugby Football team of No. 45 (Bomber) Squadron RAF, 1930. George Fachiri seated on extreme right, middle row. (The Aeroplane)

Robert Bannister Pickett, 1932. (Courtesy RAF Museum)

On 30 October Doherty and his four new recruits flew from Croydon to Paris where they went to the Spanish Embassy to collect safe conducts for their journey to Spain. The next day de Wet, du Berrier, Fachiri and Pickett were put aboard the night train for Toulouse where they were to collect their aircraft at the secret aerodrome that the Popular Front government in France, which was sympathetic to the Republican cause, had turned over to the Spaniards. As no aircraft had arrived by 3 November they flew to Spain on an *Air France* civil aircraft, piloted by the famous French pilot Lucien Cornet.

George Fachiri had with him a lucky-charm, a small crucifix, which had been given to him by a young girl in Toulouse when she heard that he was going to fight in Spain. This was nearly to have disastrous consequences for him in Loyalist Spain as being a symbol carried by the followers of Franco.

The noisy, vibrating trimotor aircraft with its load of mail and ten dozing passengers crossed the snow-covered Pyrenees at 15,000 feet and then dropped lower and lower until it landed at Barcelona, where it was refuelled for its flight onwards to Madrid. It was early morning on 4 November 1936 as the lumbering machine, now flying at 300 feet over the red sun-baked earth to avoid being detected by roving Nationalist fighters, approached the beleagured capital of Spain. The armies of General Franco, numbering some 25,000 well-trained soldiers, were converging towards Madrid on a long arc from the north-west to the south-west and were now no more than fifteen miles from the city. The first sight to greet Hugh, as the aircraft landed at Barajas aerodrome nine miles to the east of Madrid, was the many burnt-out, broken-backed aircraft to be seen scattered around the field, the broken windows of the Custom House and the roofless hangars, the result of the daily bombing raids on the airfield. The transport aircraft, as soon as it was refuelled, took off again in a cloud of dust bound for safer skies.

The four new pilots were met by armed militiamen who, at once, conducted them to a car. They were taken to the *Ministerio de Marina y Aire* in the centre of Madrid, where they signed their contracts for a month's service as pilots, renewable with the agreement of both parties on a month to month basis. After all the necessary forms had been signed and formalities completed with the Sub-Secretary for Air, Colonel Antonio Camacho Benitez, the deals were clinched over a whisky and soda.

Hugh and the others were then taken by a group of militiamen through the crowded streets of Madrid to the Hotel Florida, where many of the foreign pilots flying for the Republic were staying. Journalists from all over the world were also there to report the battle for the city expected to start any day. One of the first men to greet them was Eric Griffiths, from New Zealand (see Chapter 8), whose right arm was in plaster from the explosive bullet he had taken in the shoulder during an air battle. Soon they were introduced to other foreign pilots, including a dashing Frenchman, Abel Guides, and a short, thickset American named Ben Leider, both of whom were to be killed later in 1937 whilst flying in Spain.

After a bath and a change of clothes, Hugh felt much better and went down to enjoy his evening meal. Sitting down at one of the vacant tables with his friends Hugh called over to one of the militiamen carrying plates to and fro, "Waiter". The man, who was wearing white overalls and carried a pistol, came over to their table looking very angry and said, "Don't ever call me 'Waiter' – I am 'Comrade' to you." He served them their dinner just the same.

During their meal the hotel was shook by several explosions nearby and the rattle of anti-aircraft fire could be heard. The bombardment continued on and off practically all night, and it was a haggard and red-eyed de Wet who emerged from his room next morning. Hugh had persuaded Eric Griffiths to stay the night at the hotel when the bombing had started – this turned out to be extremely lucky for him as the hospital where he was convalescing had fallen into the hands of Franco's Moorish troops during the night.

Hugh, du Berrier, Fachiri and Pickett made their way out into the streets of Madrid after breakfast. Here they found masses of people going about their daily duties, men clearing up the streets after the bombing raids, banners stretched across the streets bearing the slogan *"No pasaran"* (They shall not pass), made famous at the French defence of Verdun in World War I. There were also many refugees fleeing the oncoming armies of Franco. Despite the grimness of the situation Hugh and du Berrier decided to take advantage of the ingenuous nature of the young Pickett. They explained to him, most seriously, that one reason for all the crowds to be seen was that the famous English soccer club, the Arsenal, were playing a match in Madrid the following day and many of the people had come to see it. He took them at their word.

Later that day they went again to the *Ministerio de Marina y Aire* where Hugh and du Berrier played another joke on Pickett. This time they bypassed the door marked AIR MINISTER and entered by that marked NAVAL MINISTER. Pickett, who did not realise both these services were located in the same building, showed his surprise. Hugh told him, again with a straight face, that the Spanish Government had decided that they were not to be employed as pilots but they were to serve in submarines. Pickett swore violently and said "I am a pilot and only a pilot." Then, suddenly calming down, remarked "Never mind, if they give me £300 for sinking each ship as they were going to give for shooting down each aircraft, I'll accept. Aeroplane or submarine, I am only here for the money." It was some time before he discovered the trick that had been played on him.

The four men left Madrid in the evening of 5 November 1936. They were accompanied by an interpreter named Alberto and the American pilot, Ben Leider. Alberto caried with him various safe-conducts and other documents picked up by them earlier that day at the Ministry. Pickett was in a bad temper both because of the trick that had been paid on him earlier and because he thought he would be missing the 'big match' arranged for the next day.

They started their journey in a requisitioned large Chrysler car driven by Alberto through the darkened streets of Madrid. The car journey never seemed to end. No headlights were used and the car was stopped every 100 yards or so at first by groups of armed militiamen who had set up road-blocks. Here all the documents had to be shown and long explanations made as to why they were travelling from Madrid. Even when they, at last, left the city behind the journey did not improve – their chauffeur took them by a roundabout route over rough minor roads. Ben Leider, who was very serious-minded and a paid-up member of the Communist Party, insisted in giving his views on World politics and trying to convert the others to his beliefs, without any success.

At last they reached their destination, Albacete, where Leider left (to the others' relief) to rejoin his unit. The aircraft they had been promised were not at the airfield so they were given dinner and plenty of wine and were told they would be driven on to another base in the morning. Unfortunately, the Spanish official told them, there was no sleeping accommodation available and they would have to make the best of the situation. Hugh was tired – they had driven most of the night through the pincer movement closing around Madrid – and irritable. He started demanding a bed and berating the Spaniards with the smattering of the language that he had picked up. With his part-Dutch, part-Irish temperament and the effects of too much wine he became insulting. A militiaman asked if he was a *Camarada* (comrade). Hugh spat on the floor to show them what he thought of Communists. The militiamens' leader gave an order and six men picked up their rifles. It took some hard and serious talking by du Berrier, who spoke Spanish fluently, to convince them that de Wet, in the air, was an "ace" pilot but on the ground was crazy. From the way Hugh had talked to them it was obvious that he was fearless and du Berrier convinced the Spaniards that it was better for him to be killed in the air fighting the enemy rather than in front of a firing squad in Albacete.

The next morning they were taken further south to the military airbase and village of Los Alcázares, on the shores of a large lagoon formed by Cape Palos on the Mediterranean Sea. After leaving his few belongings at the hotel Hugh wandered into the deserted streets – only a few elderly people were to be seen there. Most houses appeared to be empty and had notices posted on them that they had been requisitioned by the government. The small church had a large red flag flying outside where the cross had stood. Inside, the building was filled with petrol tins and aircraft parts – fuselages, wings and tail units.

Later that morning Hugh, du Berrier, Fachiri and Pickett were taken to the naval air base at San Javier, some nine miles further north from Los Alcázares. This was one the finest airfields in Spain, a large rectangle, perfectly smooth with an excellent sod surface. Stationed here was a fighter training school where young pilots were instructed before being posted to their operational units. The school was under the command of Commandante Juan Alwal, a short, slightly built, energetic man about 30 years of age. Here the four men were to be given their final flight checkout. The school had several aircraft – two dilapidated looking Nieuport Ni-D.52 fighters, three Dewoitine D.372 fighters, several Breguet Br.19 two-seat biplane bombers, three Focke-Wulf FW.56 "Stosser" biplanes (originally sent from Switzerland to Ethiopia for Haile Selassie but never arrived; after much journeying they had been purchased by the Spanish government agents and off-loaded from a British ship at Alicante in October), a small Caudron C.600 "Aigion", used by Commandante Alwal himself, and a Miles M.2H Hawk Major (still bearing its British registration G-ADDC). The last named aircraft was one of the many British civil aircraft that found their way to both sides in the Spanish

Civil War despite all the efforts of the British authorities. The Republican markings were to be seen on most of these aircraft – a wide red band around the fuselage covering the area between the cockpit and tailplane, chordwise around the wings, and the national colours of red, yellow and purple in stripes on the rudder.

The flight tests being successfully completed on the Miles Hawk, the four pilots had the chance to fly the other aircraft. Hugh soon found that the Nieuport Ni-D.52 sesquiplane fighter, which had been the main Spanish fighter aircraft at the outbreak of the war, was no easy aircraft to fly. It swung like hell at take-off, handled like a heavy lorry, had a top speed of no more than 156mph and was armed with two light Vickers machine guns. The Breguet Br.19, also an obsolete design of 1925 vintage, was a sturdy, rather rotund looking biplane that had established an outstanding reputation for reliability in Spain. The "Dix-Neuf", built under licence in Spain together with the Nieuport Ni-D.52, had been the main bomber aircraft of the Spanish Air Force prior to the war and both sides in the conflict still operated many of them. Its 450hp engine gave it only a top speed of around 145mph. Wallowing along under the power of their single engine Hugh thought how like the pictures of the German Taubes of World War I they looked, with their swept-back wing tips. The Spaniards called the Breguet Br.19 the "Guardian Angel"; they said no one was ever killed in them. Hugh hoped fervently that this was the case.

Nieuport Ni-D.52 C1 of Republican Air Force, 1936. (The Aviation Bookshop)

At the other end of the airfield and strictly "out of bounds" to all the British pilots were to be seen several modern looking aircraft. These were some of the new Russian equipment that was arriving for the Republic together with pilots and ground personnel. The pilots were also staying at Los Alcázares but stuck together and avoided contact with Hugh and his friends. The sleek-looking biplane fighter aircraft, the Polikarpov I-15 – soon to be dubbed the *Chato* (snub nosed) by the Spaniards – were transported to Los Alcázares for assembly under Russian supervision as they were off-loaded at the port of Cartagena. They had just made their appearance in the skies over Madrid causing much concern to the Nationalists. Also to be seen later by Hugh were several sleek twin-engined bombers – Tupolev SB-2, named *Katiuska* by the Spanish Republicans. Hugh could not help but admire this fine piece of craftsmanship no doubt capable of speeds exceeding those obtainable by any of the single-seater fighters operating at that time in Spain. He was told that these aircraft were modifications of the American Martin 139 bomber – a fable fostered by the Spaniards by issuing photographs of the American bomber with Spanish markings superimposed. The Russians had become the great hope of the Republicans and saviours of the Cause.

A week later, on 13 November 1936, Hugh and George Fachiri were transferred further north to Valencia leaving du Berrier (who was being used as an interpreter and translator by the Spaniards because he could speak so many languages) and Pickett at San Javier. The battle for Madrid was still raging with the eyes of the world on the events in Spain. In true mercenary style and because, no doubt, of the obsolete aircraft they were told to fly both Hugh and George Fachiri refused to fly on operations until they had received some of their agreed salary in order to meet expenses.

Hugh and George Fachiri were to spend several weeks flying out of Manises airfield at Valencia. It was a very gentlemanly sort of war with transport every day to take them to lunch. They both refused to wear uniforms and flew in open shirts and slacks. Their main job was to provide the dawn patrols – fighter defence against bombing attacks on Valencia flying the antiquated Nieuport Ni-D.52, which Hugh came to loathe. They also piloted the lumbering Breguet Br.19 on coastal patrols, with a Spanish observer-rear gunner-bomb aimer in the rear cockpit, carrying a 225lb bomb under each wing if any likely targets presented themselves. Hugh was later to describe a typical uneventful patrol.[11]

Ten miles from the shore. Ambling through the blue sky in an old Bréguet 'Dix Neuf.' Indifferently I glance seawards, not because I expect to see the rebel warships for which I have been sent to search, but really for lack of another pastime.

I am tired of staring vacantly at the dash-board, littered with all its corroded, its inanimate instuments. They look at me blankly, fixed as the eyes of a plaster cast.

Twice I have kicked the compass – pretty hard – just to see if that would increase its permanent deviation of approximately 100 degrees. Nothing happened. My course 10 magnetic; the instrument between my knees registers 106. That would land me somewhere near Algiers.

White gulls circle about the fishing boats scattered on the patched,the chequered sea. White wisps race across the surface, footmarks on a floor of green. Far out beneath the wing-tip a P. & O. – no mistaking its dark hull – ploughs its way homeward. I should like, for memories of the past, to go closer. I should like to have a good look at her. I dare not. Were I alone it would be a different matter. The recollection of that awful moment of suspense before the two bombs had splashed into the sea! That had been three days ago. Flying over an in-offensive tramp steamer of God knows what nationality, the man in the back seat had tried his luck. "No, no. I shall not go near that liner," I say to myself.

Humming like a determined bee, the Gnome-Rhône keeps in time to the rattle of the ill-lifting cowling, the aluminium engine-cover ever threatening to break away from the frail slit-pins to hurtle by in the slip-stream. What old, lazy, comfortable aircraft these are! Feet on the dashboard, I close my eyes and sense the drone of the engine, the steady vibration. I can feel the contours of my face, the sun hitting the raised flesh. The noise of the exhaust, the cylinder explosions fade – fade to form a background for the small sounds; the small voice of the tappets. Now I am slumbering.

The rattle of a machine gun. No, it is not a dream, and I swing about in my seat. My companion is squirting his gun at two distant shapes below; two destroyers chalking a thin line across the sea. The Spaniard grins with all the naïveté of a child when a stoppage puts an end to his game.

The air war was not always so quiet for Hugh. He met the German Heinkel He 51 biplane fighters flown by the Nationalist Air Force. This aircraft, which had been supplied in some numbers to Franco's forces, was greatly superior to the Nieuport with a top speed of over 200mph. Hugh later told of one patrol.

Far below, dreamily meandering, like fat carp in a Flemish pond – the five Bréguets. It seems that they hardly progress at all; it might almost be that the earth moves away from them. A little distance ahead, the pilot of the 'Vickers' – as the Spaniards call it; it is actually a sort of bastard 'Vildebeest' built in Spain and powered with an Hispano-Suiza motor – is now doing his best to keep in touch with the other bombers, his engine so well throttled back that he must be nearly stalling.

It is a clear and lovely day; the broad province of Valencia spreads out beneath us: the garden of Spain. Clouds rest lightly on the distant mountains. It is warm and very comfortable in my Nieuport. Close on either side are my two companions.

We have soon left the bombers far behind, and we hasten on to reconnoitre the postion they are to attack: a battery of howitzers on the Teruel front. All along our track are small villages and in the streets are people talking; sometimes three together will turn their faces upwards; small dots, pale and luminous.

It is good to have had reliable information that there are no enemy air bases in the vicinity; for ours is a pretty moth-eaten fleet. For once, I think, I shall have a flight over the lines unmolested. I am thinking thus when Narrango swings out in front of me. It does not take me long to see what he is drawing my attention to. It takes me less time to turn the flight back. Full throttle, noses slightly down, getting every ounce out of the Nieuports, we head back for those far glinting shapes, the Bréguets. Frightened? No, just common-sense; much the same instinct as stops people walking on live rails. Three dark blobs far away – fifteen rebel fighters – that is all I had seen; that is all I had waited to see.

Now as the heavy Delage drags me away to safety, I am thinking what a glorious opportunity this would have been for a suicidal maniac. For a moment I slip down into my seat to peer at my reflection in the dark face of the altimeter; I want to see if I have a sort of 'wind-up' expression stamped on my features, and if I have, how to avoid it. Regrettably there is nothing new – just the same ordinary face that I shave every morning. I am a trifle disappointed.

My two companions give way as I throttle in close up to the 'Vickers.' I am so near I can clearly see the sunken cheeks of the Rumanian gunner, gypsy-like in his scarlet helmet of knitted wool. It does not take the pilot very long to understand the meaning of the crossed arms I lift from my cockpit. The red dusty bombs under the wing lift high as he banks his machine into a turn; there they hang, like large, excessively large sausages upon an inverted counter.

So we turn for home. The Bréguets seem to go even slower now that we are in a hurry. We can just keep pace with them by holding the Nieuports on the brink of a stall. Gazing back, I can see the enemy lined out across the sky, hard in pursuit. Maniscs seems miles away. Distantly the sea smiles wanly upon our wish. The fields, the plantations, the coloured roofs, the winding roads all seem to urge us on – frantically – as futilely as the crowd on the 'rails.'

Thirteen Heinkels; no mistaking them now. No, I am not feeling sick inside, I have noticed that one does not feel that way when practically certain that it is 'all up': there is only a great emptiness in me. I am thinking how foolish it all is.

As we climb, the Bréguets drop away close to the ground. There with a good back gunner – they are two-seater bombers – they are assured of a large degree of safety; in fact, they are often more secure than some of the multi-gunned bombers. Bellies close to the hard earth, no single-seater fighter is able to attack them from underneath; the enemy is made to operate within the gunner's field of fire.

Sixteen white St Andrew's crosses is the pattern I see dropping on to the Bréguets. Half rolling we have hardly started our dive when we find ourselves involved with the other flight of Heinkels; they are there suddenly all about us. Five of them black against the sun. Gone. Dragging round, holding our formation, again we see them a mile away above us. We climb desperately. Then it seems all aircraft everywhere. The sharp dagger-like noses of the Heinkels, broad plate-like tail-planes of the Nieuports; the instant glimpse of an undercarriage. The far horizon, the checkered land, aircraft and little clouds plunging in an out of the pool of blue sky between my planes. A burst at a flashing enemy, then up with the nose again; climbing, climbing, the stench of my engine getting hotter and hotter.

Something is telling me all the time that the combat cannot last for long. We are close to Manises, our aerodrome; the enemy far into our territory. If only we can hold out for a little longer against the numbers and speed of our opponents! Into a turn. A burst at a mottled machine. Holding her in the turn – the other two Nieuports, I see them still in the air, moving sluggishly compared with the German fighters.

It comes suddenly, my opportunity – a Heinkel climbing. I am between the sun and him, perhaps he has not seen me.

Whipping stick and rudder over I aim at the side of my foe. He has not seen me; he continues climbing. And by God I shall have him! I am certain of it. A tremendously good feeling within me, a deep satisfaction. I feel I should like to be suspended like this for ever, grasping all the wealth of joy in the one transparent moment. The roaring engine. Cold draught.

Close ahead of me he is still climbing unconsciously. The moment has come. He is there, a small, small fly imprisoned in the window of my sights.

I close my hand on the trigger.

There is deathly stillness. Not the slightest shudder. Both my guns are jammed. I sweep far past my target. Away below I once more see the St Andrew's crosses, now heading away.

A dull thunder as though there is somebody hammering the centre section. A spray of liquid hits my chest, saturates me coldly. God! Petrol! The pungent scent, the coldness of it – unmistakable. I can see it pouring from a bullet-hole in the starboard tank, whipped away in the slip-stream. I have undone my harness. Tensely I wait for the flames and the next burst of fire from the enemy. All seems strangely silent since I switched off the motor – the whistle of the wind in the wires, the rush of it along the fuselage, the dead propeller in front of me. we are gliding steeply. I cannot see my attacker; I feel that he must now be underneath me. But glancing this way and that at last I see the whole enemy formation heading away. It is over!

Now all my faculties are concentrated upon getting the crippled machine to the field; during the engagement the wind has carried us nearer to it. I can see it fairly close. Though my machine is losing altitude very rapidly I feel that I can make it; in any case there is nowhere else to try to get to.

A long steep glide takes me there. Soaked in petrol I am thanking my lucky stars that it was not an incendiary that got the tank. I put her down with a wallop on the field.

The 'Vickers' is already there. Three of the Bréguets are also in. As the mechanics drag my machine to the tarmac I learn that only one of the bombers was forced down. To me it all seems too amazing to be real; it is like some fantastic dream in which all of our wishes come true. Thirteen Heinkels against nine old crocks and they only got two of us. What different thoughts I had had on seeing them closing in behind!

Wandering past the hangar I can hear the deep back-firing of a Gnome-Rhône – the last of the Bréguets coming in; vaguely I wait for the rumble of the wheels.

It happens just as I reach the door of the canteen. The first thunder of the explosions I hardly hear:

73

what seems more shocking is the awful silence that follows, the tinkling of falling glass that sounds very far way. A dull throbbing in my head. I am running back from where I have come, quite mechanically. Back to the field, back to the disaster. And then – 'Why?' I think to myself, 'Why go back there?' 'Yes, why should I drag myself there?' Sitting upon an empty oil-drum I repeat the question to myself, but I can find no reasonable answer.

I know that there are people running past close by me, hurrying and calling. I know that something dreadful has happened. I know well enough; I do not have to be told that the Bréguet piled up on landing with her load of bombs, bombs that should not have gone off even so. The pilot was probably wounded: misjudged his height from the ground.

A dumb, rather stupid stillness settles on my brain. I do not disturb it. I believe that I am at one hundred other places but where I am; I am therefore happy.

Occasionally Hugh had the chance to fly the French Dewoitine D.372 parasol monoplane fighter on patrols. This was the best fighter he flew in Spain, being highly manoeuvrable, with a top speed of 236mph and a wonderful climb. It was a match for the Heinkel He 51 and even the superb Italian biplane fighter, the Fiat CR.32, in the right hands. He also flew another French fighter, the gull-winged Loire 46. He thought that this was "far too pretty to be a fighter" although, when the engine cut out (which was often) it glided as steady as a rock. This aircraft had exceptional climbing ability but lacked power. Unfortunately, Hugh never had a flight in the solitary Hawker Fury, which only the commanding officer was allowed to fly. On one occasion, however, Hugh flew a captured Fiat CR.32, arguably the best biplane fighter in Spain, on a test flight. He was able to examine the four different kinds of ammunition in the machine-gun belt of the Fiat fighter, firstly, an incendary, next a soft-nosed expanding bullet (the nickel shell had a small incision in the nose so that when it struck a solid object the lead would be squeezed out of the aperture), then a nickel bullet with an explosive charge and a standard bullet. He was now able to appreciate the reason for the terrible wounds inflicted to any pilot unlucky enough to be hit in the air battles. He was also able to see the new Russian monoplane fighter, the Polikarpov I-16, that had just arrived in Spain. These machines, capable of over 250mph, with a retractable undercarriage and enclosed cockpit, were the forerunner of the next generation of fighter aircraft. This barrel-like little aircraft soon became known to the Spanish Republicans as the *Mosca* (fly).

During a lull in the battle, Hugh borrowed a Breguet to fly himself, plus a bouquet of roses, to a girl-friend in Alicante. George Fachiri actually flew the aircraft, with Hugh in the rear cockpit clutching the roses and some bottles of beer. Fachiri attempted to take off cross-wind and nearly wrecked the whole party by pranging a hangar. Fortunately both men escaped but the aircraft was badly damaged. Hugh drank too much from time to time and word reached du Berrier, still at San Javier, that he had scared the townspeople of Valencia by buzzing the housetops after a bout of drinking. On another occasion Hugh bombed one town only to find that his own troops had occupied it that morning.

Back at San Javier the tall, sour-faced Pickett was as eccentric as ever. He flew in a blue linen suit and borrowed beret. His only luggage seemed to be a shirt and razor tucked into a tiny bag. Usually half the shirt dangled out of this bag, which he carried around with him. He would hang around the group of pilots at night, taking no part whatever in their talk or sports. Obsessed with the idea that they were talking about him, he would glare and finally saunter over and whisper, "You don't like me, do you?" The fellow so assailed would look up with much surprise, whereupon Pickett would walk away and repeat the performance on someone else. He also made himself unpopular with the Spanish authorities by one day performing aerobatics at roof level over the house of a young girl-friend in Alicante.

On 22 November 1936, Vincent Doherty arrived in Los Alcázares with two newly recruited British pilots, Sydney Holland and Walter Coates, together with five Americans. The following day du Berrier confirmed the flying proficiency of the British pilots, and all of these new arrivals, except one of the Americans, were sent north to the Basque front as bomber pilots (see Chapter 5). A day or so later du Berrier and Pickett were transferred to La Rabasa airfield, Alicante, to help to protect the town after a heavy bombing raid that had been mounted by the Italians based on the Balearic Islands. By this time "Bobby" Pickett had seen enough of the Spanish Civil War and decided to return home to England when his contract expired in early December. Towards the end of November he paid a visit to the British Consulate in Alicante and asked to see the consul, who was not amused when Pickett gave him the clenched fist Communist salute to open the conversation and then asked to sign the visitors' book.

Hilaire du Berrier and his Nieuport Ni-D.52 fighter at La Rabasa/Alicante, November 1936. (Courtesy Hilaire du Berrier)

On the morning of the 29 November, du Berrier, Pickett and a Spanish pilot, (flying Nieuport Ni-D.52s) were on patrol over the Mediterranean Sea about twelve miles off Alicante. Suddenly, through the broken clouds below, du Berrier, flying Nieuport No 3-86, sighted a large trimotored aircraft. Certain that this was an Italian bomber on its way to bomb Alicante, du Berrier dived down and let off a stream of machine-gun bullets which seemed to strike the large aircraft. It dived away towards Alicante in a steep glide and made an emergency landing at the airfield. Imagine Hilaire du Berrier's chagrin when he landed at La Rabasa to find the aircraft that he had forced down was a Wibault airliner of *Air France* flying on the regular Toulouse-Tangiers-Casablanca route. It had a line of bullet holes across the wing midway between the cabin and fuel tank; an aileron was also damaged but, luckily, none of the passengers or crew were wounded. International complications, of course, ensued and *Air France* threatened to cease operations to Spain. Investigations followed by the Spanish authorities, but du Berrier and the other pilots decided to pin the blame on Pickett, both because he was leaving in a few days and because it was well known that he was crazy. Pickett was given his discharge and left Spain for England in early December.

Meanwhile Hugh had decided to renew his contract when it expired on 4 November 1936. George Fachiri, however, it is believed, decided to return home and had to obtain an emergency certificate from the British Consul as his passport had been retained by the Foreign Office in England.[12] Du Berrier also wished to stay on in Spain and went to the new Air Ministry in Valencia to discuss possible terms for a renewal. Unknown to him, however, he had been denounced to the local Soviet as an anti-Communist and a member of the French monarchist party, *L'Action Française*. He was arrested, interrogated for several hours, and it looked very likely that he would face a firing squad. Luckily for him, however, Colonel Alberto Bayo (who later trained Castro's guerrillas in Cuba) from the Air Ministry found out where du Berrier was being held and insisted that he was released to his custody. The fortunate American spent the night at the Air Ministry and was put on a train, under military guard, bound for France and safety the following morning.

Whilst his friend recovered in Paris from his near escape from death, Hugh successfully negotiated a renewal of his contract and continued to fly patrols from Manises airfield during December. At the end of the month he again renewed his contract as he soon spent the money he had earned. During his final month in Spain Hugh did little flying except for flying fighter aircraft from France to Barcelona, his activities being reported to British intelligence authorities by George Steer, *The Times* correspondent in Spain, in early February 1937.[13] This allowed him to visit Paris where he joined du Berrier. One day, at the Lutetia Hotel, where du Berrier was always to be found, Hugh caused quite a stir when he tried to pull his French girl-friend out of a lift — she was leaving him because he had been drinking — but he did not have a stitch of clothes on at the time and was oblivious to the lift full of passengers.

On one of his train journeys to and from Spain Hugh met a Greek arms dealer named Zacharoff (no relation to the great Sir Basil) who was one of the many shady characters trying to sell the Republicans second-hand weapons. This time it was Czech Letov and Avia aircraft. Zacharoff persuaded Hugh to act as his agent in Spain. But nothing came of his efforts to sell these aircraft to the Republicans.

Perhaps it was inevitable that, with his continuing liaison with discredited du Berrier, his thinly disguised anti-Communist views — which he was not backward in expressing after a few drinks, that de Wet too would come under suspicion as a spy. Indeed, at one time Hugh offered his services to the British authorities but was considered too unreliable to be used to report on events in Spain. Finally Hugh was arrested, interrogated, and spent a week in prison in Valencia until released and given 48 hours to leave the country. When he reached Paris, on his way home to England, de Wet called in to see du Berrier. His clothes were in a mess, with the lining of his jacket split open in the search for hidden documents — even the soles of his shoes had been pulled off by the Spanish interrogators. According to du Berrier, Hugh ordered six bottles of 1914 champagne, lay down on the floor and started to drink.

In Paris, du Berrier, not discouraged by his adventures in Spain, had another idea about how to use his talents — and that of his friends. With Charles Sweeny he set up the *L'Escadrille Étrangere.*

This was to be a private Foreign Legion of the air, available to all those who could afford it, to fight anywhere in the world. The aircraft to be used were Dutch Koolhoven FK.51 two-seater biplanes. Du Berrier managed to obtain sufficient funds to meet initial expenses by selling the story of his Spanish adventures to the French and American press.[14]

The possible first use for the new venture soon came to their notice. One day in March 1937 Sweeny came to see du Berrier and told him that he had received a confidential tip-off from the French War Ministry that the Japanese were going to start hostilities in China. He suggested that du Berrier went out to "try to get all of us in". Du Berrier thought immediately of de Wet and Vincent Schmidt (who was in Spain at the time flying night bombing missions from Barcelona for the Republic). He wrote to tell Hugh what was happening and took ship for Asia in mid April en route for Shanghai.

Back in England once again Hugh was finding that "starvation was the greatest danger in aviation". He wrote to du Berrier:

28/5/37.

Dear Hal,

How do you find China? All that you expected?
When are you coming back to the Civil War?
I heard from Freddie* the other day, he has gone to Mexico or some such place; I hope to follow him when my exchequer is a trifle more satisfactory, but at the moment I am as usual "flat broke", I think is the expression. In short in a few days I shall be on the Basque front, where I have been posted on my old contract and this time, thank God, I shan't have jittering George to put me into a state of chronic nerves.
The first trip was a ghastly show what with one thing and another — I shall never forget watching you take off in that Nieuport for the first time, I felt like a murderer. I hope that

I shall never have to be witness to a similar show for at such times I always forget that people like you and I don't die.

Isn't it funny how each time we think it is going to be the last, that we are going to have done with adventure to settle down quietly in some small corner of the world, in a little white fisherman's cottage or some secluded chalet. But we never do. And should it ever happen I believe it might prove the greatest adventure of the lot being in itself so novel. But now I am afraid I have become resigned to my wander lust; what I can't cure I suppose I had better put up with as best I may, and all said and done there are worse things than "being a little boy all one's life", which reminds me: I am enclosing a list of toys that might interest your Chinese friends – they can all be moved as soon as the credits are put up, the man I am dealing with has a Chinese licence having done business with them before and is a very reliable fellow. You need not add anything onto the prices quoted for the arms and ammunition as those figures cover you for a commission of 5% approximately 70,000 pounds sterling, in the case of the aircraft you would require further particulars of performance et cetera with which I will furnish you should you find an interested party; for your own information you could count on making something like 1,000 pounds per machine for yourself if you can sell them, and I don't see why you should have much difficulty – all of them will do over 240mph and what's good enough for the RAF ought to be good enough for the chinky-boys. See what you can do. I can sell you a complete gas factory as well if interests anybody. I haven't got any battleships or forts but I think the old Jaime Primero† should be coming on the market some day soon. Did you see that the Espana† had a bomb dropped down its funnel by a Breguet and went to the bottom like a brick, the up-draught from the explosion nearly wrecked the aeroplane as well, I am told. Were you in France when the Italians were chased all over Spain by a handful of militiamen?

Well that's that, and what a feat of energy. All going well I shall be seeing you in Tahiti, where we might rent a houseboat, but would it be any fun without those railway fireworks?

Write me here as I shall leave my forwarding address with Molly. I shall send you another line from Santander.

Hugh.

Hugh did not write to du Berrier from Santander and little is known about his attempt to rejoin the Spanish conflict except he never flew and may have been thrown in prison again before leaving Spain for good. By the summer of 1937, however, he had found his way to Paris again where he lived a precarious existence as an artist in Montmartre, spending his days at the café Chez Eugene, forming friendships with such Montmartre characters as "Ivan the Terrible", a Russian guitar-player, and demonstrating an ability to chew up wine glases without cutting his mouth. Here he also started to put down on paper some articles about his adventures in Spain. The first appeared in *Blackwood's Magazine* in the issue for November 1937 under the title "From a Pilot's Diary". This incorporated stories told him by Eric Griffiths in November 1936 about the first British pilots in Spain. He brought back his own arrival in Spain to the beginning of August 1936 and wove in these stories with his own experiences.

Meanwhile in China du Berrier had been unable to persuade the Chinese authorities to take advantage of his offer to provide an instant "air force". The Japanese, however, launched their invasion of China in July 1937 and in August du Berrier met Claire Lee Chennault, also newly arrived from the USA as an adviser to the Chinese Air Force. China wished to hire foreign pilots, on a temporary basis, to fill the gaps created by the Japanese assault and to set up their own international volunteer unit. Du Berrier recommended de Wet and Schmidt to Chennault and the Chinese embassy in Paris sent de Wet his fare from England but, after buying his ticket, Hugh arrived at Calais without his passport – he had forgotten it. The Chinese refused to send any more money so de Wet never reached China. Vincent Schmidt, however, arrived there and became the leader of the 14th International Squadron (see Chapter 13). Du Berrier had also informed Robert Bannister Pickett that he could find lucrative employment in China and was to meet him, en route for Shanghai, at Hong Kong in 1938. Hilaire du Berrier himself flew a Douglas Dolphin aircraft between Hankow and Nanking for the government towards the end of 1937.

Back in France Hugh continued to work on further articles about Spain for *Blackwood's Magazine* and these appeared in this journal in the early months of 1938. He included further stories told him by Griffiths and tales he had heard of Spanish, Russian and other foreign pilots in Spain together with his own memoirs. These articles were also published in the French magazine *Revue de Paris* in July 1938 and plans made for publication in book form by Blackwood in the UK and Doubleday & Company in the USA. The book finally appeared towards the end of the year under the title *Cardboard Crucifix* in Britain and *The Patrol is Ended* in the USA. Hugh had used his imagination to embellish the story and had produced a book that was more a novel based on fact than a straight autobiographical account. His natural poetic and almost surrealistic style of writing, together with his penchant for black humour, brought to the manuscript an unusual yet gripping flavour. He did not realise it at the time but the account he gave of the British pilots would be closely scrutinised many years later and taken at face value by historians writing of the air war in Spain. Practically all the names he used for the pilots were fictional, although the characters were all based on actual persons. It would have caused him great amusement that all the "definite" accounts of the air war in Spain written in recent years in Spain, France and Mexico should include many of the names he uses (see also Chapter 12). One critic, C. G. Grey in a review of the book in *The Aeroplane* magazine in December 1938, said "This is by a long way the best book that has yet been written on flying."

Whilst all the preparation went ahead for the publication of his book Hugh was on his travels again. The impending crisis in Europe during the summer of 1938 with Hitler hurtling threats towards Czechoslovakia caused de Wet once more to put aside pen and palette. He hastened to Prague where he offered his services to the Benes government as a pilot. The offer was politely refused so Hugh settled down to enjoy life at the Hotel Esplanade in the ancient city of Prague and continued his writing and painting. He made many friends amongst the Prague intelligentsia and the many foreigners living in the city. One day he was approached by an acquaintance and asked if he would be prepared to act as a courier and agent for the French intelligence services. Unknown to de Wet his friend du Berrier had himself become involved with French intelligence operations with *Renseignment Guerre*, an espionage service set up by Colonel (later General) Raoul Salan. When he received a postcard sent by Hugh from Prague he commended de Wet to his French friends as a Sandhurst man and Francophile and suggested their associates look him up in Prague. Du Berrier figured that his friend could do with the money.

In October 1938 Hugh first met and soon fell in love with a petite, beautiful Russian refugee in Czechoslovakia, Alla Fyodorovna Hepnerova. He moved into a flat in the ancient half of the city and they were married at the beginning of March 1939. Hugh continued to send information to his French superiors in Strasbourg. One of the methods used was to buy a ticket from Prague to Pilsen, some 50 miles to the south-west; before the journey he had put the copies of stolen documents inside one of the little wedge-shaped cushions such as fitted into slots in the first-class compartment of the express train. He would substitute his cushion for the one already in the compartment, get out at Pilsen and take the next train back to Prague. Hugh then informed the French by sending an innocent seeming postcard to an address in Strasbourg that told them the number of the carriage and compartment so that the documents could be retrieved. On one occasion a Czech colleague was betrayed to the Gestapo. Hugh was given the job of eliminating the betrayer – a meeting was set up in a woodland cottage near Prague where he met the Gestapo agent. From that meeting only Hugh was to return.

The sell-out to Hitler at Munich the previous autumn left the remaining rump of Czechoslovakia open for the Germans to take whenever they felt like it. On 15 March 1939 the German army marched into Prague and the democratic republic of Czechoslovakia became the German Protectorate of Bohemia and Moravia. A few days later Hugh saw Adolf Hitler himself driving through the streets of the conquered city.

Hugh's services for French intelligence now assumed a more serious, dangerous and organized nature. His days were now fully occupied with establishing, with as much accuracy as possible, the disposition, nature and movements of the occupying German forces. On one of his periodic trips to France at this time Hugh was arrested, searched, interrogated and held for twenty-four hours at the German frontier station of Brentheim. Fortunately they did not find what they were looking for – the documents were hidden inside the roller of his typewriter. He tried to persuade Alla to go to England for her own safety but she would not leave him. Hugh continued his espionage activities in Prague, Bratislava and Vienna. It was only a matter of time before he would be betrayed, like so many of his colleagues.

On 7 July 1939 Hugh was arrested by the Gestapo in the lounge of the Imperial Hotel in Vienna. A search soon revealed that he was carrying photostatic copies of German secret documents concerning their fortifications along the River Waag. He was taken to the headquarters of the Gestapo in Vienna at the Hotel Metropole. From that moment began a tale of suffering that almost defeats imagination.

Hugh was tortured by the Gestapo in all the ways they usually employed to break down a suspect. Also, knowing that de Wet was an artist, they stubbed cigarette ends on his hands which they used as ashtrays and broke his fingers in a desk drawer. Still he kept silent, but one day he was suddenly confronted with his wife, who had travelled to Vienna to try and warn him that he had been betrayed, and fallen into the hands of the Gestapo herself. They threatened her with torture in front of his eyes. Back at Rossauerlande Prison that night, where they were both being held, she hanged herself.

In his despair de Wet went on hunger strike, then attempted to kill himself and ended up in the mental wing of the University Hospital of Vienna. Once he had recovered somewhat from the physical and mental pain he had endured de Wet was returned to a cell at the prison. The interrogations stopped for a while and he was left alone to suffer the deadening routine of captivity. The outbreak of World War II passed him by. He was then moved to Landesgericht, the central prison of Vienna. He remained there until October 1940 when he managed to escape by sawing through the bars of his cell window with a small piece of rusty hacksaw blade he found in the courtyard of the prison during the exercise period one day. He was soon recaptured, manacled and a month or so later taken to Berlin for a show trial before the Nazi People's Court and charged with being a spy for the French *Deuxième Bureau*. On 21 January 1941 the court gave its verdict – guilty of espionage and high treason. The sentence was death. The report in the Nazi Party newspaper said that de Wet heard the sentence of death with indifference and left the court with a polite bow to the judges.[15]

Hugh was to spend the next two-and-a-half years in solitary confinement at Plotzensee Prison in Berlin with his arms chained across his chest. Prisoners were executed two or three times a week by an electric guillotine down the passage from death row but the fatal knock never came to his door. During this period he caught tuberculosis which resulted in him losing his fetters for a time. In June 1943 the prison was bombed and he and thirty other surviving prisoners were transferred to Brandenburg Prison and put in irons again. The remaining 180 prisoners remaining at Plotzensee, there being no cells to accommodate them, were hanged to prevent them escaping. Executions continued at Brandenburg in a courtyard below his cell window. Twice a week batches of fifteen prisoners were executed and the pace increased to between 60 to 120 a week as the war drew to its close. Still death passed him by although on one occasion he put on the paper shirt of those to be decapitated only to be returned to his cell again.

When the Russians approached Berlin he was amongst 18 prisoners selected as negotiable hostages to be taken to Hitler's redoubt in Bavaria. Handed over to the SS in Halle-an-der-Saale the officer in charge allowed him to escape to the American lines. He was not to know for many years that the only reason he had not been executed was that the British were holding a German agent as hostage against his life.

De Wet's agony was not yet over as the Americans thought that his story was too good to be true so put him back into prison again until the intervention of an USAAF officer, who had read Hugh's book on Spain, had him released to the British sector. The British too assumed that he was some sort of dangerous war criminal on the run and sent him to

England with an aeroplane load of Nazi suspects. There, at last, he managed to persuade somebody to take him to his bank in St James's, London, where the manager identified him to everyone's satisfaction – he had an overdraft!

Hugh found austere post-war London to be a strange and drab place after the heady days of the thirties. When he had recovered a little from his terrible ordeal, although his health was never the same again, he wrote an account of his experiences in captivity which was first published in *Blackwood's Magazine* in 1947-48 and then, in book form, by Blackwood in 1949 under the title *Valley of the Shadow* (not his chosen title – he had intended the book to be called *The Gap*). This was later dramatized and broadcast by the BBC with the actor Edward Woodward as de Wet. Hugh was also the subject of an early "This is Your Life" on BBC. Television in April 1956. Amongst the guests were George Fachiri and the Lutheran pastor at Plotzensee Prison in Berlin, Dr Harald Poelchaul. Fachiri had been in several sales jobs after leaving Spain and had served in the Army as a private soldier at Wrotham in Kent in World War II. He died in Worthing in 1968.

After the war Hugh achieved wide success with his painting and sculpture, despite the injuries inflicted on his hands by the Gestapo. Amongst his portrait busts were those of Dylan Thomas, which is at the Royal Festival Hall; Ezra Pound, in the possession of the publishers Faber & Faber Ltd; Lord Horder, at the Royal College of Surgeons, Roy Campbell, Robert Graves, Edmund Blunden and John Cowper Powys. His little studio off Kensington High Street was visited by artists, boxers, politicians, businessmen and authors.

Hugh travelled again to Paris and the south of France. On one occasion he paid a visit to Spain. He still had the ability to charm and turn the head of any woman he met. His engagement to Sir Winston Churchill's daughter, Sarah Churchill, was announced in the press in 1970 but the marriage never took place.

Hugh was never to meet his friend of the thirties, Hilaire du Berrier, again. Du Berrier too had suffered in World War II, being held captive by the Japanese and tortured by their secret police, the *Kempetai*, from 1942 to 1945, for his intelligence activities on behalf of the Free French. He too survived but did not learn until it was too late that de Wet had not been executed by the Germans. Du Berrier now lives in Monaco.

Hugh Oloff de Wet with Sarah Chuchill, 1970.
(S & G Press Agency Ltd / Daily Telegraph)

By the mid seventies de Wet was very frail, the ordeal in Germany and many years of fairly heavy drinking having taken their toll. Hugh had his own still in the kitchen of his studio and brewed a concoction that was practically pure alcohol. He died on 16 January 1975 after being ill for a considerable time.

Hugh Oloff de Wet was born several centuries too late – in Elizabethan days he would have sailed around the world with Drake. A modern day Cervantes, also an artist and soldier, Hugh would not fit into our modern cynical world of the eighties.

CHAPTER 4 – SOURCES/NOTES

Much of the information regarding de Wet's career as a soldier-of-fortune comes from his own books/articles and from the writings and memories of Hilaire du Berrier. Details of his early years and service career came from Philip Denny, Librarian, Monkton Combe School; M.G.H. Wright, Deputy Librarian, The Royal Military Academy, Sandhurst, and Ministry of Defence RAF records. Information about his imprisonment in Germany and later life come from his own writings, newspaper reports and interviews with de Wet by Gerald Howson, shortly before his death. Roger Law of the BBC also filled in several gaps in the story by kindly providing me with a copy of the 'This Is Your Life' typescript on de Wet. Unfortunately many of the documents listed in the *Index to the Foreign Office Archives* at the Public Record Office concerning his career in Spain are missing.

1. One source states that de Wet enlisted in the Bolivian air Force during the Gran Chaco War. This, however, cannot be confirmed. See *Brigades Internacionales de la Guerra de España*, by Andreu Castelles.

2. *From Mules to Jets: A Short History of Aviation in Ethiopia*; Addis Ababa 1981, with additional information from Ole G. Norbø.

3. *Waugh in Abyssinia*, by Evelyn Waugh; London 1936.

4. *The Aeroplane*, 18 December 1935.

5. *The Aeroplane*, 1 January 1936, and various newspaper reports.

6. *Black Eagle*, by H. Julian (as told to John Bulloch); London 1964. *The Black Eagle*, by John Peer Nugent; New York 1971.

7. *The Brown Condor: The True Adventures of John C. Robinson*, by Thomas E. Simmons; Silver Spring, Maryland 1988.

8. *Popular Flying*, May 1937, and *Evening Standard*, 17 December 1936.

9. F0371 File (1936) 20580.

10. Information regarding Fachiri and Pickett from Ministry of Defence RAF records; Bryan Matthews, Archivist, Uppingham School; RAF Museum and Mr R. Fachiri. Also from AVIA 2/1976 Part I file at Public Record Office.

11. 'More from a Pilot's Diary', by H. Oloff de Wet; *Blackwoods Magazine*, February 1938 & 'Spanish Turmoil'; *Blackwoods Magazine,* June 1938.

12. *Index to Foreign Office Archives* (1936/7) – documents missing from files.

13. FO371 (1937) 21284. As told to George Steer to Lt-Col Arnold of British Intelligence, on his return from Spain, February 1937. "An individual called de Witte [sic], a frequenter of an American bar in Paris (Tommy's or Bobby's) has, for a considerable time, been flying fighter aircraft from France to Barcelona. He is believed to be ex-RAF, and have some connection with the British Legation in Addis Ababa". 11 February 1937.

14. *Petit Parisien*, January 1937.

15. Report on trial given in the *New York Times*, 8 February 1941.

FOOTNOTES

* American pilot Frederic Lord (See Chapter 5).

† Jaime Primero referred to by de Wet was the Republican battleship *Jaime I*. The *España*, a Nationalist battleship, was actually lost in the Bay of Biscay in April 1937.

CHAPTER 5

Death of a Gentleman – The Suicide Squadron

Sydney Henry Holland was born on 17 March 1883 at Petworth in Sussex where his grandfather, Prebendary Holland, was rector. At the outbreak of World War I, Sydney volunteered for service in the Army and in 1917 was serving in the Royal West Surreys. In the same year he married the daughter of Mr W. Powell Breach of Steyning and joined the Royal Flying Corps as an observer.

He was sent to the observers school in June 1917, eventually joining No.9 Squadron in France in September. This unit was equipped with R.E.8 aircraft and carried out corps reconnaissance duties over the lines. Sydney returned home in February 1918 and joined No.1 Armament School shortly afterwards before attending No. 1 Flying School. He was posted to the newly formed No. 139 Squadron at Villaverla in Northern Italy with the rank of Lieutenant (Honorary Captain). With this squadron, equipped with Bristol F.2b Fighters, he flew patrols over the front in north-eastern Italy until the end of the war. The squadron was disbanded in March 1919 and the following month Sydney was, in the impersonal terminology of the armed forces, "placed on the Unemployed List".

At 36 he found, like so many others, that there were little opportunities at home for ex-service flyers. His responsibilities also increased as his first child was born in 1919 and another shortly afterwards. By nature an adventurer he decided, therefore, to go abroad to South America and leave war-weary Britain behind.

Eventually he arrived in Buenos Aires in Argentina where he carried out any flying duties he could obtain. His friend Charles Grey, editor of *The Aeroplane* magazine, would later say that "Holland was one of those steady-going pilots who could get an aeroplane out of anything if it could be got out, and he would fly a machine anywhere it could be flown". Sydney also became an expert photographer and was soon able to put this talent to good use. He became a pilot with Major S.H. Kingsley and the River Plate Aviation Company and also flew joyriding flights on his own account.

During this period he produced an excellent air map of the city of Buenos Aires entirely by himself with the use of his camera. When he had somebody else to fly the aircraft whilst he worked the camera he could never get the pilot to fly where he wanted to go – if he flew the machine himself and left somebody else to work the camera the other man never took the photographs where he wanted them. So at last he did it himself, flying his own line, holding the control-column between his knees while he took the photographs over the side, and then changing the dark slides with one hand while he flew the aircraft accurately back on to his line again at exactly the right height. After all the slides had been shot off he would go down, develop the plates himself and enlarge the prints to precisely the scale to which he was working. The only help he had was a young

Argentinian who used to hang the prints out to dry and see to the packing of photographs and the cleaning of the studio.

Sydney sold so many of these photographic maps of Buenos Aires and did so much air photography survey work that he made quite a reasonable living for a while. Further air surveys were carried out in Brazil on behalf of the Aircraft Operating Company at Rio de Janeiro. Here Sydney's latent spirit of adventure managed to get him into trouble again because one day he photographed a restricted area – there was one of the periodic revolutions going on at the time in Brazil – and was arrested and thrown into prison. He remained there until his long-suffering wife, who had followed him out to South America, managed to persuade the Brazilian authorities to release him. His fondness for filibustering, however, caused him to get involved in the revolutionary activities himself.

Sydney Holland, 1933. (Courtesy RAF Museum)

Sydney sneaked out of Rio at night and managed to get to his de Havilland Moth aircraft, which was under guard on the aerodrome, took off and flew the aircraft to a strip where he picked up one of the leaders of the Paulista revolutionaries and took him to São Paulo. In São Paulo nobody wanted any air survey work done so he took to ferrying Chilean-built Curtiss fighters from the Mato Grosso to São Paulo. The aircraft were flown over the Andes by Chilean pilots and landed on Brazilian territory, after which they were flown by Sydney and an American pilot over hundreds of miles of jungle and forest. He took no part in any of the fighting himself but later enjoyed telling his friends back in England of the air battles he had seen. The government forces eventually defeated the Paulistas which made Brazil no longer a safe place for Sydney to be in so he took ship to England leaving his devoted wife to realise his assets in Rio and get most of the money out by sheer diplomacy.

Back in England they went to live at Crawley with their two children. Sydney set about obtaining his Royal Aero Club private pilot's 'A' licence at Surrey Aero Club. He obtained it in January 1933 (No.10933) and followed this with his commercial pilot's 'B' licence (No.1552). This enabled him to continue his photographic survey work and to obtain employment in civil aviation. Eventually he became a pilot with Wrightways Limited of Croydon and flew on the regular newspaper services from Croydon airport to Paris. A fellow pilot with the air charter company was to become a close friend and was to share his last fatal adventure with him.

This airman was Walter Scott Coates. He was born at Leverington, near Wisbech, Cambridgeshire, on 20 March 1896, the youngest of four children. After an idyllic childhood living in his farm house home, playing in its lovely garden and the surrounding fenland countryside (where he learned to become a good shot in his teens hunting game birds) he, like so many of his generation, was drawn into the horrors of World War I. He enlisted into the ranks of the Army Service Corps in March 1915 and five months later left Avonmouth bound for Alexandria in Egypt, where he served until August 1916. During his time there he picked up a local remedy for boils which later on, back in England, he was to advertise and supply locally. Selected as suitable officer material he returned to England and was appointed to a temporary commission as 2nd Lieutenant with the Machine Gun Corps in December 1916, joining 147 Company in France the following April. He served there until September 1918, being promoted to Lieutenant during this period. After his return to the UK he was attached to the Royal Air Force from the beginning of November, attending No.1 School of Aeronautics, and took his first steps towards a flying career. However, the end of the war soon came and Walter rejoined the Machine Gun Corps before being released in January 1919. He finally relinquished his commission in September 1921.

Walter married in 1920 and settled down to live at Harrold Bridge, Lincolnshire, about four miles from his birthplace. Although he had always wanted to be an engineer he became a farmer growing potatoes, sugar beet, cereals, strawberries and mustard. He showed his practical ability and inventive mind by wiring the remote farmhouse for electric light which was supplied from accumulators. He used a cat as his assistant by tying the wire to its hindquarters – putting it under the floorboards and holding a kipper the other end. A daughter was born in 1923 to the young couple, and for several years Walter pursued the life of a farmer and family man.

The love of speed and aviation had never left him. He became a motoring enthusiast and enjoyed driving as fast as possible in a series of cars and on motor-cycles. In 1928 he bought his first aeroplane, a de Havilland D.H. 60 Moth, and joined the Norfolk & Norwich Aero Club, obtaining his Royal Aero Club 'A' licence (No. 8450) in October of the same year. In 1931 he also decided to renew his links with the RAF and was appointed to a commission in the Reserve of Air Force Officers. During this period Walter spent less and less time on his farm and left his long-suffering wife and the foreman to carry on with the harvesting and other work as best they could. When he did come home he often used to fly his aircraft over from Norwich and try to land on the paddock by the house, but only once achieved this as the farm animals were quite terrified by the strange noise.

Having never really been interested in farming Walter decided to give it up and to try to obtain a career in aviation. After obtaining the necessary flying hours and going through the required tests and stiff medicals at the Air Ministry in London, he eventually obtained his 'B' licence (No 1661) which enabled him to become a commercial pilot. In the late summer of 1933 disaster struck, however, as Walter had a serious air crash which led to one of his feet being amputated. This was, of course, a great blow to Walter and his ambition to pursue a flying career but, typically, he overcame this handicap in a remarkable way. He soon discharged himself from hospital and came home to Harrold Bridge on crutches. He dosed himself with aspirins and brandy for a few weeks and fretted at being an invalid; he had an allergy to doctors. He gradually recovered sufficiently to have a temporary artificial leg and later an artificial foot.

Farming was not good in the depression in the early thirties so the farm and house was let and the family moved to Wisbech where they remained for about a year. During this period Walter, still chaffing at his enforced inactivity, walked from King's Lynn to Wisbech – about fourteen miles – for a bet. He arrived home in the middle of the night in a terrible state and spent quite a few days recovering.

In 1934 Walter and his family moved to London. There he bought a share in a garage near to his house and took up flying again by giving joy rides from a field at Elstree. He still could not settle down to a normal existence and went out to the Middle East to help lay an oil pipe line. By the spring of 1935 he was flying for Crilly Airways Limited on their passenger service between Norwich-Leicester-Bristol, and later that year on their Sunday services from Norwich to Ramsgate. By now Walter and his wife had become estranged and were living apart – his new way of life had meant he had been home only on rare occasions in recent years. In 1936 Walter left Crilly Airways to become a pilot for Wrightways Ltd. Soon he became good friends with Sydney Holland, with whom he had much in common.

When the Spanish Civil War broke out in July 1936 the newspapers were soon full of stories of how Captain Cecil Bebb of another air charter company at Croydon had flown General Franco from the Canary Islands to Morocco to start the revolt (see Chapter 2).

They were also soon made aware of how many of their fellow charter pilots were being paid large amounts for flying civil aircraft, bought in Britain by agents of both sides in the conflict, to Spain. Sydney wrote to his friend Charles Grey and told him that he too had had an offer to fly some aircraft to Spain but on 19 August the British government finally implemented an embargo on all war materials to Spain and announced that any pilot ferrying an aeroplane to a Spanish destination would have his licence suspended or cancelled. In early November both Sydney and Walter were suddenly dismissed by Wrightways for failing to observe air navigation regulations. For Sydney especially this was a serious blow, with a wife and two children to support, as he was no longer a young man – he was 53 years old although very young for his age. Walter was 40 years old, and jobs were not easy to find in civil aviation.

Walter Scott Coates with Crilly Airways' de Havilland D.H.84 Dragon aircraft, 1935. (Courtesy Mrs Magaret Walters)

Hearing that the Spanish government were looking for pilots to fly and fight in Spain the two mens' love of adventure overcame the prudence of middle-age; they paid a visit to the Spanish Embassy in London and offered their services. Like de Wet, they were greeted by Vincent Doherty who had returned to the UK to recruit more pilots. Despite their age he was impressed by both men and their enthusiasm. Sydney Holland could also speak Spanish well after his years in South America. Doherty arranged that they could go to Spain via Paris

On 16 November 1936 the two men left for Paris by Imperial Airways, accompanied by Doherty. The Foreign Office had been made aware of their impending journey to Spain by the police, but noted that they "had no power to refuse them passports but they are committing an offence under the Foreign Enlistment Act".[1] After arrival in Paris they joined up with other foreign volunteers and were then flown to Barcelona.

They received an enthusiastic reception, and were then taken to Los Alcázares for flight tests before signing contracts.

They arrived at the Hotel Incarnation at Los Alcázares on Sunday, 22 November 1936. Doherty took Sydney and Walter into the bar and introduced them to five American pilots who had also just arrived in Spain and the debonaire Hilaire du Berrier, who had been asked to check out their flying ability. Hilaire du Berrier recently gave his recollections of this meeting:-

> "I liked Holland at once. He was a small man with greyish hair, a quiet cold way about him, and turned out to be an inveterate gambler. Holland had brought his mandolin with him, and when not playing dominoes for a peseta a point he was playing it."

Of Walter Coates he noticed his prematurely greying hair but not his artificial foot — which shows how well he had disguised the fact that he had one. Du Berrier also took an instant liking to Walter.

The following morning du Berrier took Sydney and Walter over to the naval air base at San Javier and showed them over the controls of the Nieuport Ni-D.52 they were to be tested on. Sydney went up first and soon showed the onlookers that he was a good pilot. Commandante Alwal, in his report, listed him as capable but old. Walter also completed his test successfully. Both men, at this time, hoped they would be sent to fly with a fighter squadron.

The two Britons, together with the new American pilots, were taken to the Air Ministry at Valencia to sign contracts. These varied in some details from those of de Wet, Fachiri and Pickett. The salary was £220 a month, to be paid into a bank in England appointed by the Spanish Embassy in London; living and hotel allowance amounted to £24 a month; first-class return fare home; a premium of £300 paid for each enemy aircraft brought down; £1,000 in event of total incapacity from wounds; £1,500 to be paid to their nearest relative in case of death. Their contracts, signed on 27 November, were renewable on a monthly basis.

Sydney had already fallen out with Freddie Lord, one of the American pilots, who had offended him that first evening at the hotel in Los Alcázares when Lord drank too much. He was then very annoyed when it was announced by the Spaniards that both himself and Walter were to be sent to the same base in the north of Spain with four of the five Americans — Lord, Bert Acosta, Gordon Berry and Eddie Schneider Jr. Only Edwin Semons, who had helped recruit the others in the USA and had journeyed to Spain with them, did not go to the Northern Front.

Frederic Ives Lord, then 36 years old, had earned a high reputation for himself during World War I when, after joining the RFC in Canada, he had gone to France with No 79 Squadron flying Sopwith Dolphin aircraft and had become a flight leader at the age of only 18. He was credited with nine 'victories' over German aircraft before being shot down himself and wounded. For this he had been awarded the DFC. Upon release from hospital in the spring of 1919 Lord had volunteered for service in Russia where the British and Americans had intervened on behalf of the White Russians still fighting against the Communists.

For his service in this disastrous campaign he was awarded a bar to his DFC. Lord's career since those exciting days had included barnstorming in the USA, being a salesman, acting as combat adviser to the Mexican Government during the 1929 revolution and attempting to run his own airline between Texas and Mexico. This hard-living, hard-drinking opportunist was always on the lookout for wherever money and adventure could be found so that it was natural that he jumped at the offer to fly in Spain.

Bert Acosta, 1928 (via Richard S. Allen).

Bertram Acosta was a similar type of person to Lord. The oldest of the group at 41 years old, he had achieved world-wide fame in 1927, when he was one of Commander Bryd's pilots during his trans-Atlantic flight, after many years of test and record breaking flights in the USA. The career of the suave, good-looking Acosta with his olive complexion and clipped moustache then went from one disaster to another. Business ventures failed, he went to jail for non-payment of alimony and, in 1929, he was grounded for five years for a drunken stunting spree. Acosta's life then went from bad to worse; he took up serious drinking and lived from hand to mouth. Finally in 1935 he started to fly again but by the autumn of 1936 he was broke again and only too eager to accept an offer to fly in Spain.

Gordon Berry, a 39 year old flying and drinking companion of Acosta, who had also served in the RAF towards the end of World War I, and Eddie Schneider Jr, the youngest of the Americans at 25 and a former holder of junior flying records in the USA, completed the motley group who were to fly with Holland and Coates. It is no wonder that both Sydney and Walter felt ill at ease with these wild American airmen — especially the former, who was very much the typical old-school English gentleman of the military type and in Spain partly in order to get enough money to send his children to a good school.

On 28 November 1936 the group of pilots left Valencia for northern Spain. They flew in an American Douglas DC-2 transport aircraft (the Spanish Government had obtained several prior to the war) from Barcelona. The aircraft flew directly over the Pyrenees and veered over to the French side as it approached the Insurgent* lines in the west. It continued for a time over France, then kept in the clouds over the sea before landing at Santander. The pilots then completed their journey to the Basque capital, Bilbao, by rail. The Basques had achieved self-government in October 1936 and immediately had set about organising their own armed forces, independent of the Central Government. The Spanish Government, however, had sent a squadron of the newly-arrived Russian pilots with their Polikarpov I-15 aircraft north together with what other personnel and aircraft could be spared.

At Bilbao the British and American pilots were quartered in a chateau that had originally belonged to the Marquis de Lamiaco. They were then taken by car through the pouring rain to Sondica airfield, about ten miles from Bilbao. Here they were shown the aircraft they had to fly, a dilapidated collection of old military and hastily acquired commercial machines. The aircraft of the Basque "air force" were a Miles M.2H Hawk Major, a Miles M.3B Falcon Six, a General Aircraft Monospar ST-25 Jubilee (these had recently been obtained from Britain);[2] an older model Monospar ST-12 (this had been delivered to Spain in 1935 for aerial mapping duties); a Fokker F.VIIb/3m trimotor; a Vickers (CASA) Vildebeest (which had been sent from Barcelona to the Basques); a few old Breguet Br.19 recce-bombers; an ancient cabin Farman F.291/1 and other oddments. Most of the aircraft were unarmed but bomb racks had been fitted to the Hawk and Falcon carrying four 25lb bombs. The Monospars and the Farman carried, besides the pilot, an observer/bombardier, whose job it was to throw out by hand the eight bombs stacked on the cabin floor. Each observer carried a machine-gun on his lap — the idea was that, if attacked by an enemy aircraft, they would try to shoot it down by the arm-held gun from out of the cabin windows.

Miles M.3B Falcon Six (G-ADLS) of Basque Air Force prior to going to Spain. (A. J. Jackson Collection)

The base was commanded by a Spaniard, Manuel Cascón Briega, who had started the war as the leader of a fighter group near Madrid and claimed the first aerial victory back in July. He soon made it obvious to the newcomers that he regarded them as purely mercenary troops, whom he could send to death without compunction. He did not even regard them as valuable fighters who were considered worth a good salary and kept the few armed Breguets and Nieuport Ni-D.52s available for the Spanish pilots leaving the British and Americans to fly the decrepit civil aeroplanes. The airfield at Sondica was being extended and only a narrow and dangerous strip was left for use which was itself liable to flooding in the wet weather encountered in the Basque winter. Even their quarters were cold and damp, and food at the airfield consisted of soup and cabbage. It was no wonder, therefore, that before long they were all ill to some extent.

Cascón informed the new pilots that their duties would be to fly bombing raids over enemy territory to the south to support an offensive toward Villareal. Protection would be given to the makeshift bombers by Russian fighter aircraft based at another airfield at Lamiaco, a short distance away. The Spaniards did not issue any flying suits to the Britons and Americans so they had to fly in their civilian clothes with only their overcoats for protection against the cold and damp. Later on the Russians, hearing of their plight, found some flying equipment for them to use.

In late October or early November a Soviet ship had arrived at Bilbao bringing fifteen Polikarpov I-15 *Chato* fighter aircraft from Leningrad along with thirty-four Soviet pilots and mechanics to assemble and fly these aircraft for the Government's Northern forces. The Russians were under the command of Major Maranchov (who used the nom-de-guerre *Borés* whilst in Spain). Several of these aircraft together with their pilots and ground crew were deployed to Lamiaco airfield, which was a converted polo field. The Soviet pilots, all of central European or Baltic extraction, were all experienced. The unit was fully self sufficient, well equipped and disciplined – a complete contrast to the situation at Sondica.

Events at Sondica had started badly for the volunteers when Cascón ordered one of the Americans (Lord) to go up in a Breguet in poor visibility and bomb the Insurgents' airfield at Vitoria, some forty miles to the south. He went up but soon returned saying that it was hopeless to try and find Vitoria because of the fog. The Commandant immediately pulled out his revolver and ordered him up again, saying that he would shoot him unless he did. Sydney Holland and Walter Coates did not believe that Cascón would carry out his threat but the American was obviously impressed. He walked towards his machine but the Spanish mechanics told him that the aeroplane was no longer fit to fly and that they would shoot the Commandant if he tried to carry out his threat. This incident only added to the ill-feeling between Cascón and the foreign volunteers. Further problems also arose between the Spaniards and the group because of the Americans' behaviour on the ground, typified by a series of drunken brawls. This also added to the tension between Sydney, Walter and the Americans and was not the right sort of preparation for the trials ahead.

Day after day the volunteers flew twenty or thirty miles into enemy territory, dropped their load of bombs and flew back as fast as they cold, dodging into the clouds to avoid being spotted by Insurgent aircraft. Luckily the weather was uniformly bad which gave plenty of cloud cover. However, on 12 December 1936, the squadron was sent on a mission to bomb Lacua airfield at Vitoria. Sydney was the pilot of the Monospar ST-25. With him in the aircraft was a Spaniard, Gumersindo Guiterrez Merino, the observer / gunner, and a Soviet airman (possibly a Czech). The motley group of aircraft took off at dawn from Sondica and made their way south. Unfortunately the different speeds of the machines meant that, by the time Vitoria was reached, the aircraft were spread over a distance of ten miles so that the job of the few Russian fighters escorting the bombers was made extremely difficult. It was obvious that they could not guard all the bombers at the moment they reached the aerodrome. The first two bombers dropped their bombs, wheeled to the right and made off.

General Aircraft Monospar ST-25 Jubilee. Similar to aircraft that Sydney Holland was flying when he was killed in Spain - former British registered aircraft G-ADSN. (The Aviation Bookshop)

By this time the *kette* (flight) of Heinkel He 51B fighters of the German *Legion Condor* J-88 stationed at Vitoria had been alerted. They came up just in time to catch Sydney Holland in the Monospar who had just dropped his bombs. His observer fired the machine-gun through the broken windows of the aircraft but, with no rear vision it was futile. The aircraft slowly nosed down as Sydney was hit by the bullets tearing into the Monospar, burst into flames and plummeted to earth. Walter Coates, flying the next bomber in line, watched with horror as his friend was shot down. He then dropped his bombs and made for home protected by two Russian fighters. The two Americans, Acosta and Lord, were also witnesses to the death of Sydney Holland. Bert Acosta, flying the Miles Hawk Major, was saved from the same fate because the Germans thought his aircraft was part of the fighter escort and veered away. The Monospar was almost completely destroyed in the crash and all three crewmen were killed. The aircraft had fallen in Insurgent territory and news of the death of Sydney Holland was soon released to the world's press. His contract was found on his body together with an unposted letter to his wife in which he commented on the lack of efficient organisation among the Government forces. Details from his contract and the story of his last flight were published in the *Daily Mail* the following week through their correspondent in Nationalist Spain, Harold G. Cardozo.[3]

The volunteers continued to fly for about another week or so but, luckily, no more fatalities occurred. All the pilots had had enough of the Spanish war by then and were anxious to get home. Just before Christmas the Americans left for Paris via Barcelona and Port Bou. Acosta, Berry and Schneider soon returned to the USA where Acosta and Berry made headlines telling their story to an eager press. Acosta's accounts became more and more unbelievable as time went on including such items as shooting down German fighters with a revolver. Lord remained in Paris for some time with his wife and co-operated with Hilaire du Berrier with his account of the Basque fiasco – this appeared in the Paris press in January 1937.[4]

Walter Coates, glad to see the back of the Americans, soon followed them home via Paris. It was a pleasure to have a bath again, to be warm and to eat good food. Whilst in Paris he met one of the British civil pilots who had been in Franco's Spain (see Chapter 2). This man told Walter how the German pilots he had met were depressed by the performance of the German aircraft compared with the Russian fighters and bombers.

Walter gave his account of the air war in Spain (anonymously) to the press in London, which was carried in the *Daily Telegraph* on 13 January 1937. He also went to see Sydney's wife and family and arranged with the Spanish Embassy that they honoured his contract with respect to the money due to her on Sydney's death. He then continued his career in civil aviation and married again after divorce from his first wife in 1938. When World War II broke out in September 1939 he was still in the Reserve of Air Force Officers, and thus was recalled to duty with the RAF. Because of his age he did no combat flying but became a ferry pilot and served in various maintenance units before becoming a test pilot with Phillips & Powis Ltd, by which time he had been promoted to the rank of Flight Lieutenant. For the last few months of the war he was attached to General Aircraft Ltd, as a test and glider pilot – ironically the same company that had made the Monospar in which Sydney Holland had died. Walter remained in the RAF until released in 1947 when he went to live in Norfolk. He died in 1959.

What of the strange band of Americans that had flown in the Basque country with Walter? Acosta died of tuberculosis in 1954 after years of alternating bouts of drinking with attempts to dry out – a sad end to a once famous flyer. Lord returned to the USA in 1937 after abortive attempts to get into the lucrative sale of arms to the Spanish War and did a national lecture tour, with his wife, to raise funds on behalf of the Spanish Republic. When World War II broke out he tried to talk his way back into his old RAF squadron, No 79, by the use of a 'doctored' birth certificate. Higher authority caught up with him, however, and he became a ferry pilot. He died in 1967, murdered by a vagrant in California. Eddie Schneider was killed in an air collision in 1940 and Gordon Berry died in New York in 1943.

Perhaps Charles Grey's obituary for Sydney Holland 'Salute to an Adventurer', that was published in *The Aeroplane* could be applied to them all: "I for one lament the death of a friend, who, according to the pacifist standards of today perhaps not an estimable character, was at any rate a man."[5]

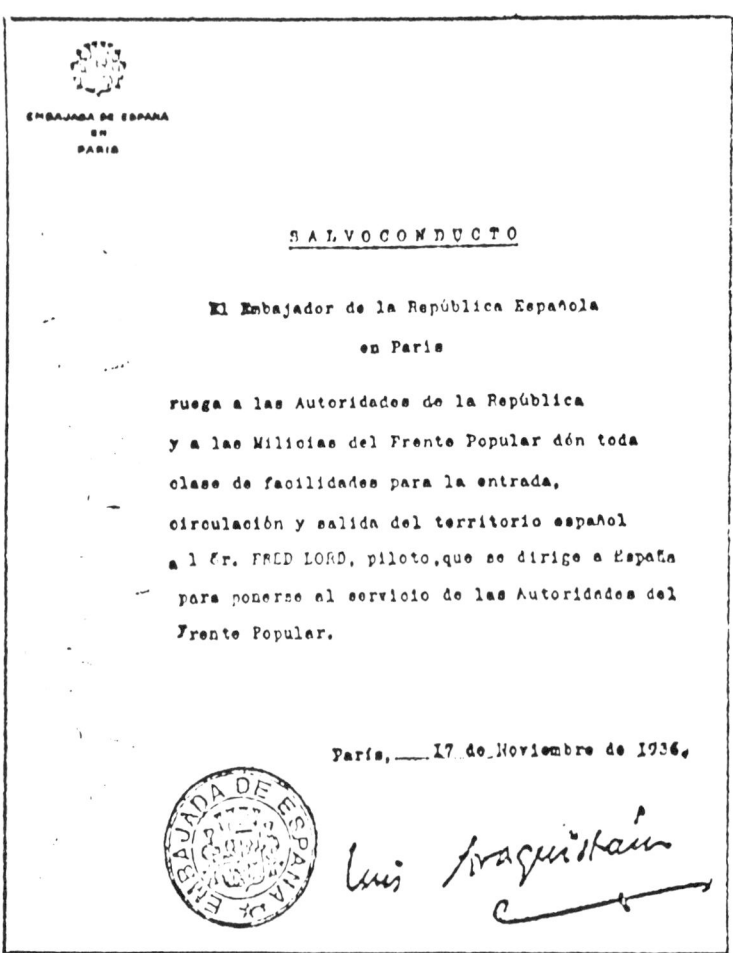

Safe Conduct issued to American pilot Fred Lord by Spanish Embassy in Paris.

Translated it reads: "Safe Conduct. The Ambassador of the Republic of Spain in Paris requests the Authorities of the Republic and the Militia of the Popular Front of all ranks to give facilities of entrance, travel in, and departure from Spanish territory to Mr Fred Lord, pilot, who is going to Spain to put himself at the service of the Authorities of the Popular Front." The signature is that of Luis Araguistain, Spanish Ambassador to France.

CHAPTER 5 – SOURCES/NOTES

Walter Coates's daughter, Mrs Margaret Walters, kindly provided much information regarding her late father whom she remembers as having great charisma and zest for life. Hilaire du Berrier again provided much information and other details came from contemporary magazine/newspaper articles. Also from Ministry of Defence RAF records and the RAF Museum. Information regarding the American pilots came from Richard S. Allen and Allen Herr.

1. F0371 File (1936) 20586.

2. 'Contraband Wings of the Spanish War . . .', by G. Howson; *Air Enthusiast Ten,* July-September 1979.

3. *Daily Mail,* 16 December 1936.

4. *Le Journal,* 18 January 1937.

5. *The Aeroplane,* 23 December 1936.

FOOTNOTE

* Contemporary term used for Nationalist or rebel forces.

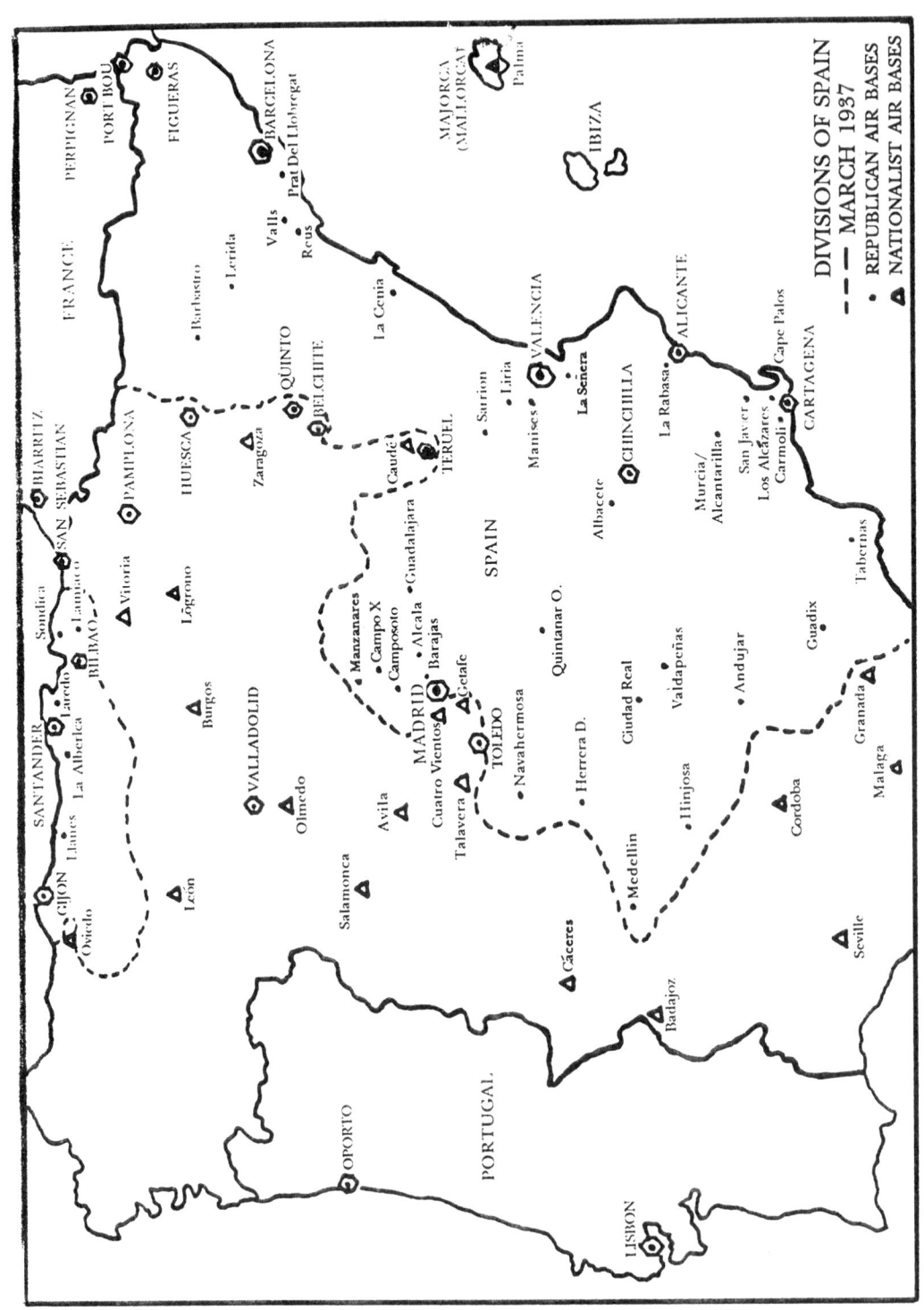

DIVISIONS OF SPAIN
— — — MARCH 1937
• REPUBLICAN AIR BASES
▲ NATIONALIST AIR BASES

CHAPTER 6

The Stormy Petrel in Spain

Charles Kenneth Upjohn (or Apjohn)-Carter was born at Dalhousie, in the foothills of the Himalayas in India, on 17 September 1900. His father was a major in the British Army and, as soon as Charles was old enough, sent his son to England to receive the obligatory public school education at Wellington College. Here, at the age of 16, Charles sustained a fractured skull when falling down a flight of stone stairs which resulted in his spending several months in hospital and affected his mental stability for some time. Charles did not continue his education after leaving hospital but managed to obtain a commission in the Royal Flying Corps in July 1917 by giving an incorrect age. In the following months he learnt to fly but, as he had not really recovered from his accident, was discharged on medical grounds at the beginning of March 1918. Thwarted in his chosen career he re-enlisted in May of the same year only to desert two months later before the authorities caught up with him as being medically unfit for duty. In October 1918, he again re-enlisted but deserted four days later. According to his own later account he also married in 1918 but left his wife after only ten days. Later claims in obituaries that he had become a squadron commander in World War I, won the Military Cross, DFC, and Croix de Guerre have not been confirmed by the Ministry of Defence.

Charles's actual career from 1918 until the mid-thirties is difficult to establish due to the various lurid accounts that appeared subsequently in magazines, newspapers and his own autobiography. The latter, under the title *Stormy Petrel,* was published by Hurst & Blackett in London in 1936. It reads more like a crime novel than a serious autobiography and is written in a racy journalistic style. For this book and other later writings he used the nom-de-plume of Charles Kennett, by which name he was to be better known in later years.

Charles tells his avid readers that he emigrated to Canada after leaving the RFC with a view to farming in Alberta but soon spent all his money on easy living. He drifted over the border to the USA, finally finding himself in Los Angeles, where he became a pilot for "Marco", a local racketeer who "ran all the booze from Santa Barbara down to San Diego" – this being the era of Prohibition. He claims to have flown cocaine from Mexico to the USA in an old war-surplus S.E.5 fighter aircraft and to have carried illegal Chinese immigrants over the border into California. After a period spent at sea as an engine-room wiper during which he visited Argentina, Charles says that he returned to the USA and eventually became a pilot for the US Air Mail, flying between Reno-Sacramento-San Francisco, before being dismissed because he was not an American citizen.

Never one to be disheartened by such set-backs Charles next says he joined the US Army Air Corps and eventually was posted to the No 29 Squadron based at Nicholls Field in the Philippines, where he flew de Havilland D.H.4Bs. There he again fell out with authority and decided to desert by flying from Luzon to Kowloon in Hong Kong, a journey of some 680 miles, in a Curtiss Oriole, a solo flight not previously accomplished. Charles says he made it by refuelling the aircraft on the Kaipong Islands from spare cans of petrol carried in the Oriole. After crash landing near Hong Kong he then found his way to Canton, where for some time during 1923-24, he was a flying instructor for the "Air Force" of Sun Yat-sen, together with other foreigners. Riots at Canton made him leave, and he worked his passage to Sydney in Australia aboard a merchant ship.

On his arrival he obtained a job as a pilot with a Queensland air transport company and flew mail, medical supplies and freight in the outback. Surviving a crash in which he broke his left arm, leg and ribs, his next venture was to set up an air charter company. This, unfortunately, soon failed because he lost his flying licence after another crash when it was found he had been drinking.

Prospecting for gold in New Guinea, a period of being a golf professional in Queensland, a suspended prison sentence for passing false cheques, trying his hand at school teaching, radio announcing and journalism all followed during the next few years before he left Australia bound for Europe as a quartermaster on another merchant ship.

Charles did not stay long in England, however; he was soon off again, this time as an able-seaman on an oil tanker bound for Mexico. He eventually ended up in Miami where he joined up with yet another local gangster, "Red O'Connor", running liquor to Cuba, before returning to Europe where he became an interpreter/guide with a travel agent in Paris for a while.

Kennett then came home to England and married for the second time (his first wife had died in the Twenties). He tried, unsuccessfully, to launch his own aviation company on the south coast and spent some time as a lorry driver.

Charles's obituaries also claimed that he had surveyed the Paris-Casablanca route for *Air France* in 1930-31. How much can be believed? Attempts have been made in America to substantiate his claims of flying the US Mails and serving in the USAAC, but no supporting evidence has yet come to light. Captain W.E. Johns perpetuated much of the above by publishing rehashed extracts from *Stormy Petrel* in his aviation magazine *Popular Flying* during 1936. In one editorial[1] he described them as "awful confessions". Perhaps he had a puckish sense of humour and knew the taste of his readers?

What actually happened to Charles Kennett during these years? Unfortunately documents giving biographical information on him listed in the *Index* to the Foreign Office files at the Public Record Office have disappeared and all we have left are newspaper reports of various court cases that he was involved in during 1936-37. According to these sources Charles had been abroad from 1926-31 (in Australia?). Returning home he had been sentenced to several terms of imprisonment in 1931 and 1932 for obtaining credit and goods by false pretences by passing false cheques. There was a case of fraud in 1934, and in 1935 he was bound over for twelve months for similar offences.[2] Reviews of his book were not altogether favourable and Charles was getting into severe financial difficulties by mid 1936. He was also having problems at home – whilst staying at a hotel he had spent some money and did not want his wife to know so he told her that the cash had been stolen. She called the police who soon found out the truth and, probably due to his record, charged Charles with 'causing a public mischief by telling a false story to the police'.[2] All these misfortunes can, probably, be traced back to his fall and fractured skull back in 1917 which had left him as erratic, eccentric and occasionally unstable. Charles admitted himself in *Stormy Petrel* that in the early Thirties he was attending a London clinic for psychological treatment. The 'public mischief' case came up before the courts in July 1936 and Charles pleaded guilty but was bailed to appear again at the next session in September and his term of probation extended for two years. But by September Charles was not in England. He was flying in Spain.

Charles Kennett, 1936.
(Popular Flying)

Shortly after the court case Charles learnt of the many British civil pilots who were making a lot of money by ferrying second-hand aircraft to both sides in the Spanish Civil War, which had broken out in mid July. He claimed to have delivered a de Havilland D.H.84 Dragon himself but this cannot be verified. His friend, Captain W. E. Johns, later referred to a story Charles told him about his delivery flight. In order to fly the aircraft non-stop to Barcelona the seats in the Dragon were pulled out and a sixty-gallon tank put in their place. This was filled from time to time by a mechanic who went along for the flight. Running into bumpy weather the petrol started sloshing about and the rocking motion of the loose tank took the aeroplane all over the sky, in a kind of regular swing that frightened the pilot considerably. True, or another of his stories?

The Air Ministry had now become very concerned about the number of British civil aircraft finding their way to Spain and, during August 1936, issued a *Notice to Airmen* warning them that they would have their flying licence cancelled or suspended if found guilty of making false declarations to Customs in attempting to deliver aircraft to either side in the war. For a while this action prevented further aircraft flying direct from Britain to Spain but soon determined men found other ways to get around any official restrictions.

In the meanwhile it was reported in the press that the Spanish Republic were seeking British pilots to deliver aircraft from France and to pilot them in action against the Insurgent forces. The acute shortage of experienced pilots available to the Spanish Government (many of the most experienced officers had gone over to the rebels) had meant that already, since the early days of the war, it had been only too pleased to accept mercenary pilots from all over Europe, especially France, as well as a few foreign left-wing volunteer airmen, many of whom were refugees from the fascist regimes in Italy and Germany.

Charles Kennett, with his growing financial problems, decided to offer his services to the Spanish Republic – at a price. He went to the Spanish Embassy in London and there met Antonio Ramos Oliveira, a left-wing writer and journalist, who had been sent to England specifically to recruit Britons to fly in Spain. Charles produced references stating that he had 8,000 hours flying experience and was a highly qualified airman.[3] His ability to speak French also impressed the Spaniard who decided that he would be an ideal man to recruit other British pilots. During the next few days Charles found there was no shortage of men willing to risk the perils of flying in Spain for the adventure and the money on offer, even if they had only a hazy idea of the background or the issues about which the Spanish were fighting. Finally, on 31 August 1936, Charles and four other pilots were each given £15 as an advance against their salary by Oliveira and, accompanied by the Spaniard, caught the late afternoon Paris boat-train from Victoria. It had been a gloriously hot late summer's day and the five men, ostensibly bound for a holiday in Paris, sat in different compartments of the train – the Spanish wanted to keep their departure as secret as possible.

Unfortunately Charles had already given the following statement to the *Daily Express* air reporter which appeared in the following morning's newspaper: "I saw there was big money going to Spain. A Spanish agent was in London with nearly £40,000 to get pilots. We met and I was asked to collect seven experienced pilots to fight the rebels. This morning I had six. Two fell out. An urgent cable came through from Madrid. The rebel air raids are damaging the civil morale. English pilots are needed to turn the raiders back. Each of us is going to strike the best bargain we can with the Madrid authorities. We are signing contracts in Spain. I am asking £200 a month – in advance. It's money down for me. Madrid has four Hawker Furies. Four of us will fly those, escorting the fifth, who will fly a big de Havilland bomber. . . I have over 7,000 hours' flying experience. My senior pilot has 3,000. Two of my men are ex-RAF. One was doing a gunnery course a few weeks ago. I engaged the last man this morning."[4] Never one to miss a chance for self-publicity was Charles Kennett.

When the group arrived in Paris the Spaniard obtained rail tickets for Toulouse whence they were to make their way – still as tourists – to the border town of Port Bou, on the Spanish frontier. At Toulouse one of the Britons, Peter Crawford, was given his ticket to return to England – apparently he had been drunk most of the time since they started their journey and had behaved in a disorderly manner. Luckily for Charles it would appear that Oliveira had not yet heard of the story in the *Daily Express*.

After the four Britons crossed the border into loyalist Spain the enthusiastic welcome they received soon made up for any problems so far encountered. It surprised even Charles Kennett and was a complete eye-opener to others, especially the youthful Brian Griffin, only nineteen years old. Travelling first-class by rail to Barcelona it was almost a triumphal procession right up to Madrid where they arrived on 2 September 1936.

In Madrid nearly every male over fifteen years of age seemed to be armed and many of the young women, smart, with faces made-up, were also wearing the uniform of the militias, overalls of white, khaki or blue. On their heads were forage caps and over their slim shoulders they wore bandoliers of cartridges, and pistols at their hips.

The four Englishmen were taken to the Air Ministry where their contracts were finalised and signed. By now the Spanish authorities knew of the publicity engendered by Charles's interview in the *Daily Express* but, it appears, he managed to talk his way out of the situation, as usual. Next stop was the Hotel Florida in Madrid's Gran Via. Walking into this elegant hotel they were greeted with a babel of noise as this was where all the foreign pilots flying with the squadrons around the capital were quartered including those with the *Escadrille "España"* organized by the famous French writer, André Malraux. At the hotel at this time there were Frenchmen, Swiss, Czechs, Austrians, Italians as well as the odd Briton or American who had come over to Spain very early during the conflict.

That evening wine flowed freely, toasts were drunk and plenty of food was consumed. The realities of a civil war seemed very far away. It was, therefore, a rather subdued quartet who arrived at Getafe aerodrome, some ten miles south-west of Madrid the following morning. After being kitted out in the smart blue uniforms of the *Aviación Militar Español,*[5] with gold star and wings, blue overalls and green tasselled field cap, they were introduced to the aircraft they had to fly – the Nieuport Ni-D.52 fighter and Breguet Br.19 bomber. On the tarmac could also be seen a few Dewoitine D.372 fighter aircraft and a Hawker Fury. However, they were soon informed this was reserved for the Spanish pilots. Charles tried out a Nieuport but, like de Wet later on, found they were slow and under-powered. As for the lumbering Breguet Br.19s, the group of British pilots nick-named them "cows", as they looked like one on the ground and handled like one in the air.

That evening Charles and the others returned to Madrid and went out for a meal at a restaurant with the flight operating captain of the aerodrome. He left them at the table while he went to get the necessary food ticket. Whilst he was gone there was a slight commotion at a nearby table. A young man, who was with his mother, suddenly stood up and went to leave the building. At the door he was confronted by three armed men who, ignoring the pleas of his distraught mother, dragged him away after a brief interrogation. The woman, sobbing, collapsed where she stood in the doorway. Charles asked their interpreter why the youth had been taken away. The answer came that he was just a Fascist and would be shot in the morning. The four Englishmen now realised that the rumours they had heard back home of the summary executions carried out in Spain were not just newspaper stories.

Back at the airfield the Englishmen found that they would be flying with various other foreign pilots and some Spaniards in a mixed Nieuport-Breguet squadron led by Antonio Martín Luna. Also at Getafe were other Spanish units of Nieuport fighters and Breguet Br.19s. The *Escadrille "España"* of André Malraux, with its own fighter cover, which used mostly Potez 54 bomber aircraft, was based mainly at the civil airport of Barajas to the east of Madrid. The four British pilots – soon joined by others from the UK – found that their job was to patrol the Talavera front to the west of Madrid where the Insurgent forces were slowly advancing towards the capital. The average number of patrols was two per day – at dawn and 4pm. If on the early patrol, they stayed at the aerodrome overnight, unlike many of the other foreigners who insisted on returning to Madrid for a night's drinking and carousing so that in the morning the orderly had to go round to take the names of those available for duty. The bombing patrols consisted of the Breguets 'protected' by the Nieuports and the solitary Fury. The "cows" would move slowly into line to take off and then, to the thunderous roar of their Hispano engines, they would wallow slowly into the air. At about 8,000 feet the aircraft would head off towards the Insurgent lines where the bombs were dropped, usually without any visible effect – only a few melons or so were normally hit.

At this time there was only limited fighter opposition but this was soon to change for, on 11 September 1936, a well-trained Italian squadron flying the exceedingly robust little biplane fighter, the Fiat CR.32, joined the battle. Led by Captain Dequal, who used the nom-de-guerre *Limonesi* in Spain, and including the future top 'ace' pilot of the Nationalist Air Force, Joaquín García Morato, this squadron made an immediate impact. On the first day the Fiat squadron encountered the British pilots, young Griffin was killed over the Talavera front (see Chapter 7). Charles was convinced that the two Spanish pilots flying on the patrol with Griffin had deserted him when the Fiats had attacked and later related how he had told the commander of the squadron at Getafe exactly what he thought of the two airmen, of Spaniards as a whole and of their country – a very risky thing to do. Luckily for him they seemed unmoved by his outburst but within twenty-four hours he was ordered to fly an aircraft down to the southern front near Cartagena, probably to remove him from the scene.

Another reason may have been that, back in England on 11 September, Oliveira had been detained by the Special Branch at Folkestone whilst on his way to take up the position as press attaché at the Spanish Embassy. He had been searched and several secret documents concerning the recruitment of Charles and his group found on him, including references they had supplied regarding their flying history, capabilities and character, together with names of their guarantors[6] – hardly the sort of information that the Spanish Government wanted the Foreign Office in London to get hold of.

The next morning Charles took off from Getafe in a Breguet Br.19, with a Spanish gunner in the rear cockpit, bound for Los Alcázares on the south-east coast of Spain. On the way they only sighted one enemy fighter aircraft but, luckily for them, its pilot only fired one burst from long range which did no damage before veering off, because he was a long way from his home base and did not want to chance having to force-land in Republican territory. They reached the coast without further incident, but by now it was dark and Charles found he was lost and flying over the sea. He turned back. After twenty minutes he saw the lights of an aerodrome. Charles thankfully put the Breguet down and discovered they had landed at San Javier, the naval air base a few miles north of his true destination. Here they stayed the night before setting out in the morning for Los Alcázares.

At Los Alcázares, Charles reported to the commandant and, after having his papers examined, he was told that he would be flying on the afternoon patrol and shown the aircraft in the hangars. Here, apart from the usual Nieuports and Breguets, were several ancient looking biplanes which turned out to be World War I vintage Martinsyde F.4s, the remnants of the small number supplied from Britain in 1921-23, and a few Vickers (CASA) Vildebeest bombers. At one stage it looked as though he would be expected to fly one of the Martinsydes. It was a relief when he heard he was to continue to fly a Breguet Br.19. For the rest of his stay in Spain he was to fly as a bomber pilot on the Granada front.

Whilst at Los Alcázares, he met Juan Ortiz Muñoz, a short, stocky Spaniard who impressed him both as a pilot and as a man. Ortiz had made a name for himself in the early days of the war by leading a small party of men from Los Alcázares to take the San Javier air base, which had been taken over by officers sympathetic to the rebels. Another Spaniard who impressed Charles was Alejandro Gómez Spencer, who was in charge of the flying school at San Javier at the time. Spencer was under suspicion of being a fascist sympathiser because of his aristocratic background and bearing but, although always closely watched, he was not arrested because his services were considered too invaluable. Charles also became friends with his interpreter at Los Alcázares, a pilot named José Selles Ogino, but always known as 'Chang', as he had been born and reared in Japan and could speak Japanese, English and Spanish with equal fluency.

Life at Los Alcázares and San Javier was the peculiar mixture of enjoyment and tragedy that only airmen in war know. Every day the pilots would lie on the beach in the hot sun, bathe in the Mediterranean Sea and enjoy café life but, almost every day, one or more of them would not return from a patrol. Charles later described a typical dawn patrol on the Granada front:-

> "The batmen knocked us up at 3.30 a.m. 'Tres y media', he always said, and we would spring out of bed. A quick shower to wake us up, then a stiff cup of coffee, while an interpreter explained the orders for the patrol. Always it was the same orders; 'You must penetrate into the ring of mountains surrounding Granada, bomb the fortifications and return.' Always the same result was achieved. We would be forced to unload our 'eggs' long before we reached Granada. The patrol would consist each morning of about 30 planes. Flying in ten flights of three, we would set out with orders to deal death and destruction to the insurgent base which we never really expected to reach."

Nationalist spies would warn Granada and the bombers would be intercepted, usually long before their target was reached, by the Insurgent fighters.

> "About half an hour's flying time from Granada we would suddenly receive those dreaded taps on the shoulder from our gunners, followed by a burst of firing underneath us as an insurgent plane swooping up to attack our blind spot . . . Groups of three or four of our planes would huddle together for mutual protection, and back we would fly towards home. Usually we left two or three of our companions' blazing wrecks below, before, with the distance increasing between them and home, the

107

Nationalists would finally give up the chase. With torn wings and pitted fuselages we would limp home, having unloaded our bombs on whatever piece of land seemed to be a good place to drop them. If we managed to hit some outpost of the Nationalists we counted ourselves exceptionally lucky."[7]

Every now and then Charles and 'Chang' Selles would borrow a car and go into Cartagena, the naval base, in the evening. Early one morning, whilst on the way back to the airfield for the dawn patrol, they witnessed the execution of a group of suspected fascists in the village of Pacheco – a sight that shocked Charles as it was the first time he had seen himself the realities of the Spanish Civil War.

So the days went by. Charles spent his days flying and taking it easy between patrols in the local café, where he would try to listen to the British news bulletins from London. At Los Alcázares the mess was a babel of languages with pilots from Spain, Russia, France, Belgium, Rumania, Cuba, Switzerland and Czechoslovakia. Another Britisher also joined Charles there after a few days. Charles's worst moment in the air came when he had to land back at the airfield one day with live bombs still in their racks on the Breguet – he had been unable to drop them. Luckily they stayed in place during the landing but Charles had to stand his gunner a large cognac afterwards when he told him how near they had been to disaster.

His month's contract was nearly up when orders came through that he had to take an aircraft and report to Madrid at the Air Ministry. Charles left almost immediately in a de Havilland D.H.84 Dragon which was being used to take airmen to and from Madrid and the southern fronts. After an uneventful flight he landed at Cuatro Vientos aerodrome, just north of Getafe, and was taken into the city. By now it was too late in the day to go to the Air Ministry so Charles went to the Hotel Florida for the night. After a meal he decided to try and find out what had happened to the group of British pilots while he had been down in the south. After enquiries he found that two more had been killed, two wounded and another injured in a forced landing.

The next day he went to see the Air Minister who asked him if he would sign on for another month. Charles had already decided to get out of Spain as soon as possible but told the Spaniard that he would return to England and try to obtain more aircraft for the Republic – a promise he was to keep. Charles arranged that he would be flown to Barcelona later that same day and obtained the necessary papers to leave Spain. Before he left Madrid he visited the hospital where the two wounded British airmen were recovering. In hospital they were having a wonderful time – the nurses and doctors could not do enough for them. Flowers were sent in to decorate the small private ward in which they lay. Fruit, wines and even whisky was sent in for them. Typically Charles was the first person to sample the whisky – the two men were not fit enough to sample the spirit so the bottle had remained unopened for several days until he arrived.

Soon Charles was looking down at the war-ravaged land of Spain as the transport aircraft took him towards Barcelona. From there he caught a train to the border at Port Bou and thankfully put behind him the danger and horrors of the Spanish Civil War.

Charles was back in England by 5 October 1936. We can imagine the welcome he received because his wife had gone to court at Kingston the previous week to explain why he had failed to surrender to his bail; the case had been adjourned until the November sessions. After seeing her, Charles went to the *Daily Express* offices in Fleet Street with Pat Mertz, another of the British pilots in Spain who had returned to England with Charles. An interview with them appeared in the following morning's newspaper together with a photograph in which they are wearing *Aviación Militar* uniforms. Whilst he was there Charles sold two rather lurid articles to the newspaper about his adventures which appeared in the issues for the 7 and 8 October under the titles *Girls are in Death Squads in Madrid* and *British Airmen's War Thrills*.

The next few weeks were spent milking as much publicity and cash as possible out of the story of his adventures in Spain. His friend, Captain W. E. Johns, bought an article which appeared in the November 1936 edition of *Popular Flying*. He also contributed a series of four articles to the journal *Guide & Ideas for Competitors*.[8] These last four articles are about the best and least exaggerated of all his writings.

On 15 November 1936 Charles obtained his Royal Aero Club private pilot's 'A' licence (No 14572) at the Herts & Essex Aero Club. It appears he did not have a previous licence in Britain. Also in November he had to attend court to answer the charge of causing a public mischief and not appearing at the September hearing. His term of probation was extended for two years and he was fined £7. Accounts of these hearings used his real name of Upjohn-Carter so many were unaware that Charles Kennett was one and the same.

Charles next made the headlines on 31 December 1936 when reports appeared in several daily newspapers that he had been rescued from the sea off Le Havre in France after his aircraft had crashed into the Seine estuary. True to form the full story appeared in the *Daily Sketch* about a week later[9] – Charles had sold them his exclusive account of how he had returned to Spain to collect a fortune in jewels before crashing in the sea on his way home. How much truth there is in the following story is not known (a re-hash also appeared in *Popular Flying* the following November) but no evidence has been found to substantiate this yarn and, unfortunately, relevant documents listed in the *Index* to the Foreign Office files at the Public Record Office are missing.

According to Charles, whilst he was flying in Spain, he had been approached to bring £50,000 of gold and jewels to safety in England. Towards the end of November he had set out from an aerodrome in Kent (West Malling) in a de Havilland D.H.80A Puss Moth (G-ABWA) bound for Spain. He was held up by bad weather for several days in France but at dawn on 12 December had taken off from Perpignan heading straight for Valencia, his ultimate destination being Albacete. At the pre-arranged rendezvous he was unable to land as the ground was covered in snow. Another meeting place was arranged at Chinchilla, and he made a second attempt but this time was attacked over the sea by Nationalist flying-boats, and having escaped these, by Nieuport fighters of the Loyalists. He again managed to escape but flew back to France and landed at Mariagne, near Marseilles.

De Havilland D.H.80A Puss Moth (G-ABWA). (via R. T. Jackson)

He then arranged to see the Spanish Consul at Marseilles and told him that he wanted a safe conduct to Valencia in order to discuss supply of aircraft for Spain. This was soon arranged, and Charles flew to Chinchilla where the valuables were stowed in the fuselage of the Puss Moth behind the cabin. The Spaniards had, however, discovered they had been tricked and Charles's aircraft was attacked by several fighter aircraft which he managed to outwit by flying close to the ground, twisting and turning around trees and buildings, until he reached the sea. The Loyalist aircraft finally gave up the chase and he made a safe landing at Montpellier, where he found that the window behind his head had been smashed by a bullet and there were further bullet holes in the wing and cabin.

Despite being arrested by the French authorities and having his aircraft searched nothing was found. He was eventually released and sent on his way. Further delays due to fog and bad weather whilst travelling north over France prevented his early return home but, finally, on 30 December he took off from Le Bourget aerodrome, Paris, on the last leg to England. With him was a passenger whom he had picked up at Le Bourget, none other than the sour-faced young pilot, Robert Bannister Pickett (see Chapter 4), on his way home from Spain. Above the clouds Charles set course for Lympne airfield in Kent.

Suddenly the compass swung 180 degrees and he was unable to control the aircraft – the steering geer had failed. The only chance was to land as quickly as possible, but now they were over the sea and lost. The sun had set and darkness came. His luck held, however, and Charles finally managed to put the Puss Moth down in the sea near a lighthouse. The two men fought their way out of the cabin in the freezing December sea and managed to swim to a breakwater nearby. Here their cries for help were heard and they were taken to a cottage near the shore.

They found that they had landed near Le Havre. The following day the port authorities there towed the remains of the aircraft into the harbour but, although Charles arranged for a diver to examine the seabed where the crash had occurred no trace was found of the missing gold and jewels.

For the rest of 1937 and into 1938 the Spanish Civil War continued to figure large in Charles's life. Many were the schemes that were thought up by himself, Robert Pickett, Vincent Doherty and others to beat the Government's ban on the export of aeroplanes to Spain. Charles was in trouble again with the authorities when in mid-February 1937 he took delivery of a General Aircraft ST-25 Monospar Jubilee (G-AEGX) at Hanworth for delivery to the Potez airfield at Meautle in France – the General Aircraft Company had been granted leave to export some Monospars because they had been fitted out as ambulances – but failed to obtain the required Customs clearance at Lympne.[10] This subsequently led to him being fined, but the aircraft duly turned up later in Spain, for the company to which Charles had handed the aircraft over, the *Société Française de Transport Aeriens*, were agents for the Spanish Republican Government.

He found himself again in hot water when trying to deliver another ST-25 Monospar (G-AEVN) to France in the following June.[11] This time he was refused Customs clearance because he did not have the necessary Board of Trade licence although he told the Customs at Lympne that he had only loaned the aircraft from a Mrs Montefiore, the registered owner, for a week's holiday in France. The scheme having failed he flew the aircraft back to Heston with Robert Pickett, who was in on the plot. Pickett himself had purchased another ST-25 Monospar (G-AEWN) but managed somehow to obtain an export licence towards the end of July. Charles then was involved in abortive schemes to export two Beechcraft B.17 aircraft to the Spanish Republicans but these also came to naught.[12]

After the end of the Spanish Civil War in 1939 Charles was said to have become an instructor in a flying school in Scotland and, in 1940, to have been one of the first batch of British volunteers to go to Finland's aid against the Russians during the "Winter War". A few months later he is said to have become a senior instructor in the Empire pilot training scheme in Canada. From then until 1942, when he was grounded by ill-health, he was either an instructor or an RAF Ferry Command pilot. By the spring of 1943 Charles was living in New York City and had become a US citizen. A photograph of him appeared in the US "pulp" magazine *Flying Aces* in May, 1943, in full RAF uniform. It was stated that he was waiting for a commission in the USAAF and that he held the rank of Squadron Leader in the RAF. From 1944 Charles, with his Canadian (third?) wife lived in St Albans, Vermont, until his death from a heart ailment at the early age of 46 in January 1947 in St. Luke's Hospital in New York City. The following week obituary notices for Wing Commander Charles Kennett, MC, DFC, Croix de Guerre, appeared in both *The Times* of London and *The New York Times*. These referred to his war services in the RFC and RAF as well as his flying in the USA, China, Australia and Spain.[13]

General Aircraft Monospar ST-25 Universal (G-AEWN) of Robert Pickett - this aircraft also went to Spain. (Courtesy Michael J. Hooks)

The Ministry of Defence in Britain have only been able to confirm that Charles served for the short period between July 1917-March 1918 and that they have no record of any MC or DFC decorations being awarded to him. Nor do they have a record of him as serving in Ferry Command in World War II.

Hero, villain, charlatan, adventurer – the dark-haired, smooth-talking ex-public schoolboy, Charles Kennett was probably a mixture of all of these. He certainly proved Abraham Lincoln's adage that you can fool some of the people all of the time. One of the only men who could have put matters straight, Robert Bannister Pickett, died before he could be contacted at Barton in Lancashire in 1978. He had continued to fly after World War II having renewed his flying licence in 1953.

CHAPTER 6 – SOURCES/NOTES

1. Popular Flying, October 1936.

2. *Evening Standard,* 25 May 1937, and *Middlesex Chronicle,* 29 May 1937.

3. FO371 (1936) 20577. Unfortunately many documents listed are missing from files.

4. *Daily Express,* 1 September 1936.

5. Pre-war name for the Army Air Force. The Republican Air Force became known as the *Fuerzas Aéreas Republicanas Españolas* (F.A.R.E.)

6. Ibid 3.

7. 'Flying the Doomed Patrol', by Charles Kennett; *Guide & Ideas for Competitors,* 31 October 1936.

8. *Guide & Ideas for Competitors,* 24 & 31 October 1936; 7 & 14 November 1936.

9. *Daily Sketch,* 8 January 1937.

10. Public Record Office. Air Ministry Files. AVIA 2/1976 Part II (1937-38).

11. Ibid.

12. Ibid.

13. *New York Times,* 13 January 1947, and *The Times,* 14 January 1947.

CHAPTER 7

The Wages of War

The story of the main group of British airmen who flew in Spain during the autumn of 1936 has been distorted ever since by historians and other writers who took the account given by Oloff de Wet at face value. The true story of these men and of the tragic deaths of three of them, however, is as interesting as any fictional account.

We have already seen how Charles Kennett left for Spain at the end of August 1936. He was accompanied on his journey by four other pilots of widely differing backgrounds and motives for going there. The youngest of the four was Brian Douglas Griffin, born at Charlton, London, on 26 January 1917. Always keen to be an airman, he had been accepted for a commission in the Royal Air Force in December 1935 and began his training as an Acting Pilot Officer at No.7 Flying Training School, Peterborough, in the following month. For various unknown reasons his service was terminated in mid-July 1936, shortly before the outbreak of the Spanish Civil War. Short of funds, idealistic and very keen on flying he was only too happy to accept the offer of a contract to fly in Spain for the Republic against the Fascist rebels – one can imagine how the worldly-wise Charles Kennett would have brought much influence to bear on such a young man who, no doubt, had read of Kennett's exploits in *Popular Flying*. The fact that he had only some 130 flying hours to his credit did not deter him at all.[1]

The other three men were older. Peter Crawford, in his reference given to the Spanish Embassy, was said to have been a Sergeant-Pilot in the RAF with seven years service and about 380 hours of flying experience during the day and 75 hours at night. His speciality was as a machine-gunner. Little or nothing else is known about Crawford except that he may have served in No. 27 Squadron, RAF, at some time although this cannot be confirmed.[2]

Claude Warsow, born in Southsea on 9 October 1903, was the youngest son of a local cigarette manufacturer. Educated at St Helen's College, Portsmouth, he had served a Short Service Commission in the RAF from 1926 to 1931, spending all but the last eighteen months of his service in the Middle East (Egypt and Palestine) with No. 45 (where he served with George Fachiri for a brief period) and No. 14 Squadrons flying de Havilland D.H.9As. He then returned to the UK and flew the twin-engined biplane day bomber, the Boulton & Paul Sidestrand, with No.101 Squadron for the rest of his service. In January 1931 he was placed on the Reserve List but in October 1932, for unknown reasons, was "removed from the service". Claude married in the spring of 1933 but could not settle down to civilian life. The marriage did not last long. He parted company from his wife, who was much younger than himself, in the early summer of 1935, three months before their first child was born. When he heard that the Spanish Government wanted pilots to fly and fight in the Civil War, and of the large salaries being offered, Claude must have thought that the chance he had been waiting for had come – to make a good living out of what he liked best and had been trained for whilst in the RAF.

Edward Hillman, 1937.
(Courtesy RAF Museum)

The last man in the group was of a very different type. Edward Arthur John Hillman, born at Laindon, Essex, on 10 May 1913, was the eldest son of Edward Hillman, the civil aviation pioneer. His father, a "rough diamond" who was seldom seen working other than with rolled-up shirt sleeves, had been a coach operator who went into civil aviation partly because of government restrictions on his road services. He founded Hillman's Airways in 1932 and operated on a low cost structure, offering cut-price air services, with low wages to its staff and no difference in status between pilots and coach drivers. In December 1932 he began operating the prototype and first three production model de Havilland D.H.84 Dragon aircraft – he had asked de Havilland to design this aeroplane for use on a cut-price Paris service. Hillman's was also the first airline to operate the de Havilland D.H.89 Rapide in 1934.

Young Edward (or Sonny as he was known) joined his father to help run the company and soon became a director. His duties were mostly on the ground, but he learnt to fly without actually obtaining a pilot's licence. Unfortunately in 1934, when Edward was only twenty-one years old, his father died leaving him to face all the business commitments and debts as well as providing for his mother, an invalid, and five younger brothers and sisters. Hillman's Airways were bought out by British Airways in December 1935 but many financial and family problems remained for Edward. One of his friends was Tom Wintringham, a member of the Communist Party and a journalist. By the late summer of 1936 Wintringham was in Barcelona as correspondent for the *Daily Worker*, the British Communist Party newspaper.

Edward's financial problems grew worse during 1936, and when he heard of the large sums being offered by the Spanish Government for pilots he decided he had to go there. A visit to the Spanish Embassy, complete with a recommendation from Wintringham that he was a first-class pilot, resulted in him being offered a contract. Edward shut up his semi-detached house in Gidea Park, Essex, and left his bride of a year for the unknown dangers of the Spanish War. Ever the dutiful family man, he asked the Spanish Embassy if £20 per week of his salary could be sent to his wife during his absence.[3]

These then were the four men who accompanied Charles Kennett on the boat train from Victoria station on 31 August 1936. The contracts they had been offered were very similar to those of de Wet and Fachiri later. The Foreign Office later released details from that of Warsow:[4]

Mr Claud Warsow shall be paid the sum of £220 a month, payable in England to the Bank which he may designate, through the Spanish Embassy . . . Mr Warsow shall also receive an allowance of 850 pesetas per month during his stay in Spain, and the cost of his outward and homeward journeys, first class. These payments shall be made in April [sic] . . . Mr Claude Warsow is insured[5] against physical disablement for the sum of £1,000, and in the case of death for the sum of £2,500. These sums shall be paid in the same manner as the monthly payments.

Peter Crawford never signed his contract because he was sent back to England by the Spaniard, Oliviera without ever reaching Spain, as he had been 'habitually drunk and behaved in a disorderly manner' on the journey. He was given 300 francs at Toulouse for the return trip.[6]

Kennett, Hillman, Warsow and Griffin signed their contracts in Madrid and were admitted to the aerodrome at Getafe on 3 September 1936, accompanied by Oliveira. They were joined there after a few days by several other Britons, four of whom had left London on 7 September – their departure was duly noted in the *Daily Express* the following morning with the fact that they had been promised about £30 spending money on the trip out.

It is believed that this second group included Vincent Doherty, Keith Lindsay, Edward Downes-Martin and Eric Griffiths (see Chapter 8) or, possibly, Pat Mertz.

Vincent Philip Joseph Gerald Doherty, to give him his full name, was born in Cape Town, South Africa, on 7 July 1909. He was the son of a well-known Cape Town timber merchant and became a fine all-round athlete at college where he played both cricket and rugby. Although not more than average height he was solidly built, as befits a rugby player, with a pleasant personality. In 1930 he came to England and obtained a Short Service Commission in the RAF. After learning to fly at No. 2 Flying Training School at Digby in Lincolnshire he was posted to No. 100 Squadron at Donibristle in Fife where he flew firstly Hawker Horsleys and then Vickers Vildebeeste torpedo bombers. In February 1933 he was posted to the Far East and joined No. 36 Squadron at Singapore again on Hawker Horsleys and later Vildebeestes – an aircraft he was to see again in Spain. By April 1936 Vincent was back at the RAF Depot at Uxbridge. *The London Gazette* of 18 August announced that "Flying Officer Vincent Philip Joseph Gerald Doherty is dismissed the Service by sentence of general court martial August 1st, 1936". The reason for his service being terminated is not known but in August Vincent married an English girl he had met whilst in Singapore and they bought tickets to return to Cape Town towards the end of the month. But flying was in his blood and, when he too heard of the money on offer in Spain, Vincent told his new bride shortly after they returned from their honeymoon that he was going to deliver an aircraft to Spain, but she need not worry as he would be back in three days.[7]

Keith Oliver Davis Lindsay, born in London on 11 December 1910, was another ex-RAF pilot although he only served from March 1936 to mid-August 1936, when his Short Service Commission as an Acting Pilot Officer was terminated. He had spent his short time in the service at No. 11 Flying Training School, Wittering, Peterborough. Little or nothing else is known about Lindsay but he probably went to Spain for the same reason as others in the group – money.

Little is known regarding the young, blond pilot, Pat Mertz, who turned up at the *Daily Express* offices with Charles Kennett in early October 1936 (see Chapter 6). Available records, however, show that a Patrick John Henry Mertz, born at Hastings on 16 March 1917, served in a non-commissioned capacity with No. 604 'County of Middlesex' Squadron, Auxiliary Air Force, from February 1935 to March 1936. During this time Mertz became a pilot flying the Hawker Hart and Demon light bombers that this weekends-only unit was equipped with. In March 1936 he was transferred to the RAF Class F Reserve.

Edward Gawin Downes-Martin, the last of those who left London on 7 September 1936, did not go to Spain for the money – he had plenty enough already – but for the adventure and because he was bored. Born at Teddington on 19 May 1909, he came from a well-off family. Always of an adventurous turn of mind he was deeply interested in motor boats and before he began flying, he was in business in Christchurch, Hampshire, where he worked as a marine engineer. Edward loved speed – on one occasion he drove his power boat at such a fast rate that the engine caught fire and he had to be rescued by lifeboat. In 1932 he learnt to fly at the Wiltshire School of flying at High Post airfield near Salisbury and obtained his Royal Aero Club private pilot's 'A' licence (No.10487). Later in the year, following a "lightning" romance, he married a professional ice skater from Bournemouth at Christchurch – a wedding much publicised locally at the time, especially as the newly married couple flew off to France in his own two-seater Kleem aircraft for their honeymoon. In March 1934 Edward again made the headlines locally when, with two other men, he set out from Poole Harbour on a mystery voyage – about which rumour associated romantic possibilities including a search for hidden treasure – in *Sea Hawk*, a 20-ton yacht. In early May, however, the quest came to an early end as word reached Britain that the yacht had caught fire and burnt out at a small port near Vigo in Spain.

By mid-1936 Edward was bored with just hanging around the house with nothing to do – he had lost interest in motor boats and, being of independent means, did not have to work for a living. His wife continued to act as an instructress at the ice rink at Bournemouth so he was often left on his own at their house at Burton.

After a weekend in London, Edward told his wife he wanted to go to Spain as a pilot. The fact that he had no military training whatsoever did not deter him at all. His wife, of course, was very worried about him but knew he would be really miserable if he did not get his way. Edward, perhaps had a premonition of what was to happen because he told her just before he went after hurriedly packing, "I hope it's a nice death. If I have to die, and it does seem possible, I don't want it to be agony. I would rather have it that way than you having to meet me in pieces at Waterloo"[8]

Edward Downes-Martin, 1932. (Courtesy RAF Museum)

These were the men who gathered together at Getafe airfield near Madrid in the second week of September 1936. Vincent Doherty had sent his famly in Cape Town a letter from Paris to tell them that he was on his way to take part in the Civil War in Spain. Downes-Martin was later reported to have flown a Junkers [sic] aircraft from Paris to Barcelona before joining the others in Madrid.

This influx of Britons to join the "International" Squadron at Getafe must have caused much curiosity to the Spanish pilots and those of other nationalities based at the aerodrome. One of the Spaniards stood out from all the others. Tall, slim, with an unruly mane of jet black hair, Andrés García Lacalle, although only a Second Lieutenant at the time, was already the "ace" fighter pilot of the Republican Air Force having shot down several Nationalist aircraft in the battles over the Talavera front in August. He generally flew the solitary Hawker Fury fighter then available. There were three of them originally supplied to Spain but one had crash-landed near the Portuguese border and had been captured by the Nationalists; the other had been damaged in a test flight and had to be sent for repairs at the Hispano factory. In the Fury, for which Lacalle had an almost idolatrous affection, he would escort the Breguet Br.19s and, in reality, also the Nieuport Ni-D.52 "fighters". Many years later, when living in exile in Mexico, he wrote down his memories of the British pilots at Getafe in September 1936.[9] It is interesting to compare these with the pilots' own accounts and the semi-ficticious version given by Oloff de Wet in his book, *Cardboard Crucifix*.

Hawker "Spanish Fury" at La Rabasa/Alicante, 1937. (Archivo Aeronautico/Juan Arráez Photo)

119

Only just over a week after he had arrived at Getafe with Kennett, Warsow and Hillman the nineteen year old Brian Griffin was killed. Lacalle remembered that a youthful pilot, well-dressed, slight of stature and with a pleasant personality, who impressed him by immediately aligning the machine guns of his Nieuport Ni-D.52 and generally showing that, despite his lack of years, he had received some military training. The fact that this young man always wore yellow gloves also stayed in his mind. De Wet identified him as "Cartwright", who was killed on 27 August 1936. It would appear that de Wet obtained this information from Griffiths who could only have arrived at Getafe around 10 September. It is thought that Brian Griffin went on patrol in his Nieuport on 11 September over the Talavera front with two Spaniards and was jumped from above by Fiat CR.32s of the newly arrived *1a Squadriglia* of the *Aviación del Tercio*, based at Cáceres, under Dequal, and received a burst of machine gun fire in the back. The poor youth never had a chance as, Lacalle observed, the Nieuport was no match at all for the agile Fiat, which also had a speed superiority of over seventy miles per hour. Griffin's aircraft fell behind the Loyalist lines and his body was brought back to the airfield for burial.

One of the first Fiat CR.32 fighters to arrive in Spain in August 1936, in insignia of Aviación del Tercio.
(Patrick Laureau Collection)

The effect of Griffin's death on the remainder of the British contingent can be imagined. Kennett accused the two Spaniards of deserting him and was posted to the southern front. The others were reminded, in no uncertain manner, of the realities of war when they saw the sadly mutilated body of Griffin. He was buried in the Carabanchel Military Cemetery at Madrid with full military honours and many of his fellow airmen attended the funeral.[10] The first report of Griffin's death did not appear in the British press until the 17 September, as news of his death was not immediately released for security reasons.

The British pilots who remained at Getafe continued to fly on bombing raids in the Breguet Br.19s or escort duty in the Nieuports. Occasionally they had the chance to fly one of the more modern French fighter aircraft used by the Loyalists – the Dewoitine D.372 and the gull-winged Loire 46 (a few of the latter had arrived in the second week of September). Downes-Martin wrote to his wife in England, "I am flying the Loire 750hp single-seater plane. The only bother is that it lands at 100mph."[11] Lacalle, unfortunately, never came to know the British civil pilots at Getafe because they tended to keep themselves apart from the others, only remembering one who stood out from his companions, being well over six feet in height and, obviously, very strong – the Spaniards called him "King Kong". Could this have been Downes-Martin?

Dewoitine D.372 of Republican Air Force at Cuatro Vientos Aerodrome, late August 1936. (Archivo Aeronautico/Juan Arráez Photo)

Some of the former RAF pilots did mix with the Spaniards and the other foreigners at Getafe despite the language problems. Doherty, especially, was soon asking Lacalle for his advice and became firm friends with the Spaniard. He also discussed tactics with one of the French fighter pilots who often visited the airfield. This man, Jean Dary (or

Darry), very good-looking in a bronzed, grizzled kind of way, had been in Spain since early August. He was in his early forties and had been a fighter pilot in World War I, claiming six "victories". He spoke perfect English. One report later said that he had attended Harrow public school in England.[12] He had been attached to the British Royal Naval Air Service (RNAS) for a period during World War I. Dary had already made a name for himself in Spain as a tactician and leader. Doherty's willingness to learn from others and his skill as a pilot soon made him the most popular of the British contingent with the Spaniards – he was one of those lucky individuals who seems to have impressed everyone he met in Spain from Lacalle to, later, du Berrier.

Doherty and Griffiths, both being 'colonials', also became good friends whilst at Getafe. Lacalle recalled that Doherty had another close friend amongst the group of Britons, a man who was taller than himself, lean and muscular, calm, thoughtful, a man of few words who always smoked a pipe and wore a plaid shirt. This may have been a description of Claude Warsow.

On 21 September 1936 the Nationalist forces advancing towards Madrid broke through the Republican lines at the village of Maqueda, the last important defensive position separating Franco from Madrid. The Nationalist army, however, then swung southeast towards Toledo to relieve the beseiged fortress of El Alcázar, which had been held against Republican forces (mostly undisciplined militiamen) by about 1,200 men, a mixture of Falangists, Army Oficers, Civil Guards and Army cadets, under Colonel Jose Moscardó since the rising against the Government in July. The news of this epic seige had done much to improve Franco's image around the world and even the most rabid Republicans admired the fortitude of the defenders. With the Nationalist army rapidly approaching Toledo the Republicans made one last attempt to take the fortress and, at the same time, the airmen were given the task of trying to help halt the advance of the Spanish Foreign Legion and Moorish Regulares of Franco.

Dawn of 25 September was gloriously clear and sparkling, although very cold for the season. Yet another bombing raid was organised on the Toledo front and several Breguet Br.19s wallowed their way towards the lines escorted by three Nieuport Ni-D.52s, one flown by Edward Downes-Martin. Suddenly they were attacked by six Fiat CR.32s. He tried to follow the only method to survive in such a contest, as later recalled by Kennett "of going into a vertical turn whilst the Fiat chased round and round trying to get his guns on you."

But the outcome was usually certain. Downes-Martin was hit in the back of the neck by an explosive bullet. His aircraft plunged to earth. Before the British contingent recovered from this loss another pilot was killed and two more were seriously wounded – the following day Claude Warsow was flying a Nieuport on another bombing raid towards Toledo (according to Kennett this was the first time he had been on patrol in one of these as he usually had piloted one of the Breguet Br.19s). Again they were jumped by the Fiats of Dequal's squadron and, although Claude tried to dive away, a fatal move in the Nieuport, two of the Italian fighters were soon on his tail and his aircraft fell 8,000 feet, a blazing mass of wreckage on the brown plain.

The same day Doherty and Griffiths were on patrol over the lines escorting another bombing raid. Vincent Doherty, luckily for him, was flying one of the French parasol fighters, a Dewoitine D.372. Suddenly his patrol was attacked by six Fiats who came hurtling down on them with machine-guns blazing.

> "I felt my left arm suddenly go useless as a spurt of blood from my shoulder hit the windscreen while my left leg remained jambed under the joystick helpless with another bullet wound. I began to feel faint as I lost blood but managed to pull the joystick over and get away despite fifty bullet holes in the fuselage."[13]

Doherty's flying skill and military training had saved him. Knowing that the Dewoitine could outclimb the Fiat he pulled the joystick back with his one good hand and climbed steeply away. He nearly fainted twice on the forty mile flight back to Getafe aerodrome but managed to make a perfect three-point landing there before fainting away. He came to to find the aircraft swarming with mechanics and ambulance men who were trying to get him out of the cockpit. At last they managed it, put him into a car and rushed him to the infirmary, where his wounds were immediately attended to. Lacalle rushed over to see Doherty and comforted him as much as possible in the condition he was in. By this time Griffiths, also badly wounded, had landed at the airfield.

An explosive bullet had to be extracted from the South African's leg and the edges of the huge gash stitched together. Lacalle recalled, all those many years later, the courage of Doherty during this operation as he lay there, fully conscious, with beads of perspiration standing out on his forehead. All this time Griffiths patiently waited his turn to be treated without a sound despite the pain he must have been suffering. The fortitude of these two men remained for the rest of his life with Lacalle. Shortly afterwards both Doherty and Griffiths were transferred to the hospital in Madrid.

The end of the month soon came and the contracts of the British pilots who still survived ended. Little is known of the experiences in Spain of Pat Mertz, Edward Hillman and Keith Lindsay. It was reported that Lindsay too had been injured in a forced landing after his aircraft had been riddled with bullets.

Hillman had been very lucky – a bullet went through the shoulder of his leather flying jacket but only just nicked the skin. If he had been taller than his 5ft 8ins it would have probably killed him. On another occasion he crash landed his aircraft after a battle near a village and was captured by the inhabitants who thought he was a Nationalist pilot. Edward, unfortunately, could not speak Spanish and it looked likely he would be executed there and then. He kept repeating – "But I am your friend – I am your friend", as he stood before the firing squad. Then one spectator, who knew a little English, said to stop. As soon as they realised he was an English volunteer the mood of the villagers changed completely and he was feted, filled with food and drink and taken in triumph back to his airfield.[14]

Pat Mertz too had a near escape – one day he flew his Breguet back to the airfield riddled with bullets with the gunner dead in the rear cockpit. All he had to show was a scar on his left cheek from a near miss. It is likely that Mertz, or perhaps Hillman, were stationed with Kennett at San Javier/Los Alcázares later in the month.

Kennett visited Doherty and Griffiths in hospital before returning home, as mentioned previously, and brought home a letter from Doherty to give to his wife in London. A doctor at the hospital told Kennett that the South African would be incapacitated for four weeks and arrangements had been made to transfer both him and Griffiths to the British Embassy as soon as the Insurgents entered the city – as it seemed certain that they would in the next week or so. But he was wrong – although at that time it seemed that the sacrifice paid by Griffin, Downes-Martin and Warsow had been in vain, the Alcázar having been relieved by the Nationalists on 27 September, but by swinging southeast to relieve the fortress, the advance of the Franco forces had been delayed for three weeks, and once lost, the momentum of attack was not easily resumed. On 6 October the Nationalists recommenced their offensive towards Madrid but the Republic had been given sufficient time to regroup its forces and to hold a defensive line at the outskirts of the city. The loosely composed militia groups were soon stiffened by the arrival of the first of the International Brigades, comprising anti-fascist volunteers from nearly every country in Europe and also from America. Despite boasts to the contrary Franco was not to enter Madrid until 1939.

Kennett and Mertz, as already recorded, were back in London by 5 October 1936 and selling their story to the press. Edward Hillman, however, did not get back home for another day or so when he too was interviewed by the press. Unlike Kennett and Mertz, however, he obviously had enjoyed himself whilst in Spain despite the danger and told of his intention to return after a holiday at home. His wife, however, must have made him see sense for he never returned again as a war pilot.

The families of Downes-Martin, Warsow and Griffin were left to mourn their loss. Again the Spanish authorities at first refused to release news of the death of Downes-Martin and Warsow but the Foreign Office in London were notified after a couple of days from British diplomatic sources in Madrid[15] and reports of their deaths, together with interviews with their wives appeared in the press.

Vincent Doherty made a remarkably early recovery from his wounds in hospital; after only a couple of weeks he was on his feet again. One day in early October he received a visitor from the Air Ministry who asked him if he would return to London as soon as he was fit enough to interview further British pilots who wished to fly for the Spanish Republic. Doherty was also asked if he would approach the Air Ministry in London with a request that Spanish pilots should be allowed to receive training at civil flying schools in England.

Doherty arrived in London in October and recruited Hugh Oloff de Wet, George Fachiri, Hilaire du Berrier and Robert Bannister Pickett to fly in Spain. He also tried to arrange for thirty Spaniards to be trained for their pilot certificates at Air Services Training at Hamble in Hampshire and visited the Air Ministry on 28 October to plead his case, just two days before he flew off from Croydon with the four British pilots. While he was at the Air Ministry he gave his impressions of Spain and the aircraft being used by both sides in the conflict to the Air Staff. These impressions were later sent to the Foreign

Office. It is very interesting to read these comments in light of present knowledge.[16]

Interview with British Pilot on return from Spanish War.

Mr. V. P. Doherty (ex-Flight Lieutenant), who has recently returned from service with the Spanish Government Air Force, visited this Office on the 28th October. He is recovering from a wound in the shoulder received in combat with a C.R.32 Italian Fighter, and is at present trying to arrange for Spanish pilots to receive training at Civil Flying Schools in England. When he has recovered sufficiently, he intends to return to Spain.

Doherty is a Roman Catholic and an anti-communist, but in spite of this he has a strong sympathy with the Spanish Government supporters, and spoke highly of the spirit in the Spanish Air Force and in the Spanish Government Forces, with the exception of the anarchists who he states are quite indisciplined and unreliable.

The following is a resumé of the statements made by Doherty.

Strength of Government Air Force.

The small part of the Government Air Force which remained loyal, has been greatly reduced in numbers, in spite of foreign acquisitions, as a result of enemy action and crashes. The following was the strength at the Madrid Aerodromes on the 20th October:-

Fighters.

4 Dewoitines 370.
1 Fury.
1 Loire.
1 Boeing.
3 Nieuports 62. [sic].
9 Russian Fighters – type unknown.

Heavy Bombers.

4 Potez 540
1 Bloch 200.
1 Junkers 86.) converted
1 Douglas.   ) converted

There are also a number of heavy bombers which are not used.

The type of Russian fighters is uncertain. They carry 6 wing mounted machine guns, and Doherty stated a moto-cannon (this is discredited in A.I.) Full speed 270 m.p.h., retractable undercarriage, enclosed cockpit.

New consignments of German aircraft have not recently arrived in Spain, at any rate not through Lisbon, because of the refusal of the dockers to handle ammunitions for the insurgents. Further large consignments of French aircraft, including 12 Potez heavy bombers and 18 Dewoitine Fighters are expected to go to Madrid immediately.

Fighter Tactics.

The senior French pilot, named Dary was the principal expondent of fighter tactics. He had devised frontal attack on Junker Bombers which had resulted in two being brought down. The method was to approach from ahead on a shallow dive, and when underneath the Bomber, to make a tight half-loop and half-roll, and fire into the Bomber from underneath. Neither the front gun nor the rear turret gun in the Junker could depress sufficiently to engage a Fighter climbing close under the body of the aircraft.

An engagement with the leader of an enemy formation was a serious matter. The leaders of the Heinkel Fighters were particularly tenacious. The Heinkels were of equal performance with the Dewoitines but were not so manoeuvrable. The Italian C.R.32s were inferior in performance to the Dewoitines but usually stronger in numbers. They appeared to be well lead, but their followers were lacking in fighting qualties. They appeared to be content to make one attack and then to get away. It was usually possible to overtake the retreating C.R.32s and several had been brought down in this way.

It was customary for the insurgent Fighters to patrol in formations of three, with another formation of three above them, ready to support.

The Government Fighters were usually inferior in numbers but on one occasion all the available fighters were massed for an offensive patrol. They sighted, but were unable to reach a combined formation of nine C.R.32s and three Heinkels. The insurgent aircraft did not give them an opportunity to fight.

The insurgents had one Arado Fighter mounting a moto-cannon: this was only seen on two occasions, and it is believed to have crashed. On the occasion Doherty saw it, it made one dive on a Dewoitine Fighter and, according to the Dewoitine pilot (who escaped by parachute after his machine was destroyed) the Arado fired at him for a very brief interval. There was a violent explosion in his aircraft which went down in flames, and the rear part of the fuselage broke off. Doherty confirmed this story from his own observation.

Bombing.

Bombing by the Government Air Force was, with the exception of Potez Bombers, carried out without bombsights. The Potez have bombsights and are reported to be bombing accurately with heavy bombs. (Types and weights not known.)

Insurgent Air Force is unlikely to be employed on sustained heavy bombing of Madrid, in spite of warnings to that effect, unless the Insurgents are unable to capture Madrid in the near future.

Two successive raids were made on Getafi Aerodrome by two Junker Bombers during one moonlight night. Forty-eight bombs were dropped. Two unexploded 250-lb. German bombs were found. Two bombs which burst alongside one of the hangars blew in the side of the hangar which was made of corrugated iron. Four aircraft were destroyed on the aerodrome.

Miscellaneous.

The Spanish aerodromes are provided with dugouts. Living quarters and bedrooms have wooden shutters to prevent escape of light, and slatted metal shutters to keep out splinters.

Doherty was wounded with what he called an explosive bullet. He states that this type of bullet is in general use. It does not contain explosive matter, but a hard steel core within the lead bullet. On impact the bullet "fragments" violently. A number of fragments were extracted from Doherty's shoulder and leg, and the result of two of these bullets striking his aircraft was that a large number of airframe members were damaged. The bullet makes a small hole on entry and a large hole on exit.

A captured Italian pilot reported that there is a reserve pool of Italian pilots at Majorca, which is constantly maintained at a strength of 100.

Result of Foreign Intervention.

Doherty stated that he believed that the Spanish Government hoped that Russian intervention would result either in intervention being stopped all round, or else in war between Russia and Italy. In the latter case the Government hoped that they would be able to deal with Franco unsupported in their own time. He said Madrid is well supplied with provisions, and if Franco was not quickly successful in his attack on Madrid, it would take a long time to starve out the capital.

Co-operation with Catalan Government.

He thought there would be no difficulty about co-operation between the Madrid government and the Catalan Government. It had been arranged if necessary, for the Air Forces at Madrid to go to Barcelona.

(There is no reason to suppose that Doherty had any means of knowing the actual relations between the two Governments or personalities within the Madrid Government).

Future Intervention.

Doherty said that he would like to be able to forward information to the Air Ministry when he gets back to Madrid, but he did not wish to go to the British authorities in Madrid. The French pilot Dary returns to Paris regularly, and he thought that Dary would be willing to take letters to the Air Attaché, Paris, if this was desired. For the time being Dary is to be found by addressing letters to South Africa House.[17]

Doherty left for Spain on 30 October 1936 without knowing the outcome of his request for the training of Spanish pilots in Britain under the Civil Training Scheme then in operation. Despite the plea of the Spanish Ambassador nothing came of the scheme because the Foreign Office were against it. Spanish Republican pilots subsequently were sent to the Soviet Union for training.

After escorting de Wet and the others to Spain, Doherty returned to Britain where he recruited Sydney Holland and Walter Scott Coates before going back with them to Spain. For the next few months he seems to have spent his time between Spain and the UK trying to acquire aircraft for the Republic with such as Kennett, Lindsay and others. The trail then goes cold and, despite many enquiries in the UK and abroad, no further mention has been found of this most courageous and skilful of pilots.

A few days after returning from Spain, on 11 October 1936, Edward Hillman flew low over his house in Gidea Park in a Miles M.2H Hawk Major (G-ADDC). He was so low that the registration letters could easily be seen. Subsequent police investigations revealed that this aircraft, together with another Miles M.2H Hawk Major (G-ADDU), had taken-off from Brooklands, their destination registered as Oxford, en route for Dublin. The aircraft never reached Oxford, or indeed Ireland, and were never seen again in England.[18] The Miles Hawk (G-ADDC) was at San Javier naval air base in Spain in early November. The other also reached Republican Spain, for it appears Hillman and Leslie Charles Lewis, the co-owner of the aircraft, had flown them via Abridge Flying Club to France. For the low flying offence and for not having a flying licence Hillman was fined £50 at Romford, according to subsequent press reports.

In July 1937 Hillman finally obtained his 'A' Licence (No.15164) at Southend Flying School. He then became a flying instructor at Rochester before going to Nottingham in June 1939 where he joined the Royal Air Force. After two years non-commissioned service he was commissioned in 1941 and spent much of the rest of World War II in Flying Training Schools and Operational Training Units. He also served in No. 520 Squadron at Gibraltar on meteorological duties and ended the war with No. 525 Squadron as a Flight Lieutenant flying Dakotas to Allied bases on the Continent. He did not leave the service until March 1946 when he joined Swedish Airlines for a two-year contract but remained with them for eight years as a Senior Captain. In 1962 Hillman started his own air conditioning company in Sydney, Australia, and died suddenly at Brookvale, NSW, in July 1975.[19]

Of the others, Lindsay dropped out of sight after being involved with Doherty in the attempts to procure aircraft for Spain in 1937. Pat Mertz soon heard the final price for his escapade in Spain – he had to resign his RAF Reserve service.[20] During World War II he served in the RAF as aircrew from February 1941 to the end of the war and remained in the service until October 1948, reaching the rank of Warrant Officer. His subsequent career is not known. Crawford also dropped out of sight.

The postscript to this story is best left to Andrés García Lacalle who, in 1973, had this to say of these men. "Without restriction, all the British pilots came to join us at a most critical and difficult time. The tragic fate that befell nearly all of them is not to be wondered at."

CHAPTER 7 – SOURCES/NOTES

To unravel the story of these men has been extremely difficult and many questions remain unanswered and will probably continue to remain that way as records and official documents that could supply this information have disappeared or are still withheld. The first mention from a Spanish source would seem to be in the book by Miguel Sanchís in 1956 (see Bibliography) who mentions Martin-Drew and Warsew [sic].

1.   FO 371 File (1936) 20577. Unfortunately, many documents listed are missing from this file.

2.   Ibid.

3.   Ibid.

4.   FO 371 File (1936) 20545.

5.   The company that insured pilots in Spain was C.A.M.A.T. of Paris.

6.   Ibid 1.

7.   *Daily Express*, 6 October 1936.

8.   *Daily Express*, 30 September 1936.

9.   *Mitos y Verdades: la Aviación de Caza en la Guerra Española*, by Andrés García Lacalle; Mexico 1973.

10.   Ibid 4..

11.   Ibid 8.

12.   FO 371 File (1937) 21284

13.   *Cape Argus* (Cape Town), 3 October 1936.

14.   Information from Mrs Georgie Hillman.

15.   FO 371 File (1936) 20547.

16. Ibid.

17. The 'unknown' Russian fighter mentioned was the Polikarpov 1-16 *Mosca*. Of the other aircraft mentioned, the Junkers 86 was, in fact, a Junkers Ju 52; the Boeing fighter was the Boeing 281, one of which had been supplied to Spain before the war; the Arado with a 'moto-cannon' remains an enigma.

18. FO 371 Files (1936) 20586, 20587, 20589.

19. Ibid 14.

20. Ibid 7.

CHAPTER 8

Eric Griffiths – The Fighting Kiwi

In about 1907 a young man from Birmingham, Percy Griffiths, emigrated to New Zealand and settled down in Wellington. He married a local girl of French extraction, Nancy Dorant. A son was born in the early autumn of 1912. Later the same year the young couple and their baby son undertook the long sea voyage to Britain in order to visit Percy's family. By this time Nancy was pregnant again and a second boy, who was given the names Eric Neville, was born in Birmingham on the 9 September 1913. Soon it was time to return home to New Zealand and the family took ship for Wellington in the late summer of 1914 as the clouds of war were looming over Europe. The news of the outbreak of World War I reached them as the ship was passing through the Suez Canal.

Back home in New Zealand the family prospered. Percy built a house in Eastbourne, Wellington, and followed his profession as a jeweller. As soon as they were old enough the two boys attended first Muritai School and then Wellington College. Eric soon showed himself to be a high-spirited lad with a volatile personality who tended to hit first and ask questions afterwards. He also began to show a growing interest in aviation and was determined to obtain his flying licence. This led to him missing classes in his final year at Wellington College to attend flying lessons at Wairarapa Aero Club, where his instructor, Flight Lt Jack Buckeridge, soon found that Eric had a natural aptitude for flying. The failure to attend his classes at College, however, led to Eric failing to Matriculate which would later prevent him obtaining a Short Service Commission in the Royal Air Force.

After leaving college, Eric spent several months in 1931 as a mechanic on a joy-riding tour with the famous New Zealand pilot, Squadron Ldr M.C. McGregor, DFC and bar. "Mad Mac", as he was known, had flown over 3,000 hours and served in France with the Royal Flying Corps in World War I. He had also flown the first New Zealand Mail from South Island to North.

Also with the troupe on the barnstorming tour was "Scotty" Fraser whose speciality was performing spectacular parachute jumps in front of the crowds of onlookers in the small country towns. Eric also acted as general assistant during the tour and filled in for Fraser sometimes on parachute jumps. On one occasion "Mad Mac" noticed there were few people coming forward for flights and asked Eric to ascertain the problem. He soon discovered that a local "bush lawyer" was claiming that the fee being charged was to high. "Mad Mac" then offered him a free flight in the Avro which the local found irresistible. Once in the air, however, McGregor asked him if he would care for a little stunting. The man acquiested so Mac turned on a full display of aerobatics, including inverted flight for a few minutes and a spin. He then landed and Eric helped the victim, now violently sick, out of the aircraft and parked him beside the airstrip. The onlookers were not in any way put off by all this and business was brisk for the rest of the day.[1]

During the tour Eric continued his flying lessons under the tuition of Squadron Ldr McGregor and obtained his private pilot's licence in 1932. "Mad Mac" continued his career and finished in fourth place in the famous MacRobertson Air Race between England and Australia in October 1934 (Handicap Race) flying a Miles Hawk with Capt H.C. Walker. Both McGregor and Fraser lost their lives shortly afterwards. McGregor, in a crash following a collision whilst coming in to land, and Fraser when his parachute failed to open during a display.

Young Eric, still only nineteen years of age, now made his way to China where he spent eight months in 1933. During this period he offered his services to several of the warlords and gave flying instruction on Moths and Avians. He also ferried many different types of aircraft, including American and British single-seater fighters, from Shanghai to the inland centres. Eric then returned to New Zealand for a refresher course in flying and obtained that most valuable asset, a commercial pilot's licence.

In the late autumn of 1933 Richard E. Byrd, the explorer from the USA, was in New Zealand making preparations for his second Antarctic expedition. Eric was engaged in early December as a mechanic on the assembly of the large biplane Curtiss-Wright Condor aircraft being taken with the expedition. This special Condor, named *William Horlick* after a principal sponsor, was to be shipped, fully assembled on floats, as deck-cargo aboard the expedition's ship, the *SS Jacob Ruppert*.

Eric impressed the Americans with his ability and the fact that he held a pilot's licence, and shortly before the expedition set sail he was told that he would be taken to the Antarctic as a mechanic. Eric decided to go hoping to get in some flying, a decision he was soon to regret as he found that the New Zealand members of the expedition did not receive the same conditions as the American members on board. All they seemed to be wanted for was to attend to the dogs with the expedition; there was also a shortage of winter clothing for the New Zealanders. Never one to dodge an issue Eric led complaints to Byrd which eventually led to him being put in the "brig". Needless to say he did not stay with the expedition, coming back to New Zealand as soon as the ship returned there.

Arriving at Wellington at the end of February 1934. Eric was determined to try to obtain a second-hand Lockheed Vega aircraft to fly in the MacRobertson Air Race planned for later that year. He was unable to raise enough capital to finance his entry in the race despite many efforts to obtain backing. Some accounts say he again went to China in 1934 but this cannot be confirmed. Other accounts say that he sold motor cars for a living but, understandably, this proved tame work for Eric. By the spring of 1935 Eric's taste for adventure led him to take ship for England to try to obtain a Short Service Commission in the RAF. On his arrival in London, however, Eric soon found that his failure to Matriculate in 1930 from Wellington College prevented him obtaining a commission. Disappointed, he looked around to see where his talents could be most of use. The Italo-Ethiopian dispute was making daily headlines in the national press by the summer of 1935. Eric became aware that the Ethiopians possessed very few aircraft and only a handful of trained pilots if war did break out with Italy. One day in June 1935 he paid a visit to the Ethiopian Legation in London and offered to organise a volunteer "air force" to fly for them using old Bristol Fighter aircraft which had been declared obsolete by the Royal Air Force and were on the sale list of the Air Ministry. The Ethiopian authorities gave their approval for the scheme and asked Eric to engage other pilots to fly the aeroplanes to Addis Ababa. Money and all facilities were to be given by the Ethiopian Government.

Eric set about recruiting pilots for the "air force" from unemployed ex-service aircrew in London. One of these, however, informed the Air Ministry of Griffith's intentions before Eric had approached the Foreign Office with the proposal, as requested by the Ethiopian authorities. In early July Eric sent the following letter to the Foreign Office:[2]

c/o New Zealand House,
415 Strand W.C.2.

July 4th 1935.

SCHEME FOR A PRIVATE BRITISH MILITARY AVIATION MISSION TO ABYSSINIA

To:- The Secretary of State for Foreign Affairs.
    (For the attention of the Ethiopian Dept.)

Sir,

As arranged verbally with you today we have the honour to submit in writing the following matter for your consideration.

The object of the scheme is to form the nucleus of an Abyssinian Fighting Air Force, with British personnel and suitable British aircraft, and military equipment. Further to organise and use this force for effective resistance to the Italian Forces should the latter attempt to invade Abyssinia.

It is proposed initially to collect 15 pilots who have had Service training, with the necessary complement of mechanics. These would be approved by the Ethiopian Authorities, and given military appointments in the Abyssinian combatant forces before leaving England.

Suitable aircraft less armament equipment would be purchased in England by the promoters of the Mission, acting as the agents of the Abyssinian Government, and flown out to Abyssinia as soon as possible.

On arrival there organisation and training for war would be proceeded with, and arrangments made for expansion of Abyssinian air power, in accordance with the development of strategical and tactical needs.

The initial aircraft which we have in mind are Bristol Fighters, which are obtainable from civil firms in this country, and which are not fitted with any armament.

In view of the International political issues involved it is proposed to use the cover of a

135

commercial undertaking in order to make certain of successfully transporting the first batch of aircraft from England to Abyssinia.

The plan proposed for this is to equip the party as a self contained aerial film expedition, proceeding to Egypt and the Sudan, with the ostensible object of making a historical film of the war activities of Col. Lawrence, and the Australian Flying Corps.

The intention is to create in Abyssinia, efficient fighting units similar in character to the famous Lafayette Escadrille, which operated with such success with the French Air Force during the war. Also ultimately to lay the foundations of an efficient Abyssinian Air Force with native personnel.

The Ethiopian Authorities have already favourably received this proposal, but have expressed the wish that the promotors should ascertain the attitude of the Foreign Office on the matter before any further action is taken.

As time is an important factor it would be greatly appreciated if we can be given an immediate indication of the attitude which the Foreign Office is likely to adopt.

I have the honour to be, Sir,
Your obedient servant
E. N. Griffiths

During the next few days Eric called several times at the Foreign Office in the hopes of learning the attitude of the British Government to his proposal. Unknown to him this scheme caused shock-waves to travel through the Civil Service and Government Departments – cries of horror were made at such a proposal. Finally, on 17 July, the Foreign Office sent Eric a letter that H.M.G. in the UK were unable to give their approval as "the avowed purpose of the proposal would contravene the regulations prescribed by the Arms Export Prohibition Order of 1931."

So Eric's hopes were quashed again. He had gone so far as to enter hospital to be inoculated and his small capital had dwindled away so he decided to join the British Army as a private soldier. He enlisted in London at the headquarters of The Rifle Brigade in early August 1935 and was sent to the depot at Winchester for his training as a rifleman. At the end of January 1936 he was transferred to the First Battalion at Gosport.

Eric's temperament was never suited for the narrow, mind-killing life of a British common soldier at that time. He had only joined up because he was temporarily down and out. Soon his individuality and quick temper caused him serious problems with the non-commissioned officers at Gosport. Amongst the enlisted men, however, he held his own – although average height, only 5'8½" tall, he weighed about 12 stone. His fellow soldiers did not believe him at first when he told them of his adventurous life to date until he produced cuttings from the New Zealand newspapers showing him joining the Byrd Expedition, etc.

By the spring of 1936, however, he had had enough of the Army. His conflict with authority finally culminated in the RSM of the unit "meeting with an unfortunate accident one dark night". Eric walked out on the Army in April 1936 and, in the words of the Ministry of Defence, "was in a state of absence" from then until February 1937, when he was finally discharged after his father had bought him out of his enlistment.

Eric's career over the next few months has been difficult to establish as he was not a prolific letter writer to his family back in New Zealand. Several sources state that he obtained employment on the ground staff of Imperial Airways and then was engaged in air charter work between London and Paris. He also reported to have obtained employment with the Douglas Aircraft Company during this period.

The outbreak of the Spanish Civil War in July 1936, however, gave him the chance he had been waiting for. According to interviews he gave to newspapers later on Eric became involved with the shipment of British civil aircraft to the Spanish Republicans in August 1936 and, on the conclusion of his third flight, threw in his lot with the Loyalist cause. No confirmation has yet been found that he piloted any of the civil aircraft that left Britain for Spain that month but he may have gone along as a mechanic. He may also have been one of the group of pilots that left London for Spain in early September along with Downes-Martin and Doherty. By the time of his 23rd birthday, he was at Getafe airfield near Madrid, one of the group of British pilots flying for the so-called "International Squadron".

Eric soon struck up a friendship with the South African Vincent Doherty and, like Doherty, formed a tremendous respect for the Spanish people in their struggle against the armed might of the Nationalsits under Franco and his German and Italian allies. Like the other Britons he had to fly the obsolete Nieuport Ni-D.52 fighters against the German Heinkel He 51s and Italian Fiat CR.32s, both of which were far superior. Later on, however, he was allowed to pilot the French Dewoitine D.372 which allowed him to take on the opposing fighters with some chance to survive an air combat. He soon found that the Italian airmen would only take on a Loyalist patrol if the odds were greatly in their favour. Eric later claimed to have shot down five fighters and two bombers whilst serving with the Republicans, but owing to the difficulty of identification he was only given credit for only four machines, being paid a bonus of £200 for each.

On 26 September 1936 he was on patrol with Vincent Doherty over the Toledo front when they were jumped by several Fiat CR.32s. Before he had the chance to do anything Eric received a stunning blow in his right shoulder – an explosive bullet had passed right through. His arm was useless but he managed to pull the joystick back with the left hand and climb away – luckily his aircraft had not been hit. Somehow he managed to get back to Getafe and land safely.

A short time after Doherty had been rescued from his aircraft and taken to the infirmary, Eric's Dewoitine landed some distance away with the engine racing. At first no one took any notice but eventually, when they saw that the pilot did not get out, two mechanics strolled up. The first man to reach the aircraft scrambled up on the machine and had a good look, then rushed off with his companion. Shortly afterwards a procession of cars and ambulances sped toward the stationary plane, and Griffiths was taken to the infirmary.

Eric had to wait his turn as the doctor was already treating Doherty. When the doctor finally ripped off the remains of Eric's shirt and saw the gaping hole where the bullet had struck all present were amazed at how Eric could have borne the pain for so long.

Hospital treatment followed in Madrid where both Eric and Vincent Doherty were afforded the best available, as previously recounted. Eric also later received the sum of £1,000 from the Spaniards due to his injury (as promised in his contract). The fact that he had been wounded whilst flying for the Republic made him, like Doherty, a hero in the eyes of the Spaniards and nothing was too good for them. Back home, in New Zealand, the first his family knew that Eric was in Spain was when his father read a report in a newspaper that a Mr Eric Griffiths had been wounded when fighting against rebel aircraft. He knew immediately that this must be his son. . .[3]

Vincent Doherty had soon recovered enough to leave hospital whilst Eric continued his convalescence. By mid October all the surviving British pilots had returned home to the UK and Eric, with his right arm in plaster, spent most of his time between treatment at the hospital and mixing with the foreign correspondents and pilots at the Hotel Florida in Madrid. By now he was in contact again with his family back home in New Zealand and also his former girlfriend from college days in Wellington, Fay Robinson, whom he had not seen for over two years. One day he cabled a proposal of marriage to her. She accepted but her parents would not let her travel to Paris for the wedding as Eric had requested. They then made plans to marry in New Zealand when Eric had recovered sufficiently to travel – he was, however, not to return home for nearly eight months.

By early November 1936 Franco's forces were advancing ever nearer to Madrid and threatened to take the capital within days. One day Eric heard that his friend Vincent Doherty had recruited several more Britons to fly for the Loyalist cause and met them at the Hotel Florida shortly after their arrival. Eric was invited to spend the night at the hotel due to the Nationalist bombardment, which was just as well because the hospital where he was convalescing fell to Franco during the night.

The new arrivals soon went on their way but not before Eric had told them many stories of the first group of British pilots in Spain. He made them laugh with his gift for mimicry. He enjoyed speaking in an English north-country manner (probably picked up in his Army days). The courtly, dignified du Berrier, however, found it difficult to establish a rapport with the high-spirited, proletarian New Zealander.

The intervention of the first International Brigades and the stubborn refusal to surrender by the common people of Madrid stopped Franco's troops in their tracks at the outskirts of the city. When it was considered that Eric was fit enough he assisted in a training school for Spanish pilots but the Republican Government had other plans for him. They entrusted him with a mission to go to France and the UK to see if he could obtain further aircraft and war materials.

His movements over the next few months are difficult to establish but it is known, from such documents that still exist in the Public Record Office at Kew, that Eric was in England during December, when he visited relations in the Midlands and chartered an aircraft which he flew to Yate aerodrome, near Bristol, before returning to Paris with a certain Henry F. Harrington, a former employee of Imperial Airways and Air Dispatch Ltd. Harrington was strongly suspected by the police of being involved in the purchase of aeroplanes and recruitment of pilots for Spain. The reason for these surreptitious comings and goings became clear the following March (1937) when, after a tip-off, the police found a silver and red Armstrong Whitworth Atlas in a hangar on West Malling airfield in Kent, fuelled-up and ready for take-off. Ownership was traced to Eric and Harrington. The aircraft was dismantled and stayed at West Malling for several weeks, the owners not knowing what to do with it. It was finally sold to a breaker.[4]

It is also thought that Eric was involved in the attempt to fly a Short Scion (G-ADDN) to Spain in the same month. According to a story that appeared in *The Star* newspaper on 25 March 1937 and other sources, Edwin Semons (the American airman who had gone to Spain with the Acosta group – see Chapter 5) and "a New Zealander with a wound in the shoulder which he had got while flying in Spain" tried to get Douglas Lucke, a well-known British civil pilot, to fly the aircraft to Santander on the pretext of rescuing "three rich Spaniards" who wished to get out of Spain. Lucke strongly suspected this was just a way to obtain the aircraft and reported the matter to the police and the whole scheme came to nothing.[5]

According to Hilaire du Berrier, Eric visited him in Paris and later became involved with the opportunist Freddie Lord, also of the Acosta group, in a deal to sell three million pesetas worth of reconditioned war material to the Loyalists through Colonel Alberto Bayo (see Chapter 4). They convinced Bayo that they had a firm deal and could ship the material to one of the Channel Isles without customs searches. After that the shipments would be transferred to Spain in smaller boats. Bayo came to Paris to meet them in February 1937, with the intention of going on to England to inspect the arms. The British authorities would not let him enter the country so he had to return to Paris.

Throughout the winter and early spring of 1937 Eric travelled in and out of Loyalist Spain still enjoying popularity because he had been wounded fighting for the cause. By the late spring he decided he had had enough of the Spanish conflict for, at least, a time and was anxious to return home to New Zealand where his family and bride-to-be were waiting to see him. By now he had received the £1,000 promised to him in his contract after being wounded so could afford the fare back to New Zealand.[6] He sailed to New Zealand in May.

His first port-of-call in Australia was Freemantle. There, as later in Melbourne and Sydney, he was interviewed by the press regarding his Spanish Civil War experiences. He finally arrived at Auckland on 14 June 1937 to be greeted by the press and his patient fiancée. After more interviews the young couple tried to arrange to be married at the Auckland Registry Office, but discovered that it was necessary for one of them to have a residential qualification of three days in Auckland before a licence could be issued. They, therefore, finally managed to get married at Wellington a week later.

Visiting his family and friends in Wellington took up most of the next few weeks but soon Eric's wanderlust came to the fore again. Towards the end of 1937 Eric and his new bride took ship for California where he hoped to renew acquaintanceship with the film actor, Errol Flynn, whom he had met in Spain when Flynn was visiting the Loyalists. Eric thought he might be able to become a technical adviser for any films being made in Hollywood about the Spanish Civil War.

News reaching home towards the end of 1937 said that Eric was employed by the

Douglas Aircraft Company and re-enacting scenes from the Spanish conflict for the films. How much of this is true is not known but it appears that he did pay a flying visit to Mexico with Errol Flynn during his sojourn in the USA and later spoke of an ambition to ride through that country on a *burro*. Eric also busied himself to fly again using his left hand as his right arm was now virtually useless.

After several months Eric and his wife returned to New Zealand, where he decided to apply for a job as a pilot with Union Airways. He was accepted and, after his training in the Union Airways' radio school, took up his appointment in June 1938. Now perhaps, his family and wife must have thought he would settle down to a more normal existence. Eric became a co-pilot with Union Airways and in September 1938 applied for enlistment in the New Zealand Civil Reserve of Pilots. But already he was finding peace time flying was too tame for his taste and, in the words of one of his colleagues at Union Airways, that "the disciplines required for airline flying did not appeal to him". So he left the company. Hearing that there might be employment available in China in the ongoing war with Japan he decided to go there.

In early 1939 Eric showed up in Hong Kong and immediately went to the newspapers. Eric reasoned that a burst of publicity about his combat experience in Spain could get him a job with the Chinese. In April 1939, Colonel Li Fang, former secretary of the Governor of Kwangtung Province, met him with a proposition. A few days later Eric turned up at the flat of soldier-of-fortune supreme, Hilaire du Berrier, who had been in Kowloon for over a year working on one plan after another with the famous Old Etonian, Frank 'One-Arm' Sutton, who became a millionaire making trench mortars out of steel tubing for the warlord of Manchuria, Chang Tso-lin, and who later died of beri-beri in a prison camp in Hong Kong. Eric suggested he should meet Li Fang.

That evening in a shabby Chinese hotel the scheme was unfolded. Li Fang said that a guerrilla force had been set up to make lightning strikes on Japanese landing strips to hold them long enough for his pilots to take off with the aircraft. The retaining pay would be sufficient for their needs and the prize money would be high.

A few days later, Eric, du Berrier and two other pilots Li Fang had recruited for this mad scheme – an Italian named Nino Brondello and a tall Canadian called Hamilton Wright – set sail for Shanghai on the P & O liner *Canton*. In the stateroom on the ship Li Fang introduced the men to the general in charge of the scheme, Yeh Peng, formerly commander of the Hankow-Wuhan military area. On arrival in Shanghai Eric, Brondello and Wright went to live in an apartment on Wei Hai Wei Road.

Du Berrier soon moved to another address. Here he was soon in contact with Captain Rougy, a Frenchman who was connected with the French *Renseignement Guerre No 1* – a branch of their Intelligence Service. One morning there was a surprise visitor for du Berrier. It was Yeh Peng who wanted to see Rougy at once. The meeting was arranged and the Chinese general told the French captain that he would soon be named Minister for War and Commander-in-chief of the armed forces for the Japanese puppet government headed by Wang Ching-wei, but it was all a plot on behalf of General Chang Kai-shek. He would organise an army for Wang at Japanese expense and then, on a given order from the Chinese Nationalist leader, "knife the Japanese in the back". A plan of peculiarly Asiatic deviousness.

Eric and the other pilots never knew how they were being used as pawns in this scheme. Brondello (who went down at sea in a small aircraft, trying to cross the Atlantic in the early '50s) and Wright soon disappeared from the scene leaving Eric on his own. He fell out with the general's men and quickly left Shanghai for home but not before obtaining an expensive suit from the Chinese tailor, Baromon, at their expense. Du Berrier never went with General Yeh Peng either.[7]

Back home in Wellington and glad to be away from the intrigue and the politics of China, Eric found the world was drifting towards war again. Hitler was making threats towards Poland and it was obvious that New Zealand would join the rest of the Empire in supporting Britain.

World War II duly broke out in September 1939 and Eric, still on the Civil Reserve of Pilots, was appointed to the Wellington General Reconnaissance Squadron of the Royal New Zealand Air Force in the rank of Flying Officer and mobilised at Woodbourne, Blenheim. During the next three months or so he flew training missions and convoy escorts in Blackburn Baffins. In January 1940, he became a staff pilot at the Air Gunners and Air Observers School at Ohakea, flying mostly Vickers Vincents and D.H.86s. By now his flying skill had been noted by the RNZAF, for in October 1949 Eric was appointed as a test pilot at No.1 Aircraft Depot, Hobsonville, where he flew newly assembled Hawker Hinds. Test pilots at Hobsonville never numbered more than two at a time throughout the war and were usually pilots rated as "exceptional" (a very rare classification in any air force). It seemed at last that Eric had found his niche in life although he still fretted for a more active participation in the war.

In 1940 the Japanese threat in the South Pacific became more and more dangerous. Landing grounds were constructed by the RNZAF on Viti Levu, one of the Fiji Islands, and a detachment (later 'Unit 20' and then No. 4 General Reconnaissance Squadron) formed to go there. Eric was posted with the new unit to Fiji in November 1940 flying on the first operational mission in a D.H.89 Rapide to intercept and escort two ships approaching Suva, the capital of Fiji, with full loads of troops from New Zealand. The Rapides were fitted with a couple of bomb racks carrying 250lb bombs.

On 1 January 1941 Eric was promoted to the rank of Flight Lieutenant and spent most of the next few months on training flights around the islands and convoy patrols in the Rapides and later in Vincents and the four-engined D.H.86. Towards the end of the year he twice flew V.I.P.s to the tropical paradise Tonga Islands – the war must have seemed far away. Off duty hours were spent enjoying the amenities of Fiji, sun-bathing on the beautiful beaches listening to jazz records, and running around the island in his open "Vauxhall bomb". Eric became fond of Fiji finding there, especially in the indigenous Fijian people, something that reminded him of Spain. He made many friends whilst in Fiji and was popular with the officers and enlisted men alike at the airbase at Nadi (phonetically spelt Nandi).

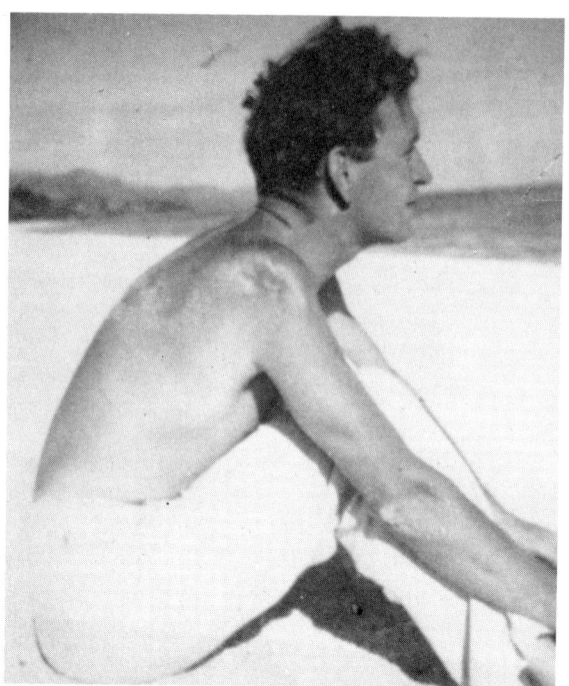

Eric Grffiths on beach in Fiji, 1941. Note wound in right shoulder caused by explosive bullet. (Courtesy Miss Dorothy Kearsley)

Eric was still a devil-may-care character known as "Griff" to one and all. On occasion he would rush into the workshop in the airbase to get the old Gipsy Moth they had started up and he would chase and burst the weather balloons the meteorological section had sent up, never waiting for the motor to warm up or testing the magnetos. After his wound during the Spanish Civil War Eric's right arm hung down nearly 2" longer than the left and the youthful 'erks' at Nadi used to delight in saluting Eric knowing that he could not raise his right arm very high. He used to bend his head over to meet his hand instead.

In early December 1941, as war in the Pacific seemed imminent, Eric received instructions to proceed to New Zealand by the first ship, but the outbreak of hostilities with Japan a few days later led to him being retained in Fiji.

The entry of the USA into the war led to news that an American fighter squadron was being sent to bolster the defence of the islands. Eric at once requested that he should be attached to the Americans in view of his considerable knowledge of the USA and his experience gained in Spain.

The 70th Pursuit Squadron of the USAAF began arriving at Suva in early February 1942 and were stationed initially beside a grass strip airfield at Nasouri, ten miles inland. Their aircraft, the sleek, beautifully streamlined Bell P-39D Airacobra, were soon being uncrated and assembled at the strip by the ground crews with the assistance of a representative from Bell Aircraft. On completion they were transferred to Nadi, and thence to a new fighter field at Nawera. By the 21 February 1942, the day Eric managed to get himself attached officially to the US squadron as "Liaison Officer", there were 20 P-39Ds at Nadi. Eric had already been in close contact with the Americans and had taken a P-39D up for a flight the previous day. The CO of the USAAF unit was Captain Henry Viccellio and Eric soon found he had much in common with some of the Americans — these included Tom Lamphier, Rex Barber, Jack Jacobson, Doug Canning and John Mitchell who later in the war shot down the bomber carrying the Japanese architect of the Pearl Harbour raid, Yamamoto.

On 23 February 1942, Eric strapped himself into a P-39D (41-7107) for another local flight. In the course of the sortie he intercepted one of his own RNZAF unit's Vickers

Vincents and could not resist the temptation to "buzz" it. Unfortunately he was still not familiar with the flying characteristics of the P-39 monoplane – never an easy aircraft to fly. The plane entered a high speed stall at low altitude and crashed out of control in to the ground about half a mile north of Nadi village, killing Eric instantly. There was no fire because Eric, as soon as he knew a crash was inevitable, had cut both ignition switches.

Bell P-39 of USAAF during World War II. (Courtesy C. F. Shores)

It was sadly ironic that the Vincent was being flown by Eric's friend, Flight Lt Ian Salmond. The groundcrews at Nadi were so upset by Eric's death that, in the words of one of them, "it was the only occasion that I can recall when all of us decided not to open the wet canteen for the night as a means of respect". He was buried with full military honours at Lautoka the following day but later re-interred in the Military Cemetary, Suva (Row 9; No. 133).

Eric Griffiths was a superb pilot who never had the chance to show his skill in the service of his own country in war, a man who did not suffer fools gladly but who had the common touch. Always candid, somewhat temperamental, intolerant of pretence and stuffiness, he made enemies as well as friends easily but he is remembered with great affection by many today.

CHAPTER 8 - SOURCES/NOTES

Much of the information regarding Eric's early life was kindly supplied by Mr R.P. (Dick) Griffiths. Many of Eric's former RNZAF and Union Airways colleagues also supplied much information. Especial thanks are due to Mrs Sally Chao, Dave Duxbury, Errol Martyn, Brent Mackrell in New Zealand and Miss Dorothy Kearsley in Fiji who also provided much information. Details of Eric's service career come from Ministry of Defence records, both here in the UK and New Zealand. I would also like to thank the editors of *The Evening Post* (Wellington) and *The New Zealand Herald* (Auckland) for their assistance in my research.

1. *Mac's Memoirs: The Flying Life of Squadron Leader McGregor,* by G.H. Cunningham; Wellington 1937.

2. FO371 File (1935) 19176.

3. *Dominion,* 5 October 1936.

4. FO371 File (1937) 21320. Also: Public Record Office – Air Ministry Files. AVIA 2/1976. Part II (1937-8).

5. Ibid.

6. The payments made to Griffiths (referred to as a "young Australian pilot") and Doherty are mentioned in the American journalist, H. Edward Knoblaugh, in his book, *Correspondent in Spain* (London 1937).

7. Information from Hilaire du Berrier.

CHAPTER 9

The File on John Wilson

Of all the British airmen who fought in the Spanish Civil War surely the story of John Wilson is the most strange – and the most difficult to establish the truth behind all the self-publicity at this distance in time.

The facts as set out in various newspaper articles in the autumn and early winter of 1936-37 state that the pale, slightly built Wilson, a student at Oriel College, Oxford or Liverpool University (or both), had left college before taking his degree and gone to Spain shortly after the rebellion of the generals in July 1936 to volunteer his services to the Republican Government. He claimed to have had military training and to have a civil pilot's licence. His home was in London or Royal Street, Liverpool (again accounts vary).

He had told his parents that he was going on a holiday in Folkestone and with only three pounds in his pocket made his way to Spain. Here his "extensive knowledge of aeronautical mechanics and considerable flying experience" soon allowed him to join the Republican Air Force. Wilson was assigned to Barajas airport in early August and survived the first bombing raid by Insurgent aircraft on the night of 2/3 August, when two bombs had fallen between the house he was staying and a bomb dump (luckily for him the bombs had buried themselves in the mud and failed to explode). A few days later he witnessed the landing of the *Lufthansa* Junkers Ju 52 (D-AMYN) at Barajas. This aircraft had taxied up to the hangars and the German pilot leaned out of the cockpit and asked some mechanics who was in charge – the rebels or the Government. The clenched fists and cries of *Viva Republica* soon told him and he quickly took off again but the aircraft ran out of fuel; the pilot had to land at Azuaga (near Badajoz) and the aircraft was confiscated by the Republicans despite threats from the German Government. The five crew members were released.

Wilson claimed to have flown the Junkers later on a bombing raid but, in fact, this aircraft was probably only used to demonstrate fighter tactics to use against the Insurgent bombers as the Spanish Government, bowing to pressure from the League of Nations, refused to let the aircraft to be used on bombing missions. It was finally destroyed, together with most of the remaining serviceable aeroplanes, during an air raid on Barajas on the night of 26/27 October 1936.

The first mention of Wilson in the British press seems to have been in the *Oxford Mail* of 25 August 1936, when it was stated that he had arrived in Madrid after receiving a bullet in the left arm (later said to have been caused by a piece of shrapnel from an anti-aircraft gun). During the first week of September, however, several of the national daily

145

newspapers carried stories received from the British United Press that Wilson (aged 21) "the hero of the Spanish Loyalist's air force" was lying wounded in a Madrid hospital after an air battle when he had fought a lone battle with three Insurgent aircraft, shooting down a Hawker Fury [sic]. His aircraft (said to be the Junkers) had been riddled with bullets and he himself had received three bullet wounds in his right side. Wilson managed to land in a ploughed field and was taken to hospital where an operation was performed.

The famous correspondent of the British Communist newspaper the *Daily Worker*, Claud Cockburn (known in Spain as Frank Pitcairn), interviewed Wilson in hospital. His version of the story is more believable; in this Wilson (now stationed at the airfield of Cuatro Vientos) had gone up on patrol as the machine gunner of an aircraft on 29 August. Before they reached their destination the aircraft had been intercepted by three Insurgent machines. In the battle that followed Wilson had shot down one of the attackers before the Spanish pilot had managed to put down their own damaged aircraft. Wilson, with blood streaming from one leg, had been helped out of his cockpit by the pilot before militiamen took him to the nearest field hospital from which he was taken later to the Military Hospital in Madrid.[1]

Wilson later said he remained in hospital for a fortnight, during which time he had received the best attention possible, but could not eat the rather oily Spanish food he was offered. He asked for some Bovril and great efforts were made to locate a jar for him. After a week on leave he returned to duty at Barajas. About this time Wilson became a well known figure around the bars in Madrid where he would recount the story of his air combats to anyone who would listen. He may have served in the same squadron as Griffin, Warsow and Downes-Martin during this period and, towards the end of September, news reached home that he had been promoted to a Captain in the Republican Air Force.

Wilson returned to England around 20 October for medical treatment and was interviewed by the press, "still wearing his blood-stained boots and pilot's jacket" at his fiancée's home at Northwich, Cheshire. He told the journalists that he had been engaged in bombing raids on Toledo and Oviedo as well as patrolling the Portuguese coast. Wilson also told of the atrocities he had witnessed in Spain and handed the reporter for the *Liverpool Evening Express* a dagger which he said he had taken from the chest of a four-year-old-boy – he had shot the man who had thrown the knife and the child's life had been saved in hospital.[2]

Shortly afterwards he returned to Spain where he took up his café life existence with Franco's forces at the outskirts of Madrid. Hilaire du Berrier was one of many pilots and journalists who remember him during these days. The American journalist, H. Edward Knoblaugh, referred to Wilson in his book *Correspondent in Spain* (as John –):[3]

> The publicity-loving young flyer from the Oxford University group, John –, was a striking example. There is no need to mention John's last name. All the correspondents in Loyalist Spain knew him well. He provided us with not a small amount of entertainment. We first came to know John when he arrived in Madrid as one of a group of English

pilots whose Communistic zeal prompted them to do what they could for the cause. Young – he was not more than 20 at the most – John had had some training as a student pilot in England. He was assigned to Getafe Airport just south of Madrid where the government planes – a sad collection of worn out Nieuports and Potez at the beginning of the war – were based.

There was nothing of modesty in John. He was a flyer and he wanted to be sure everyone knew it. His flying suit, an elaborately customed affair presented by his fellow students at Oxford, had wings all over it. There were two on the chest, one on each shoulder, and another on each leg just above the knee. Silver braided wings that showed up well against the dark flying suit. His flying cap carried another set, and a pair of silver wings fashioned in pin style was worn over John's heart.

He immediately won the soubriquet of "Wings" and his fellow pilots referred to him as "the chap with so many wings loaded on him he can hardly get off the ground in a single-motor plane".

John got wounded the second time up – a bit of shrapnel in the leg – and this brought him some publicity. The wound was not bad and the squadron commander believed a week or two at the most should see John back in service. The Government was very short of flyers at that time. Even though John was not much of a help, the presence of another escort pursuit plane gave confidence to the bombers. But John had other ideas.

The flesh wound had, as John recounted for the benefit of café admirers the thrilling battle in which he had received it, gradually grown. It had become three wounds, and incendiary bullets, not shrapnel, had caused them. John had cultivated a fine limp by this time. He wrote his own story of the "battle" in which he had participated and sent it to some English labour papers which gave it great prominence. John modestly admitted he had shot down "at least two" enemy planes before the "dozens of others had got on his tail and overwhelmed him". This lasted for nearly three months, and John made two trips to England to give 'lectures' during this time. He saved all the clippings telling about his exploits and would show them to you on the slightest provocation.

One day he blossomed out with a captain's insignia. No one knew just where he had acquired it. Those were days of astonishing promotions and we did not embarrass him by asking. He now referred to himself always as "Captain". Because he wore, in addition to a pistol, an elaborately chased Toledo poniard which his English admirers had given him, pilots and newspapermen sometimes called him "Admiral". John didn't seem to mind. He had acquired a crash helmet. With it swinging from one hand and a small riding crop in the other, he continued his gay round of the cafés. If he had ever taken a plane up again after his first misadventure none of his fellow pilots knew about it, but that didn't stop the young Englishman from accounting ever new and ever more hazardous tales of prowess as part of the Loyalist air force.

But all this eventually palled on John. He hadn't had his name in print in weeks and his old café acquaintances didn't seem to have as much time to listen to him as before. He became nervous and irritable. He decided he would go down to Albacete, where the new batch of foreign pilots was being given war training. And he decided he would take along Margarita, a café girl who had proven one of his most sympathetic listeners. The night before they were to go, while John and Margarita were in the Miami bar discussing their plans, the Cheka came and took Margarita away for questioning. Her acquaintanceship with so many pilots and officers who frequented the Miami had put her under suspicion

147

as a possible spy.

John fumed and raged as she was dragged away from the divan beside him, but to no avail. We knew that Margarita would not be harmed. She had too many friends among the militia. But John was worried. He worried all that night, and even called us at the embassy to relay his fears. The next day, John's imagination having played him false, he worked himself into such a state that he became violently hysterical. He came into the censorship offices in the telephone building with a strange, far away look in his eyes. Suddenly shouting at the top of his lungs: "Pools of blood! Pools of blood!" he fell, writhing, to the floor.

All efforts to calm him proved useless. Moaning and sobbing, he lay on the floor.

"I saw them do it!" he screamed. "They killed her – killed her right before my eyes! Margarita, my poor Margarita! There she lay, her blonde hair all blood. Blood! Great pools of blood!"

Four husky assault-guards led him away. It was only after two weeks in the quiet of a sanitarium that his serenity was restored. Then he again resumed his old haunts, pathetically seeking new listeners. He seemed to have forgotten all about Margarita. But new listeners were few. John felt he was not appreciated. He went down to Valencia, where I had been assigned to cover the activities of the transplanted government. John one day brought to the censor's offices what he termed "the outline of a fine story," a story, or rather two stories, which he apparently believed would restore him to his former place in the public eye. Acting as his own publicity agent, John had conceived the idea of his own "capture" and "escape". On a single sheet of paper he had typed, for our convenience, data which he felt should be included in the two "releases".

The first half of the page, which I have kept as a souvenir of the war, was marked: "For use December 18th."

It read:

Captain John – captured by Fascists.
Was returning to England for Christmas.
Student of Liverpool and Oxford Universities.
First airman to be wounded in the revolution.
Left Madrid hospital against doctor's orders to address meeting in London.
In October left studies and threw up career to fight in Spain.
Youngest and "baby" of the Spanish air force.
Well known throughout the British political world, especially Liverpool.

The second part John had marked "For publication December 23"

It read:

Oxford student escapes from Fascist prison.
Five days of horrifying torture.
Amazing allegations.
Beastly, barbaric treatment of women.
Fascists rejoice "Air-France" airplane down.
Franco no longer chief of the rebels.
German generals in charge of airports.
Italians and Germans erect military headquarters.

Mass supplies of planes, tanks, canons [sic] machine guns and rifles.

Italians parade in uniforms of the rebels.

Germans wear the uniforms of their own country.

Moors rejoice in cutting up children and women.

Scandalous torture of innocent people.

American citizen held prisoner without reason.

Franco under orders of two Germans and Italian chiefs.

We who had known John in Madrid folded the sheets and placed them in our pockets without comment. But one young English correspondent, just arrived on the job, cabled a long story on each of the release outlines and his newspaper, we heard, used them!

John subsequently returned to England. I often have wondered whether he went back to Spain again.

Hilaire du Berrier also referred to the "pools of blood" story of Wilson in the series of articles published in the *Petit Parisien* in January 1937. Another journalist, Keith Scott Watson, also mentions him (under the name of Captain Grotto) in his book *Single to Spain*. Watson was helping the famous British correspondent for the *Daily Express,* Sefton Delmer, during the autumn of 1936 after leaving the front where he had been with the first British volunteers. One evening in Chicote's Bar in Madrid with Delmer and some of his former comrades on leave from the front. . .[4]

A leather-jacketed, top-booted figure, strode across to our table; across his uniform he wore pilot's wings, on his peaked cap, a captain's silver star. "Ha! English, I see – you know me, I expect – Captain Grotto, first pilot. Death Squadron – have a drink?"

Our visitor ordered a round. "I don't want you to think I am out here on a money-making racket – I'm not. Party man first and last. Can't say the same for other pilots but they are good boys. You chaps been up at the front?" He didn't wait for an answer but went on with his discourse, "We'll all get it soon or late – a short life," he downed his whisky in one, "but a merry one, eh?"

I looked at Delmer, did he wink? I couldn't be certain; the others looked puzzled. "What is your bag this week?" Delmer spoke with deadly seriousness.

"To tell the truth, I haven't been up, the old wound, you know." He patted his leg. "Cabellero rang me this morning," he looked round suspiciously and lowered his voice, "got a very confidential mission, 'Grotto'," he said, "I want you to be ready. I learn that Hitler is sending the Graf Zep. to Seville – understood? It's a chance, will you take it? Not a word to anyone, of course I took it, the plane's ready, tomorrow.'

"We must drink to Captain Grotto's success,' Delmer raised his glass. the whole thing was so serious that I wondered whether I was the crazy one. A dreamy look came into the captain's eyes. "To think only six months ago at the old 'Varsity' and today shooting down Nazis – makes you wonder."

"Are you an Oxford man?" asked Delmer.

"Yes. How did you guess?"

"I knew the accent. I was there myself."

The conversation waned. Joe stood up: "Well, I suppose we'd better be 'avin a bit of old shut-eye. I 'ope that 'ot water bottle ain't leakin' ternight. The captain 'adn't better be late if 'e's goin' ter drop that bomb on Franco's 'ouse before the old eggs and bacon."

The Austrians had stopped dancing; the bar was closing, we all prepared to go. A girl pushed past the doorkeeper and looked round as if in search of someone. Captain Grotto hailed her, "Yvonne". She smiled and came over to us.

"Where 'ave you been, I look for you everywhere, such a disaster – but 'oo are your friends?" He introduced Delmer as an old college chum. Then gravely saluted the English troops in the best O.T.C. style. "These boys are doing their bit for Spain."

"*Charmant*, but we must go, *au revoir*." The captain and his consort disappeared. After seeing the English to the metro for their barracks, we walked through the still, black streets to the Embassy.

"What do you make of our aviator friend?" I asked Delmer. "Now I know why no one stops the German and Italian bombers making holes in the city."

Two days after . . . I was drinking hot chocolate in the Miami; at four o'clock it was almost empty. I was so engrossed in a book that I did not notice Captain Grotto who sat himself opposite to me.

"I've had bad news, old boy, they've taken her, the swine!"

This seemed to need clearing up: "Who's taken what?"

"Yvonne – lying there cold, her lips were warm when I left her." The air ace held his head between his hands and moaned. "I'm finished with devils, I gave my all but my life – shot down – and they take my Yvonne, I know the swine, I'll get him."

This was all very difficult. "Why not go to the police about it?" That seemed to me the most sensible course.

"Don't you understand, it was they who have taken her – she was shot as a spy."

"Are you sure she's dead?"

"Yes, I rang up as soon as I heard about her arrest. I spoke to Del Vayo. Grotto", he said, "if you'd let us know she meant a thing to you, I'd have saved her. *Claro*, they'd get me if they knew I was telling you this.'

This seemed to call for alcohol, I left after two large whiskies to give my story to Delmer. The Maestro was not over-impressed. We were discussing the coming of the M.P.s, when the door was flung open and Captain Grotto staggered in. Delmer looked annoyed. "Did you get drunk before or after the story?"

"He's not tight, unless he put in some quick work after I left him."

The captain swayed and then collapsed dramatically on the floor of the press-room. This was drama, even Delmer was impressed. "Is it poison, do you suppose?" He loosened his collar. The captain's moans increased. Ilse from the censor's office, joined the ring of pressmen around the apparently dying captain. In his tremors, his heels drummed up and down in the most alarming fashion, his eyes rolled and his arms had to be held. Ilse felt in his holster for his gun and pulled out a spectacle case. I told her the story as Grotto had told it to me. Two guards carried him away, still moaning, into the dark silence of a spare office.

"Please do not mention anything of this," said Ilse. "Our friend is a little sensational in his statements, tomorrow we shall go into the whole affair more thoroughly."

After that night the fantastic Captain Grotto disappeared from Madrid. Yvonne, we learnt, far from occupying the morgue, was quartered in the rather more congenial quarters of the Swiss Embassy.

Wilson again enters into the story on Christmas Eve, 1936. Watson was in a Valencia restaurant with a lady friend, Elvira.

> We were both terribly excited with the food. We ate Arroz à la Valenciana, a famous local dish and then fruit and coffee. I offered Elvira a cigarette, she took one; I sat there too surprised to withdraw the packet; looking around the restaurant, his peaked cap at a jaunty angle, was Captain Grotto. I turned away, but it was too late, he had seen us, he swaggered through the crowded tables to where we sat.
>
> "Ah, ha, the wounded troops!" he beckoned to the waiter, "Bring me a chair, I'll take dinner with my old friends here." Elivira looked at me in surprise, I turned to Captain Grotto, "I'm afraid we're just having a little farewell dinner, I'm leaving on the twelve o'clock train tonight."
>
> "Really, we ought to celebrate, *oiga! mas vino, comprende*? Just a bottle with me," he winked, "don't worry about paying it's on the War Office."
>
> Elvira was frigid. "How interesting, the War Office is supporting you?"
>
> "So they ought – I was brought down in flames by the Nazis, took two of 'em with me though."
>
> I turned to Elvira, "We'd better be going, the concert starts at eight-thirty – do excuse us captain."
>
> "That's O.K., not much of a one for music, but you ought to go to the Blue Angel cabaret, Jove, it's hot stuff!"
>
> We made our escape.

After the flamenco concert, Watson and Elvira went back to the hotel as Watson's train was to leave at midnight.

> Waiting at the hotel was Captain Grotto. "Come on you two love-birds," Elvira gave him a look that made him almost drop my suitcase, "not much time, you know, got a sleeper?"
>
> "No. I haven't, don't you worry about that."
>
> The captain would not be discouraged. The Barcelona train lay in the almost empty station; of Delmer there was no sign. In execrable Spanish, Grotto told the guard that I was a friend of his, a great hero and must have a sleeper. Elvira said nothing, she only smiled as the pantomime went on. At last my suitcase was piled into an empty sleeper.
>
> "Capitan Grotto; Capitan Grotto!" a uniformed porter walked along the side of the train shouting. Grotto poked his head out of the train window. "*Oiga! yo soy* Capitan Grotto!" He turned to us. "Sorry folks, I'm wanted at the hotel on the telephone," he looked around him and whispered, "it's Caballero – he can't do without me." He saluted and was gone.
>
> "Was it so wicked of me?" Elvira was smiling. "I asked Alvarez to telephone to him, when I saw he was at the hotel."
>
> "It was clever of you – a little of the Captain goes a long, long way."
>
> The whistle was blowing as I kissed Elvira goodbye. Both of us were sad at heart. There was a terrible finality about that parting, I felt as thousands had felt since the war began. The train began to move, Elvira raised her arm in the Communist salute, "Viva la Republica!" I waved until the bend of the platform hid her from sight.
>
> The door of one of the sleepers opened, a head was thrust into the corridor, "Has that awful man gone?" It was Delmer.

Although rather unkind to Wilson and though, undoubtedly, some of the conversation is not strictly accurate it still gives an idea of the flamboyant antics of the young man. It also shows how differently the same incident can be recalled and reported by various eye-witnesses.

John Wilson, 1937. (La Guerra de España en sus Fotos)

A few days later, on 29 December, Wilson arrived at Croydon airport, returning to England by air from Alicante via Paris, again saying he had come home for further hospital treatment for his seven [sic] bullet wounds received in September. He told the pressmen who met him that he had been flying home for Christmas when his civil aircraft had been brought down at Teruel and he had been imprisoned by the Nationalists. He had, of course, soon escaped to the Loyalist lines. This story duly appeared the next day in the *Daily Telegraph*. The "full exclusive" story of his adventures in Spain appeared in the *Sunday Referee* on 3 January 1937, heralded as "the world's most sensational story of mid-air murder, of parachute-jumping in a spate of bullets, of capture, and escape from Franco's executioners."

Shortly afterwards Wilson returned to Spain, but by now the foreign correspondents had had enough of his stories and the Republican authorities decided that he was an embarrassment, so they packed him off to Paris where he was employed for some time on propaganda and recruitment duties on behalf of the Spanish Republic.[5] By the summer of 1937, however, he had found his way to Berlin where Geoffrey Cox, then correspondent for the *News Chronicle* (now Sir Geoffrey Cox) who had met Wilson in Madrid, found him making the rounds of the British journalists based there trying to obtain money ostensibly to help evacuate Spanish officers to Britain, although Wilson later told that he had taken some passports to the Nazi capital belonging to men who had been killed, Germans from the Thaelmann Battalion of the International Brigades, and with the passports had brought about the release of other Germans held in concentration camps. It is known that he returned once again to Spain – by his own account in a rowing boat all the way from Marseilles to Barcelona – but became suspected of espionage activities by Government authorities there, was arrested and put in prison in Barcelona. He remained there for several months without trial. With his lack of knowledge of either Spanish or Catalan the young man became more and more desperate which, apparently, finally resulted in him going on hunger-strike because he could not eat the food offered him in jail. The exasperated Spaniards, already under pressure by the British Foreign Office, put him into hospital where he was visited by an English girl friend of the Irish poet, Ewart Milne (who was serving in the British Medical Unit in Spain). Wilson poured out all his troubles to the sympathetic girl, but Milne thought the story too unlikely to be true.[6]

Very little more is known about Wilson's experiences in Spain except from the *Index to the Foreign Office Archives (1937-38)* at the Public Record Office. Once again, however, practically all the documents listed have disappeared. It is only known that he eventually was released and expelled from Spain in 1938, possibly after an escape attempt, although it is also reported that a John Wilson was held prisoner by the Spanish Nationalists and by the Italians in the Balearic Islands before repatriation to England in October 1938.[7] This, however, may not be the same man.

Attempts to find proof of Wilson's claims made to the press in 1936 have had little success – there was a John Wilson at Oriel College, Oxford University, at this time but he appears to have been in residence at Oriel, or living at Oxford, during the period in question. Sir Geoffrey Cox, who had been at Oriel College himself, remembers that he questioned Wilson about his time there but the answers were so evasive that he soon realised that the story was untrue. No record exists of a John Wilson having been a registered student at the University of Liverpool[8] during the period and, finally, no trace can be found of anyone of that surname as living in Royal Street, Liverpool, in 1935-37. A search has also been made through the private pilots' 'A' licences issued during the Thirties but, again, no record can be found of anyone who could be the man who went to Spain. All this leads to the conclusion that, perhaps, "John Wilson" may have been a nom-de-guerre.

Recent research into documents apertaining to the *Escadrille "España"* have shown that Wilson contacted the recruiting centre set up by André Malraux in Paris on 16 August 1936 and his name is included in a listing of members of the squadron dated 10 September 1936. A photograph also exists purporting to show an English volunteer in the front gun-turret of a Potez 540/542 bomber of the unit dating from this time. From this we may conclude that Wilson may indeed have served briefly in the famous Malraux squadron but was wounded during one of his first flights.

Potez 540 of Escadrille "España", autumn 1936. (Patrick Laureau Collection)

So John Wilson remains an enigma – an odd character who certainly made an impresson on all who he met during those early revolutionary days in Madrid in the autumn of 1936. André Malraux himself seems to have used him as the basis of a character "Captain Rouse", in his famous novel of the Spanish Civil War, *L'Espoir*.[9]

CHAPTER 9 – SOURCES/NOTES

1. *Daily Worker,* 4 September 1936.

2. *Liverpool Evening Express*, 22 October 1936. *Northwich Guardian & Daily Telegraph*, 23 October 1936.

3. *Correspondent in Spain*, by H. Edward Knoblaugh; London 1937.

4. *Single to Spain*, by Keith Scott Watson; London 1937.

5. *La Guerra de España en sus Fotos*, by Tomas Salvador; Barcelona 1966.

6. 'The Statue', by Ewart Milne: *Penquin Book of Spanish Civil War Verse* (edited by Valentine Cunningham); London 1980. Wilson must be the prisoner mentioned.

7. FO369 File (1938) 2518.

8. Information from W.E. Parry, Librarian, Oriel College, University of Oxford; Keeper of Archives, University of Oxford; J.R. Bryson, Assistant Registrar, University of Liverpool.

9. Published in Britain as *Days of Hope* (London 1938). Malraux tells how this young man, who spoke only English, was badly wounded during his first flight as an air-gunner.

CHAPTER 10

John Loverseed and the Anglo-American Squadron in Spain

John Eric Loverseed was born on 4 December 1910 at Downham Market in Norfolk. He was the only son of John Frederick Loverseed, who had been a farmer for several years before turning to politics, becoming a Liberal Party agent in 1908. John's formative years were spent at Sudbury in Suffolk where his father, who was also a pillar of the local Wesleyan Methodist Church and a Justice of the Peace, pursued a successful career in local politics becoming eventually Mayor of Sudbury in 1921 when only forty years of age. Finally he was elected Liberal Member of Parliament for the Sudbury Division of West Suffolk in 1923. Liberalism, however, was in decline in Britain during the mid-twenties, as the Labour Party gradually took over as the main party of the left, and he lost his seat the following year.

Young John, who was already showing signs of a restless spirit and political views somewhat to the left of his father, was educated at Sudbury Grammar school. In 1928, however, his father died and the young man decided to apply for a Short Service Commission in the Royal Air Force. In 1929 he became a Pilot Officer on probation in the General Duties Branch of the RAF for five years Active Service. John learnt to fly at No.3 Flying Training School at Spittlegate, Grantham, being confirmed in rank and posted to No.2 (Army Co-operation) Squadron at Manston in Kent in April 1930, where he spent nearly a year flying A.W. Atlas aircraft. Promoted to Flying Officer in October 1930, John was posted to the Middle East in March 1931 and joined another army co-operation unit, No.208 Squadron, at Heliopolis in Egypt, which was also equipped with Atlas aircraft. Here John enjoyed the pleasant flying and social life available to an RAF officer abroad in the thirties.

His private life, unfortunately, was not so happy. He had married young and by his twenty-second birthday was the father of a girl and a boy (who was born in Cairo in 1932). The young couple became estranged and his wife left him in Egypt in January 1933 bringing her children back to Britain with her. John remained in the Middle East but was posted to No.14 (Bomber) Squadron at Amman in Palestine in March 1933 where he remained to the end of the year flying Fairey Gordons. Apparently, towards the end of this period, John was in trouble for "beating up a royal hunting party", returned to Britain in disgrace, and remained at the RAF Depot, Uxbridge, until April 1934 when he left the Service. He returned to his wife for a short time in 1934 but they separated the same year and subsequently divorced.

John's movements over the next two years or so cannot be established and the next reference found to him is in the book *Some Still Live*, by the American pilot Frank

Tinker, when he is mentioned as flying in Spain for the Republican Air Force during the Spanish Civil War. How did John come to go there? We can surmise that, after the breakdown of his marriage and leaving the RAF, even though he was still on the Reserve, John may have found it difficult to come to terms with civilian life. His only training was as a pilot and there were many unemployed fliers around in the mid-thirties. It is also certain that when John heard of the intervention of Germany and Italy in Spain, the bombing of Madrid and the sufferings of the people of Spain his sympathies would have been with the Republicans. No doubt also he would have read of the adventures of the British pilots in Spain during the autumn of 1936 and of the money on offer there for trained war pilots.

John Loverseed (third from right in back row) whilst with No. 208 Squadron RAF in Egypt, 1932.
(Courtesy Bill Loverseed)

It is believed that John Loverseed reached Spain in early December 1936. He probably was recruited through an agent of the Spanish Embassy in London and offered the £180 per month plus expenses that de Wet and others were promised, although it was stated by another pilot who was in Spain at this time that the Communist Party in London had assisted two Reserve Officers of the RAF to go to Spain and, in one case, to obtain a passport in a false name.[1] By late December 1936, however, John was at Los Alcázares together with several other British pilots. These included Frank George Fairhead, Percy Papps, and possibly, Arthur Russell Browne and Michael Du Cray.

158

Frank Fairhead, born in London on 6 January 1906, was a very experienced service pilot. He had served a Short Service Commission in the Royal Air Force from 1926 to 1931 during which period he had flown many types of aircraft including A. W. Atlas, Bristol F.2b Fighters, D.H.9A and Westland Wapitis. He had served in No.13 and No.6 (Army Co-operation) Squadrons; No.84 and No.30 (Bomber) Squadrons. From 1928-1930 he had served in Iraq, flying patrols over the desert. After a brief spell in Egypt, followed by a period at the School of Naval Co-operation at Lee-on-Solent, Fairhead spent the last year or so of his service on experimental flying at the Marine Aircraft Experimental Establishment, Felixstowe, and RAE Farnborough. By now with the rank of Flying Officer, Fairhead was placed on the Reserve List of Air Force Officers in July 1931. After leaving the Service he became a commercial traveller and lived in Canewdon in Essex. He continued to fly when he could but, in June of 1936, was unfortunate enough to have to crash land in a D.H.60X Moth (G-EBRT) at Ashingdon, Essex, the aircraft ending up in the branches of a tree when the engine failed. Luckily both Fairhead and his passenger were uninjured but it was discovered during the investigation after the crash that he did not hold a 'B' licence (that would allow him to carry pasengers). He was heavily fined despite his service record and plea that he had over 1,000 flying hours.[2]

Percy Papps, 1932.
(Courtesy RAF Museum)

Percy Stephen Papps was an older man (41 years of age) but a far less experienced pilot. Born in Portsmouth on 23 December 1895, it is believed that he served in the armed services in World War I. His family owned a musical instrument business in Portsmouth which he devoted his attention to during the years after the war. Portsmouth Airport opened in 1932 and, soon afterwards, Portsmouth, Southsea and IOW Aviation formed Portsmouth Aero Club. Papps, a large, stockily built man, became an early member having obtained his private pilot's 'A' licence (No.10335) at the Hampshire Aero Club at Eastleigh. He continued to fly from both Portsmouth and Eastleigh over the next few years and took a blind flying course in 1935. Why such an unexperienced pilot would want to fly in the Spanish conflict is not known but, no doubt, the attractive salary must have been the chief incentive.

159

He may also have been inspired by two Airspeed employees who "borrowed" a newly built aircraft with the intention of going to Spain, but crashed on take-off at Portsmouth Airport in late August 1936.

Arthur Russell Browne was born in Collingwood, Ontario, Canada on 17 November 1892. He learnt to fly at a young age at Camp Borden and enlisted in the Canadian Expeditionary Force for service in Europe in 1915, serving in France with the 6th Canadian Field Ambulance, In May 1917 Russell Browne was granted a commission in the Royal Flying Corps and subsequently served in No.11 Squadron in France flying Bristol F.2b Fighters. Later he became an instructor and finished the war as a Lieutenant with No.138 Squadron (also on Bristol Fighters). Leaving the RAF in April 1919 he returned to Canada, but in 1926 came back to England where he married and became a car salesman, living at Bournemouth. Over the next few years he continued to fly whenever possible and went to Spain towards the end of 1936 after being offered again £180 per month by an agent of the Spanish Embassy. No doubt with a young family to bring up the attraction of such a large amount must have proved irresistible.

The Index to the Foreign Office Archives links Fairhead's name with another former RAF officer as going to Spain at this period. Unfortunately, once again, the document in question is missing from those held at the Public Record Office. From the brief details given in the *Index*, however, it has been possible to identify this pilot as Michael Joseph Du Cray, who was born in Durban, South Africa, on 25 March 1897. At the outbreak of World War I he joined the South African forces and served in the 3rd Mounted Rifles until mid 1917 when he joined the RFC. He remained in the RFC/RAF until July 1919 attaining the rank of Lieutenant. A further period of RAF service followed in the twenties when he held a Short Service Commission from 1924 to 1933, serving in No.207 Squadron on D.H.9As, No.84 Squadron in Iraq on Westland Wapitis, No.26 (Army Co-op) Squadron on A.W. Atlas aircraft. It seems likely he may have known Fairhead from these days as they had both served in Iraq with No.84 Squadron. Du Cray also held a 'B' licence No.8446.

This group of men took the usual route to Spain – to Paris and then by train to Port Bou, just across the frontier. Papps later recorded that they experienced an air raid on the station at Port Bou as they arrived – a regular mission carried out by Italian bombers based in the Balearic Islands. The newcomers were then sent via Valencia for flight tests at San Javier airfield near to Los Alcázares. On arrival, however, they found already at the hotel a group of American pilots, also newly arrived. Both Americans and Englishmen "made the welkin ring" with stories of their flying prowess, but before things came to a head and actual blows were struck, all the pilots except two of the Americans were sent back to Valencia.

This group of Americans comprised one, Eugene Finick (aged 24), who had been in Spain since September 1936 and was a member of the regular Spanish Air Force (not being paid the inflated salaries of those who arrived later). The other Americans were Charles Koch (aged 40) and Orrin D. Bell (aged 39) – both of whom had served in the British Royal Flying Corps in World War I – Jim 'Tex' Allison (aged 31), Derek Dickinson (aged 41), Albert 'Ajax' Baumler (aged 22) and A. Caldwell Nold.[3] Baumler was to become the second most successful American fighter pilot in Spain claiming five Italian and German aircraft shot down. Later in World War II he served with the USAAF in China and had six further victories over Japanese aircraft.

By the second week in January 1937 all the British and most of the Americans were billeted at the Hotel Inglés in Valencia. John Loverseed, Papps, Fairhead and the others were given further flight checks and operational training on the aircraft at the nearby Manises airfield, the lumbering Breguet Br.19 bombers and Nieuport Ni-D.52 fighters. The temporary squadron commander of the Breguet squadron was an English-speaking Austrian volunteer named Walter Kantz; also called "Katz" though his real name was Walter Karous, and the new arrivals thought he was a Spaniard. Some of the Americans (Koch and Allison) were still haggling over their contracts with the Air Ministry whilst the Spaniards were finding that the actual flying capabilities of some of the others did not match their claims. This eventually resulted in Bell and Dickinson's "big money" contracts being reduced to the pay of a lieutenant in the *Aviación Militar*. A. Caldwell Nold (about whom little is known at present) was returned to the USA.

Most evenings John Loverseed and the others would meet the British Air Force and British Military Attaché in Valencia. Papps later recorded that they were permitted to use the diplomatic bag for letters to home. Percy Papps soon had an experience that showed him forcibly how matters stood in Loyalist Spain, for he was held prisoner by militiamen for two hours and then examined by committees of various political parties – all because he had been wearing a trilby hat (which was considered to be the mark of the *bourgeoisie*). He wore a beret after that.

On 10 January 1937 two further American pilots arrived at the Hotel Inglés – Frank Tinker and Harold Dahl (known as "Whitey" because of his very blond hair). They were both former service pilots in the USA and 27 years of age. Their qualifications had so impressed the Spaniards that they had signed contracts in Mexico before travelling to Spain. Frank Tinker was to become the highest scoring American fighter pilot in Spain with eight confirmed victories. He later wrote a book on his experiences there which is one of the best accounts remaining of the aerial war in Spain.[4]

The Spanish authorities had decided to set up a special Anglo-American Squadron to be based at Manises airfield flying Breguet Br.19 aircraft. The reasons for forming this English-speaking unit were to give operational training and terrain familiarisation, besides the obvious propaganda value of such a squadron. The unit was to be used for coastal patrols and bombing raids thus utilising the pilots until more modern Russian equipment became available in quantity. Frank Fairhead was appointed temporary squadron commander (presumably because of his experience) and John Loverseed became a patrol leader.

Formation flying practice commenced on 11 January 1937. Frank Fairhead went up first with his two wing men – one of them, a "wild Irishman" (according to Tinker) found it very difficult to keep formation and nearly rammed his leader's aircraft. It is possible that this pilot could have been Du Cray or even Hugh Oloff de Wet, judging by Tinker's description, who was still in Spain at this time. John Loverseed then took up the second flight of three aircraft with Tinker and Percy Papps. Loverseed, "an excellent pilot" (again according to Tinker) also had problems because Papps had great difficulty in keeping formation and nearly ran his aircraft into Loverseed's. Luckily, however, they landed safely with no damage done but the afternoon's flights lasting about an hour were not an auspicious start to the new squadron.

Breguet Br.19 of Republican Air Force, Sarinena Aerodrome. Note squadron transport of Alas Rojas (Red Wings) Squadron. (Archivo Aeronautico/Juan Arráez Photo)

Next morning coastal patrols started in the Breguets with the pilots flying formation on a Spanish pilot to show them the lay of the land. The aircraft carried under each wing the usual 225lb bomb with a Spanish observer/rear-gunner in the rear seat. Only a few ships were seen but these proved to be either neutral or belonging to their own side. In the afternoon a representative of the Air Ministry in Valencia visited the British and American aircrew at Manises and, after giving them a rousing lecture on the war situation, told them to elect their own squadron officers. In true democratic style a formal meeting was then held. Frank Fairhead was confirmed as commander and Tinker became squadron navigator (presumably because of his naval experience in the USA). Another American, Sam Brenner (aged 42) who had just arrived in Valencia, was also taken on as a gunner/mechanic with the squadron.

At about nine o'clock that evening an Nationalist warship appeared on the horizon and opened up a bombardment on Valencia. The aircrew immediately rushed to the aerodrome as fast as they could but found they were not permitted to take their machines off the ground until permission came from the Ministry of Marine & Air to fly. However, as the bombardment had started at nine o'clock, half-an-hour after the Ministry had shut up for the day, it was over before they could find the correct person in authority to give the word.

The following day, 13 January, the first bombing mission carried out by the Anglo-American Squadron turned out to be a complete fiasco. Six Breguets took off in the afternoon from Manises to bomb a small town near Teruel, about 75 miles north-west of Valencia. A Spaniard led the first flight of three aircraft to show the way and where to drop their bombs. Fairhead led the second flight. An escort was provided; it consisted of three of the old Nieuport Ni-D.52 fighters. When the aircraft were about half-way to the target the escorting fighters were suddenly attacked from above by six Heinkel He 51s. The Spaniard leading the first flight of bombers immediately dived down to around 50 to 100 feet from the ground (the usual manoeuvre when attacked by fighters) and made for home at top speed – about 90mph.

Frank Fairhead had seen nothing of this and continued towards the target with the remaining aircraft. After flying aimlessly around for some time trying to find where to drop the bombs they released them about eight miles further on to make sure of not hitting their own side. When the Breguets landed at Manises – luckily they had not been attacked by the Heinkels – they found that the Spanish pilot had arrived back about one and a quarter hours earlier, still with his bombs on board. Percy Papps, whose aircraft had partial engine trouble, tried to land down-wind, almost running into a Nieuport landing from the opposite direction. Suddenly a tyre of his undercarriage burst and the aircraft did a complete cartwheel completely wrecking the aeroplane. Amazingly the Englishman only suffered a bruised arm and a few cuts and scratches. His observer/gunman had a broken nose. One of the pilots of the Nieuports was not so lucky being badly wounded in the battle with the German machines in which all the Loyalist fighter aircraft had been riddled with bullets.

For the next week or so the squadron continued to carry out the duties assigned to it: bombing raids towards Teruel, usually in the afternoon, and coastal patrols, in the early morning and late evening between Valencia – Barcelona and Valencia – Alicante. On several of the bombing raids fighters were encountered but the "galloping Breguets" (as the British pilots referred to them) were not usually molested but on one of these missions John Loverseed received a bullet in the arm which put him out of action.

The bad condition of the old Breguets also gave much cause for concern – Percy Papps had three forced landings himself in January, one due to a large piece of aluminium coming adrift from under the fuselage and banging about whilst over the sea on patrol. He told the Spanish rear-gunner to release the two 225lb bombs in case of a crash-landing but the man was too petrified to act – probably remembering that two days previously another of the Englishmen had "landed" in the sea drowning his observer. Papps managed to retain control of the aircraft and land safely at Manises with the bombs still on the racks.

During lulls in the action the pilots spent their time hanging around the airfield playing dominoes and coin-pitching – an old Arkansas game introduced to the others by Frank Tinker. This consisted of digging two holes, slightly larger than the Spanish five-peseta piece, about twenty feet apart. The players would stand at one hole and toss the coins at the other one. A coin in the hole scored five points; otherwise the nearest coin to the hole scored one point. The first player to reach twenty-one would win the game. Soon everyone was getting interested in this new game, and a huge gallery of spectators would congregate to watch. Holes were dug all over the airfield and the game's popularity increased further when it was found that it was customary for the winner to get the coin that the loser had been using. Tinker of course, did well out of all this and managed to win enough money from the "Irishman" (Du Cray?) to cause him to settle up by giving him a fine pair of American flying goggles which he had.

Unfortunately the competition this gambling caused only added to the constant bickering between the British and Americans. Presumably by this time the Britons had discovered that the majority of the Americans had signed contracts which gave them $1500/month and a bonus of $1000 for any enemy aircraft shot down. At this time there were four US dollars to the £, which meant that many of the American airmen were to be paid twice the salary of the British – giving yet another reason for friction between the two groups. It was later also reported that so much whisky was drunk during this short period and so much crockery broken that the Air Ministry forbade liquor at the hotel. The pilots, however, soon found that they could get all they required at the many nearby bars.

All these problems may be reasons why the Spanish authorities were slow to advance the payments promised to the pilots. Arthur Russell Browne returned home to the UK in mid January and shortly afterwards wrote to Sir Anthony Eden, then Foreign Secretary, commenting on the recruitment in England of pilots for Spain and telling how he had not received any payment for the service put in there.[5] Despite putting his grievances into the hands of a solicitor nothing was ever forthcoming from the Spanish Embassy – all he received was a bill from the solicitor.

Before long nearly all the American pilots disappeared from Valencia. Finick was sent to the Toledo front to join a Russian two-seater bomber squadron. Tinker, Dahl, Koch and Allison were sent to Los Alcázares on 20 January and were later assigned to the 1a *Escuadrilla de Chatos*, under the command of Andrés García Lacalle. Baumler went to a Russian fighter squadron. Only Brenner remained for a while but he too returned home in February.

During the next few weeks the British pilots remaining continued to fly from the Valencia aerodromes, including escort missions (flying Nieuport 52s) to Potez 54 bombers on raids to Teruel. On one occasion one of the Potez bombers was shot up badly by Nationalist fighters killing four of its seven man crew. The Heinkel He 51s ignored the presence of the Nieuports, which were unable to offer any realistic help due to their vastly inferior performance.

The British pilots came more into contact with the Russian flying units based around Valencia during this period and, like the others from the UK who had preceded them to

Spain, came to admire their professionalism and skill. They could only envy them the outstanding performance of their aircraft because, although the Russians mixed well in a social level, they would not allow any of the men from Britain to fly their machines.

By late February 1937 all of this group of pilots had returned home to the UK, most feeling very depressed by their experiences in Spain and with little or no money to show for their sojourn there. All they had was a sun-tan and a few wounds. John Loverseed and Frank Fairhead shared a flat for a while after returning home. An interview with them appeared in a Sunday newspaper at the end of the month.[6] Du Cray disappeared from view, but Percy Papps (under the pseudonym "Cavalier") told the story of his adventures in an article that appeared in a Portsmouth evening newspaper.[7] Apparently, he had enjoyed the life and climate and would have remained in Spain longer if the cash had been forthcoming – he only received about £26 for his two months there having flown 125 hours (108 in January). Papps also sent a letter describing his experiences in Spain to an acquaintance in the Royal Navy. This letter eventually found its way to the Foreign Office and has survived to this day at the Public Record Office.[8]

Perhaps the best summary of the activities and failure of the ill-fated Anglo-American Squadron in January 1937 is given in a report by the British Air Attaché in Valencia to the Foreign Office:[9]

> The British and American pilots are diminishing in number, most of the Americans have already left and the British are beginning to follow suit. This is due to two reasons, firstly that the Government are not fulfilling the extravagant promises made to them in London and secondly that they are given aircraft to fly which are so old that they are dangerous enough without even going into action and would stand no chance against any of the Insurgent fighters.
>
> A British/American Squadron was formed in Valencia but has not been a success and now only eight pilots are left all of whom are contemplating returning. With one or two exceptions the British pilots who have come out here have been totally inexperienced and have damaged a large number of aircraft. This may account for their difficulty in obtaining their correct salary and better equipment. The few who are left are at present responsible for the defence of Valencia, all the Russians have gone to the Madrid front.
>
> They are equipped with Breguet 19s (which have no front guns) and with which they do both coastal and inland reconnaissance, and with Nieuport-62s [sic] for the fighter defence, so that the defence of the large community is totally inadequate.

Flight Lt Pearson (Air Attaché)
Valencia 13/2/1937

Of the Americans who remained in Spain, Koch and Allison returned to the USA in the Spring of 1937 due to illness and wounds received in combat. Allison later flew in China against the Japanese in 1938. Baumler and Tinker were later to be allowed to fly the 300mph Russian monoplane fighter, the Polikarpov I-16, in Spain and achieved several of their victories in this aircraft. They returned home to the USA in the summer of 1937. Dahl made headlines around the world when he was captured and sentenced to death by the Nationalists after being shot down. This sentence was later commuted to life imprisonment after his 'wife', a show girl named Edith Rogers sent a letter to General Franco pleading for his life and enclosing a photograph of herself which showed her at her best – in a white swim suit. He was released and returned home in 1940.

Derek Dickinson, who claimed to have fought aerial duel with Bruno Mussolini, and Spanish bride, c.1938. (Courtesy Richard S. Allen/Dr. R. K. Smith)

Finick was seriously burned and injured after baling out of his burning aircraft in June 1937 and spent many months in a Spanish hospital before returning home. Dickinson remained in Spain until February 1938 but his duties were mostly as an observer or on the ground, despite claims made later when he returned to the USA. One of these was that he had fought an aerial duel with Bruno Mussolini (the Italian dictator's son) over Spain – a story which has received much publicity and is still repeated in recent accounts of the air war in Spain. Bell had returned early to the USA after failing his flight test as a fighter pilot. After his book was published Frank Tinker made tentative enquiries about going to China, but was shot in mysterious circumstances in June 1939.

None of the British pilots in the Anglo-American Squadron went back to Spain. They returned to their civilian occupations whilst Europe drifted towards another general war.

Frank Fairhead disappeared from view – perhaps settling down to domestic bliss with his wife from whom he had been separated for four years. Percy Papps continued to look after his family business, whilst John Loverseed tried to make his way in civil aviation. Arthur Russell Browne applied successfully to join the RAF ex-Officers' Emergency Reserve in March 1938. In his application he stated that he had 30 flying hours in the previous three years (presumably at least some of these were in Spain).

'Buster' Browne, as he was known to his friends, soon joined the RAF again after the outbreak of World War II in September 1939 and reached the rank of Squadron Leader by the end of 1940. Most of his service during 1939-45 was with various schools of technical training. After his release from the RAF in August 1945 he obtained a job in the Army of Occupation in Germany, being in charge of transport. He died at Plymouth in 1956 at the age of 64. The South African, Du Cray, also served almost throughout World War II in the RAF. He died at Hackney in February 1952.

Percy Papps's later career is somewhat obscure. Apparently, after returning home to the UK, he applied for employment connected with non-intervention supervision of the Spanish frontier (according to the FO *Index*.) It is known that he was living in Hayling Island in the late thirties. He was still flying during World War II. He is remembered as being a ferry pilot during these years and well known for his skill in aerobatics. By this time he had apparently lost an arm in unknown circumstances. It is believed that Mr Papps died some years ago. Frank Fairhead died in Newton Abbot in November 1973 – nothing is known of his life from 1937.

John Loverseed's subsequent career after returning from Spain was full of adventure and achievement before his early death at the age of 51. John remarried in 1938 and settled in Cardiganshire in West Wales. In November 1939 he enlisted in the RAF as a humble AC2 but, with his flying experience, immediately became a Sergeant Pilot. After service at Farnborough he was posted to No.1 Anti-Aircraft Co-operation Unit in May 1940. Almost straight away, however, he was sent on detachment to No. 501 (Fighter) Squadron in France, which had been sent there after the German invasion of France and the Low Countries to back up the other Hurricane squadrons there. For a week he joined the desperate fight against overwhelming odds until on 30 May 1940 he crash-landed his Hurricane fighter (L2037) at Anglure and had to return to England for hospital treatment. He rejoined No.1 AACU in late August 1940 and remained with various flights of this unit until November 1942, the remainder of his service in the RAF being with No.1608 Tanker Training Flight, carrying out much unspectacular but valuable work giving practice to anti-aircraft batteries, searchlights and experimental flying duties. During this period much of his flying was in Hawker Henleys. Promoted to Warrant Officer in October 1941 John was awarded the AFC in the New Year Honours List in 1943 for "devotion to duty whilst flying". His flying career was now nearly over, for a new challenge was to offer itself.

In 1940 Sir Richard Acland, Liberal MP for Barnstable, wrote a book which he entitled *Unser Kampf* (published as a *Penguin Special* the same year). In it Sir Richard promulgated his views on the future of Britain after the war. Many of his social and political ideas were far ahead of his time and resulted in the formation of the *Forward March* movement, started by himself and a few supporters. Over the next year or so Sir Richard travelled around Britain making speeches to explain his ideas. The press in general poured scorn on such "eccentric" views such as being incensed at "the present hideous propaganda for hatred and revenge against Germany after the War by the same men who were hobnobbing with the Nazis while they were slaughtering and torturing the people". Sir Richard's remarks about the British colonial system and his doctrine that "private ownership of the great resources must end" were also greeted with howls of derision.

A man of similar ideals was the novelist and playwright, J.B. Priestley, who also made a name for himself as a broadcaster in 1940 with his postscripts spoken on Sundays after the nine o'clock news during the blitz on London. His 1941 *Committee* and the

Forward March movement amalgamated in July 1942 to form *Common Wealth*. This organisation articulated the widespread social determination that the post-war Britain should be wholly different from the stagnant and divided society known in the Twenties and Thirties. They became known by everyone during the late war years for their proposal for the common ownership of the land and of all the great productive resources, not so as to make "the workers" richer, but to serve as the essential foundation for a more morally directed community.

This message soon attracted much support in the country and found a ready response in very large numbers of the lower and middle ranks in the armed services including John Loverseed. The new political party began to set up local branches throughout the country and began looking for likely candidates to represent it in local and national elections. Amongst these were Tom Wintringham and John Loverseed. Tom was the leader of the British Battalion of the International Brigades in Spain in 1937, and had helped to found the Osterley Park Training School for the Home Guard in 1940. He became vice-chairman of Common Wealth. Meanwhile, John's ability to communicate, his idealism, enthusiasm, war record and political background made him the ideal candidate when a by-election for the Eddisbury division of Cheshire was called.

This rural Parliamentary constituency (now defunct) with an electorate of only about 33,000 was not, at first view, a likely seat to contest (no contested election had been held there since 1929). But John Loverseed, having been granted leave from the RAF to pursue the election, threw himself into the fray. He set up his headquarters in Chester and bought a motor-cycle to take him on his rounds. His wife left their three small children at home and joined John at Chester. John was the rank outsider of the three candidates who contested the election; the others were a National Liberal and a Liberal. His chances were dismissed by the press, but by sheer hard work and personality he managed to get his message across at the election meetings held in villages as there was no town bigger than Tarporley in the whole constituency. Sir Richard Acland has recently stated that he has never known any man who could create personal confidence so totally and so quickly at a meeting. John also received messages of good wishes from Common Wealth supporters such as Michael Redgrave, the actor. The by-election was held on 7 April 1943. To everyone's surprise John Loverseed was the victor with the slender majority of 486.

John Loverseed took his seat at Westminster a week later. He was the first elected member for Common Wealth. In June 1943 he was discharged from the RAF at his own request and concentrated on his parliamentary and constituency duties, living in Helsby, Cheshire. Unfortunately John found it difficult to make the same impression in the tough debates of the House of Commons as he did in village meetings. Common Wealth had further by-election successes but by the General Election in June 1945 John Loverseed had become a member of the Labour Party and fought the election as such. He lost his seat to a National Liberal candidate. Common Wealth was wound up in the light of Labour's win in 1945, there being many common aims and attitudes.

John made one more attempt to get back into Parliament, standing as an Independent Pacifist (against the manufacture of the hydrogen bomb) in the constituency of Herbert

Morrison, South Lewisham, in May 1955. He lost his deposit. By now he was living with his third wife in Finsbury Park. One day his eldest son, Bill, who had not seen his father since the early thirties, managed to trace him. They became good friends. John's wife died of cancer in the early sixties and he remarried shortly afterwards. Towards the end of 1962 he went into the London Chest Hospital, in Letchworth, Bedfordshire, for a heart operation. Complications set in and John died on 24 November 1962, a sad end for such a man. John was buried in the cemetery of a village near Letchworth.

Before his death, John saw his son Bill – also a pilot in the RAF – receive the AFC in 1958. He was later a founder member of the Red Arrows air display team and was leader of the team in the early 1970s. After leaving the service he has been a test pilot.

Common Wealth Politicians at Westminister, December 1943. Left to right; Lieutenant Hugh Lawson, Sir Richard Acland, Warrant Officer John Loverseed AFC. (S&G Press Agency Ltd)

It is believed that all the British pilots who were in the Anglo-American Squadron in Spain are now dead. Of the Americans, Harold Dahl flew in the Royal Canadian Air Force in World War II before being court-martialled and dismissed the service for

169

selling some surplus RCAF equipment that nobody had labelled surplus yet. He died when the old Douglas DC-3 he was piloting crashed in the Quebec bush in 1956. Jim Allison flew as a ferry pilot, piloting bombers across the Atlantic, in World War II; he died in Lima, Peru, in 1946. Baumler survived the aerial battles and died in Texas in 1973; Brenner and Bell are also known to have died in 1971 and 1943 respectively. Dickinson, Finick and A. Caldwell Nold have disappeared into the mists of time . . . Only Charles Koch survived to the 1980s. He returned to the USA in 1937 and took up his career as an aeronautical engineer and during World War II was instrumental in setting up the B-24 production line at the Ford Company's Willow Run plant. He worked until 1973 when he finally retired at the age of 79. Koch died in September 1983, the last survivor from those exciting days at Valencia in January 1937.[10]

CHAPTER 10 – SOURCES/NOTES

John Loverseed's son, Bill Loverseed, kindly provided much information regarding his father and allowed access to his service records. Also Sir Richard Acland supplied many details about John Loverseed's involvement with Common Wealth. Details of the service careers of the pilots mentioned come from Ministry of Defence records and pre-World War II editions of the *Air Force List*. Information regarding Arthur Russell Browne was kindly provided by his wife, Mrs Helen Russell Browne, whilst Wing Cmdr D.R. Bennett, Mr J. Butler and Mrs W. Jaucey supplied background details on Percy Papps.

1.   F0371 (1937) 21322.

2.   *Daily Telegraph*, 13 August 1936, and *Southend Times*, 16 October 1936.

3.   Details regarding the American pilots in Spain came from Richard Sanders Allen, H. Allen Herr, Victor Berch, Bob Miller, Dale Hopper and Dr R.K. Smith.

      Also: 'American Pilots in the Spanish Civil War', by Allen Herr: *American Aviation Historical Society Journal, Vol 22, No.3*, Fall 1977. 'On the Edge of Greatness – The Aviation Career of Charles D. Koch', by Allen Herr; *American Historical Society Journal, Vol 30, No.3*, Fall 1985.

4.   *Some Still Live: Experiences of a Fighting-plane Pilot in the Spanish War*, by Frank Tinker; London 1938.

5.   Ibid 1.

6.   *Sunday Referee*, 20 February 1937.

7.   *Evening News* (Portsmouth), 17 February 1937.

8.   F0371 (1937) 21296.

9.   F0371 File (1937) 21284.

10.   It is believed that Finick may be still alive and living in the USA.

CHAPTER 11

Harold Cosh – The Boy Who Never Grew Up

Towards the end of the nineteenth century Mr Albert Cosh from Yeovil in Somerset was appointed manager of Messrs Aplin and Barrett's creamery in Westbury, the small country town on the western edge of Salisbury Plain in Wiltshire. He married Miss Garrett, who lived in the nearby Railway Inn. In 1899 their first child was born, a boy to whom they gave the Christian names Harold Claude Garrett. Albert Cosh was one of the best known local businessmen at this time and the family lived in a house befitting his position in the community. Uitenhage House was a large dwelling with spacious gardens at front and rear and a fine view over the town towards the White Horse cut into the chalk on the face of Bratton Downs, about two miles away. In their front garden stood a flagpole as high as the building itself from which, on National days and Royal events, the Union Flag would proudly be flown.

Harold went to the local school in Westbury where he soon became the hero of the local boys. They admired him for doing things they would not have dared to do and for getting away with it. A contemporary at Westbury describes him as a combination of Huckleberry Finn and the Artful Dodger. When authority did catch him out on occasion and he was caned, young Harold never cried. He accepted the punishment as an occupational hazard.

During school holidays and weekends Harold and his friends would swim in a flooded limestone quarry near his home on the Ham and play in the disused ironstone workings beyond the railway line to London, the whole area being laced with old narrow gauge railways, remains of trucks and other quarrying relics – a real adventure playground. Another source of adventures for Harold, his younger brother and their friends were the Westbury blast furnaces that were shut down in 1908, about half a mile from Uitenhage House. Parts of the furnace structures were more than a hundred feet high and Harold would climb these not thinking of the danger involved.

Around 1910 Harold went to Trowbridge High School where he showed most interest in practical subjects such as mechanical and electrical engineering. In August 1914, however, World War I broke out and soon the whole country was gripped by war fever. Harold saw boys a few years older than himself going off to fight in France. He was anxious to join up as soon as possible, but in the meanwhile left school and commenced work at his father's creamery.

In April 1917 Harold joined the Royal Naval Air Service – his engineering interest may have helped him – and in the following August was posted on probation to *HMS Daedalus* (Eastchurch), in the Isle of Sheppey, as a Temporary Observer Officer. There he flew in Nieuport Scout two-seater biplanes. A letter that appeared in Air Pictorial in November 1966 mentioned that a Sub-Lt H.C.G. Cosh, Croix de Guerre, was observer in an aircraft piloted by Flt. Lt G.F. Smythe that took off one night to intercept a Zeppelin over the North Sea. Both pilot and observer were wounded by machine-gun fire from escorting enemy fighters.

This story or the award of the Croix de Guerre to Harold cannot be confirmed. What is certain, however, is that Harold's temporary appointment was terminated in mid October 1917. It was later stated that he was "kicked out" of the RNAS for sending out "messages in press . . . while flying in a B.E."

Harold returned home to Westbury where he was met one day by some of his former friends – he was wearing an odd sort of khaki uniform of officer's quality cloth but with no badges of rank. He told the youngsters that he was in the RNAS and left them gaping and impressed. He was very much the man graciously taking notice of schoolboys.

In December 1917 Harold rejoined the armed services as a lowly AC3 in the Royal Flying Corps being posted to a wireless school. Service records of this period are now scanty but it appears he became a Private 2 when the Royal Air Force was formed in April 1918 serving later in repair depots before being posted to the British Expeditionary Force in France in September 1918. He remained there until the following January, before returning home to the UK. He left the Service in February 1919. In later years several accounts were published of his adventures whilst with the RAF in France. He claimed to have been an observer/machine gunner, to have escaped unscathed after a forced landing behind enemy lines and, on one occasion, to have climbed out of his cockpit in flight to assist the pilot who had been wounded during an air battle, the pilot just managing to land safely. How much truth there is in these stories cannot be established.

Westbury again saw Harold in the Spring of 1919. This time he wore a Naval Chief Petty Officer's jacket together with a peaked cap bearing a badge with "RN Transport" on a roundel outside the central anchor. With all this he wore cream flannel trousers. He told his impressed audience that he was now a wireless operator at sea. This tale and the sketchy uniform lasted most of the following summer. In 1920 he again returned home where he spent several weeks riding around the Westbury and Frome area on a second-hand Triumph motor-cycle that he persuaded his long suffering father to buy for him.

That summer Mr and Mrs Cosh gave up Uitenhage House and went to live in a country cottage as Mr Cosh was about to retire from work. Harold, however, remained on in the house for a while, camping there with no furniture until the house was sold. During this period Harold was seen around Westbury in riding breeches, hunting jacket, a sort of boy scout hat on his head and carrying a riding crop. His parents gave him a small allowance and he became a well known character in the town. He managed to live fairly well without having to work as, with his laughing face and good looks he could, in the words of a contemporary, "charm the ducks off a pond".

Harold left Westbury in 1921 shortly after his mother died. He rejoined the RAF in late 1922, taking the trade of Motor Cyclist. After duty at Halton he was posted to Palestine in May 1923 where he later served with No. 14 Squadron at Ramleh. This unit flew Bristol

Fighters and later D.H.9As over Palestine and Transjordan. He reached the rank of LAC during this period – later claiming to have flown an air-mail service from Cairo to Palestine.

Harold left the RAF in November 1925. Shortly afterwards one of his former school friends at Trowbridge received a letter from him. In it Harold said that he was in the French Foreign Legion in Syria fighting the Druses and that if he ever managed to get out of the Legion alive and return home he would live a different life and settle down. His friends were touched as, knowing Harold's colossal nerve and admiring him for it, it was not the sort of letter they would have expected him to write. Harold survived the fighting in Syria during the rising against the French in 1925-26 and came back to England after two years in the Legion. He did not return home to Wiltshire and his family and friends heard no more from him for several years. It is believed that Harold took a course in marine engineering and went to sea.

The next definite reference to his movements is when he joined the RAF once more in June 1936. He spent his short period of service, lasting only until the end of the year, as an aircraftman on general duties with No. 601 (County of London) Squadron, Auxiliary Air Force.

The next time Westbury heard of Harold Cosh was in January 1938 when news reached the small market town that he had been seriously injured in an aeroplane crash near Barcelona in Spain where he had been serving in the Republican Air Force during the Spanish Civil War. This subsequently appeared in the local weekly newspaper, the *Wiltshire Times*,[1] and a copy found its way to Harold who learnt for the first time of the death of his father about a year before. In the following April the editor of the *Wiltshire Times* was surprised to receive from Spain a long letter from Harold Cosh telling of the conditions in that country, together with a bundle of Spanish newspapers and propaganda leaflets. The letter duly appeared in the *Wiltshire Times*.[2]

The paragraphs below are based on Harold's own account of his experiences in Spain.

Harold was working in an aircraft factory when he decided to go to Spain. By this time (it was the Spring of 1937) most Britons who had gone there to fly for the Republic had returned home, and the Spanish Government no longer had such a shortage of trained flyers. Most of the British volunteers who went to Spain now joined the International Brigades – notably the British Batallion – or served in other roles for the Republic. Harold, however, made contact with an ex-RAF pilot in his mid-forties known as "Captain Browne" (a surviving Foreign Office document[3] gives his name as McCarthy/alias T.K. or F.K. Browne) who was the head of an organisation fostered by the Spanish Government to recruit British airmen to fight in Spain.

"Browne" used a flat in Castledown Road, Barons Court, London, as an accommodation address for correspondence and for interviewing applicants who applied to advertisements under a box office number. He inserted advertisements in technical magazines on the lines of: *Pilot wanted. Good at stunt flying. Reply – giving types of machines and hours flown.* Applicants then received a letter from him telling them that they would be required to go abroad for air fighting at a salary of £40 a week, and if they were still interested to come for interview and bring their log-book for inspection. It soon became well known amongst flying men that "Browne" was recruiting men to fly in Spain. His cover was finally blown in November 1936 when the *Evening Standard* published a story about him. Surprisingly it seems that he continued to recruit further airmen despite all the publicity.

Harold was interviewed by "Browne" who examined his log-book from World War I, which showed 120 hours as an observer in the RNAS. Harold also answered Browne's questions about his various periods of service and passed a medical examination. He was accepted as being suitable for service in the *Aviación Militar*.

Three days later Harold left London with two other English volunteers en route for Spain. They took the usual route. First stop was Paris, the clearing house for all foreign volunteers for Spain where forms were signed and papers obtained, then by train and boat to Barcelona. Here all the volunteers were marched to the Town Hall where speeches were made, a band played the *Internationale*, the crowds sang and greeted them with raised clenched fists. The men were then quartered in an ex-nunnery whilst they were sorted out into various National sections. Harold and his two companions went with the French.

Shortly afterwards they were sent to the barracks in Barcelona of the *Compagnie Aviación* where they were fitted out with their kit. The Englishmen found the food difficult to stomach and the smell of rancid olive oil made them feel sick, but they soon became used to it. Finally a week later the three men were driven to an airfield about twenty-five miles from the city where they were welcomed by the Commandant and shown the aircraft they were to fly – which he subsequently described variously as "a Curtiss with a Pratt & Whitney Wasp engine" or a two-seater of "Russian manufacture with a 750hp radial engine". These aircraft were probably either the Polikarpov R-5 *Rasante* or RZ *Natacha* which were sent in some numbers to Spain and used for light bombing and army co-operation purposes by the Republic.

Harold was to be an observer/machine gunner. His pilot was initially another of the Englishmen who had accompanied him from London, John Hardy. Hardy had served in the RAF as a Sergeant-Pilot. Hardy firstly was checked out by a Canadian who, according to Harold, had been with the Ontario Forestry Air Service before going to Spain.

Tragedy struck the following day before the newcomers actually flew on an operational flight. The third Englishman – his name is given variously by Harold as Wilfred Sanderson or Victor Edgeley, also said to be a former RFC sergeant-pilot from World War I – was flying as observer with a Spanish pilot on a test flight when the engine of their aircraft cut out. In the subsequent crash both men died – a sobering introduction to the Spanish conflict for Harold as, with Hardy, he sorted through the dead man's effects and wrote to his family in England.

Two weeks training followed until it was considered that the two Britons were ready to take part on operations. Finally in late July 1937 Hardy, with Harold Cosh as his observer, took off on a reconnaissance mission over the lines towards Vallecas. The flight was largely uneventful with Harold just studying his maps, making notes of the position of the Insurgent forces and their transport. Hardy climbed to around 16,000 feet to avoid the anti-aircraft fire coming up at them and the shells burst far below them. Luckily on this occasion no Insurgent fighters were encountered (in fact at this time Franco had sent most of them to the Northern Front) and they returned back to their airfield without further problems. This flight set the pattern for the succeeding weeks, as patrol after patrol went by without anything really exciting happening. Harold, as well as flying with Hardy, flew with a Spanish pilot and often with a young German named Baum, who had escaped from Nazi Germany to fight in Spain.

In late August the Government forces launched an offensive in Aragón and the towns of Belchite and Quinto were captured in early September. In October, however, the war on the Northern Front came to an end with a complete victory for Franco so he was soon able to transfer the bulk of his forces south again. During early August, a period of relative calm in the south, Harold carried on flying patrols from Barcelona.

Harold Cosh in Spain, 1938.
(Popular Flying)

One morning Harold and the young German, Baum, were flying on patrol into Nationalist territory at around 18,000 feet. Harold sighted an Insurgent aircraft in the distance through the clouds – luckily for them it was another two-seater reconnaissance aircraft. Baum dived towards it and Harold let off a stream of machine-gun bullets at the other aircraft which was desperately trying to avoid combat by diving away. Suddenly there was a puff of smoke, a cloud of yellow flame and the Insurgent machine started down in a vertical dive, leaving a comet-like tail of smoke and flame in its path, and crashed. Suddenly Harold began to perspire all over and felt sick as he thought what he had done to two fellow human beings. That evening, back at the aerodrome, he forgot all this after receiving the congratulations of the Commandant and a bottle of wine.

Off duty Harold would spend his time in Barcelona; food was scarce but wine was plentiful. In fact he spent much of the 1,600 pesetas a week (£1 equalled 60 paper pesetas) he received on wine and other things he wanted – he was unable to get them changed into English currency.

Sometimes he went over to the British Consulate, whose staff gave him and Hardy good English food and real English beer, and then packed them off back to their aerodrome.

Harold was transferred to Valencia in late August. From then to early December he took part in many reconnaissance and bombing operations over the lines. Another move to Alicante followed in December where he again was involved in bombing missions. On one occasion his aircraft was forced down with oil pressure trouble behind Government lines; Harold and his pilot had to wait for three days until spares could reach them. Here Harold had a chance to see what it was like for the infantryman in the war – poorly equipped and clothed compared with the professional troops of Franco.

Several days followed spent on coastal patrols between Alicante and Valencia. One morning an aircraft returned from patrol and reported that the Nationalist cruiser, *Canarias*, together with two gunboats, was steaming south of the Balearic Islands towards the Spanish coast. Immediately every available aircraft, after being loaded with bombs, flew off to intercept the three ships. Eventually the *Canarias* was sighted through the clouds with its attendant gunboats and the aircraft dived to attack through the intense anti-aircraft fire directed at them. Harold released his two 500lb bombs but saw them splash harmlessly into the sea midway between the cruiser and one of the gunboats. The other aircraft, however, were more successful. Although no hits were obtained on the *Canarias* one of the gunboats was hit and sank about an hour later. None of the attacking aircraft were lost and they all returned safely to the airfield. On the way Harold saw a British warship, the cruiser *HMS Devonshire*, steaming towards the scene of the action. Encouraged by the outcome of the raid, the next day the squadron (which also included an American pilot) attacked one of the Insurgent aerodromes and two hangars were hit.

The food shortage was now becoming critical. For weeks the airmen had been living on beans and soup. Many days were hungry days. Even oranges were scarce. One night Harold purloined some onions and stewed them in wine for his supper.

One evening in early January 1938 Harold, with a Spaniard, Lieutenant Minguez, as his pilot left Alicante en route for Barcelona with dispatches. Towards midnight they landed for refuelling and after two hour's rest took to the air again. Dawn broke and Minguez followed the coastline towards their destination. Suddenly the engine began to miss and then cut out completely. The aircraft plunged earthwards and crashed. The last thing Harold remembered was releasing his safety belt.

When consciousness returned he found himself in bed in a small room. A bandage was around his head. His left arm and his right leg seemed to be missing (actually it was broken). He was in hospital and had been unconscious for five days since the crash. Harold learnt subsequently that he had been very lucky to survive as Minguez had died from a fractured skull and other injuries. He was told later that his parachute, which he used as a sort of cushion in the cockpit, had saved him from more serious injury as, when found, he was lying across it several yards from the wrecked machine. There had been no time to think of a parachute jump as the aircraft was at too low an altitude.

Harold remained confined to his hospital bed for about eight weeks whilst the Nationalists continued their offensive. During this time he had three operations on his leg. Eventually his condition began to improve thanks to the close attention of the hospital staff and his own strong constitution. As soon as he left the hospital Harold applied for his discharge from the *Aviación Militar,* but this was delayed for several weeks and he continued his convalescence in Valencia, Alicante and Barcelona. During these weeks he was to experience the horrors of the air warfare against a civilian target as the air raids mounted against these cities by the Nationalists, especially the Italians flying form the Balearic Islands, became more frequent and deadly. Franco had launched a full scale offensive in Aragón in early March 1938.

Finally Harold obtained his release and thankfully left Spain and its civil war behind him. He arrived back in the UK in early June 1938 and went to London where he stayed for a while with a Canadian, Major W.R.C. Dacosta, from Toronto, who had served in the RFC and RAF during World War I.[4] It is possible that Dacosta may have been in Spain himself with Harold Cosh. He had a letter published in the magazine *Popular Flying* in March 1938 which told of the adventures of:

"One of England's greatest airmen . . . a mere boy of sixteen . . . an ex-officer of the R.N.A.S." This youngster . . . "2/A.M. No. – Harold C –, was posted to 'C' Flight with a Sgt. Edgely [sic] as pilot. These two took part in many raids and are officially known to have brought down two Albatross machines. C – was offered Sergeant's rank but declined . . ."

Shortly after returning to London, Harold sent the following letter to Lord Halifax, the Foreign Secretary:-[5]

> To Lord Halifax
> June 5th 1938
>
> Sir,
> I must respectfully submit this application. And humbly request an interview for the purpose of drawing your attention to certain matters are the cause of criminal bombing of certain parts of government Spain.
> I wish to add that I have just returned from Spain after 10 months with the Aviación Militar (Spanish Air Force) – I have been at times stationed at all the parts which have been bombed. And left Alicante last Friday week. And arrived home last Saturday.
> If you so desire Sir I will submit certain authentic information in Writing.
> I have the honour to be your obedient servant
> HAROLD COSH

He was asked later in the month to submit his information in writing but, if he did, there is no trace of this in surviving documents at the Public Record Office.

Harold then submitted several long articles on his Spanish Civil War experiences that were published in the *Wiltshire Times* from June to August 1938.[6] These articles, when analysed and compared with the actual events of the period, do contain some strange statements and, for an airman, he shows a lack of knowledge of basic aircraft recognition. Harold does say, however, in the last article that appeared that he had "taken liberties with dates and with the geography of Spain . . . to give a war picture". The bombing of Valencia and Barcelona that he experienced affected him deeply. His description of the suffering of the civilian population there and the problems encountered by the ambulance and fire services foretell in detail just what was to be experienced by the population of Rotterdam, Coventry, London, Hamburg, Dresden, Berlin and so many other cities in the next few years.

Spanish sources give little or no information regarding the activities of Harold Cosh in the Civil War. Recently, however, an article published in the journal of former Republican aviators in Barcelona, *Alas Gloriosas,*[7] tells the story of an Englishman, known as "el Inglés" to his Spanish colleagues who flew in the *4a Escuadrilla del G.30* (Natachas) in 1937. Using the nom-de-guerre of "Pépe Pérez Martínez", he joined the squadron as a *Teniente Observador* after previous service in the ranks and attending an observers' course. He did not stay with the squadron for any length of time as he badly injured his left hand when he caught a ring on his finger on an obstruction in the cockpit of his aircraft when jumping from his aircraft in a great hurry – this had landed with a live bomb still in the racks which had fallen on to the ground beneath the machine. Despite his limited time in the squadron and embarrassing exit, "el Inglés" is remembered today for his happy-go-lucky nature and ironic sense of humour. From the description given it would seem almost certain that "el Inglés" was Harold Cosh. The truth of much of his own account must be in doubt (including the story of Hardy and Edgeley) but, until more evidence is forthcoming, a final verdict must be held in abeyance.

By the time Harold returned home to England he was in his fortieth year. The money he received for his articles in the *Wiltshire Times*, and for another that appeared in *Popular Flying* in November 1938 (this included a photograph of him in the uniform of a *Suboficial (Brigada) Observador de aeroplano de Aviación Militar*), enabled Harold to keep going for a few months but, by Spring of 1939, it was obvious that war with Germany was on its way and he decided to try to enter the armed services once more. He rejoined the RAF as a lowly aircraftman in May 1939 and was posted to No.927 Squadron as a Balloon Operator. He remained with this unit until February 1940 when he was discharged. Harold then, apparently, went to Ireland for a while but by March 1941 was serving in the Royal Fleet Auxiliary on RFA *Philol* as a Third Engineer Officer. It appears that he remained in the RFA until 1946 when he was serving at the Royal Navy base at Scapa Flow. In later years he claimed to have served in destroyers during World War II.

After the war Harold settled down in Bognor Regis. His endless fund of stories about his adventures proved irresistible to the youngsters he met including his nephew. Among his tales was the one of his ship being torpedoed during World War II and how the crew managed to save their ship after the captain and senior officers had been taken from the lifeboats aboard the German 'U' boat.

Harold made the headlines once more in June 1968, when it was reported in the *Evening News* (Portsmouth) that he was to be a guest of the Ministry of Defence at a garden party at Hendon to celebrate the golden jubilee of the RAF. Described as "Bognor's Peter Pan", this article retold the story of him as "the babe of the Royal Flying Corps" and his service in World War II (there is no mention of the Spanish Civil War). According to this article, Harold had joined a party of students on a trip to Red China some ten years before but had difficulty in getting out of the country.[8]

In his last years our hero grew his hair long and took to enjoying the facilities of a Bognor teenagers' club. He died in Chichester on 11 November 1973 at the age of 74.

Harold Cosh was certainly a boy who never grew up and it is very difficult to separate fact from fiction in his career, but the words that conclude his articles on the Spanish Civil War showed much foresight and are still true today. —

> I think that the war in Spain will decide within the next two or three years whether the present re-armament of the nations of the world is to be used for the destruction of life and property, for a mechanized barbarism, or for a new advance of the human spirit, and peace. Behind us are ten thousand years of war. We should now look forward to ten thousand years of peace.[9]

CHAPTER 11 – SOURCES/NOTES

Much information regarding Harold Cosh's early days in Westbury came from Lt.Cmdr R.J. Cogswell and Alan Collins. Details of his service career come from Ministry of Defence records; especial thanks are due to Harold's sister-in-law, Mrs L.A. Cosh, and nephew, Brian Cosh, for allowing me access to these. Other information came from the former editor of the *Wiltshire Times*, Mr Michael Lansdown.

1.   *Wiltshire Times*, 22 January 1938.

2.   *Wiltshire Times*, 23 April 1938.

3.   F0371 File (1936) 20588.

4.   Information regarding Dacosta from Allan Levine in Canada and Ministry of Defence (Canada) records.

5.   F0371 File (1938) 22687.

6.   *Wiltshire Times*, 18 June 1938; 2/9/16/23 July 1938; 6 August 1938.

7.   "*El Inglés de la 4a de Natachas*", by Ricardo Domingo y Bochaca; *Alas Gloriosas: Boletin Informativo Nos 21-22*, May-June-July 1982 (Barcelona).

8.   *Evening News* (Portsmouth), 29 June 1968.

9.   Ibid 6.

CHAPTER 12

Other Flyers for Republican Spain: Fact, Fantasy, Farce & Tragedy

AITKEN-QUACK, Richard Welford.[1]

He pronounced his name as "aykin kwork". Born in Harrogate, 26 December 1913. He was the son of a consulting engineer and was educated at Taunton public school. After leaving school he worked for some time in a shipping office and became a machine-gun instructor during his spare time in the Territorial Army (Artists' Rifles) before obtaining a Short Service Commission in the RAF in October 1935. He was sent to No.7 Flying Training School at Peterborough where he was a contemporary of Brian Griffin. Apparently he took unauthorised leave and his commission as Acting Pilot Officer was terminated in July 1936 – four days before Brian Griffin's service was also terminated – as he was considered unlikely to make a suitable officer.

Shortly afterwards Richard left home after a dispute with his father and tried to make his own way in the world. In the book *Under the White Rose, History of No.609 Squadron Royal Auxiliary Air Force*, by Frank Ziegler, it is stated that he flew a Boeing [sic] fighter during the Spanish Civil War for £200 a month. He later told a fellow volunteer in Finland in 1940 (see below) that he had once gone up for a practice flight in Spain with a colleague in another aircraft and the two had fired at each other in the air. He was terrified. His brother believes, however, that Richard was in the International Brigades in Spain and, with his military background, achieved non-commissioned officer rank.

According to a colleague he served with in No.609 Squadron, Richard came home from Spain on leave and, as he had by then acquired quite a large amount of money in the bank from his service there, decided not to return. By July 1937, he was living in Staines and was a "Fruit Importer's Agent". He became involved in an attempt to smuggle some brandy and liqueurs from Calais to Shoreham in a yacht. In the subsequent court case it was stated by one of the witnesses that "Franco has a price on his head. He first of all spied for Franco whilst fighting on the Government side in Spain, and later fought for Franco and spied for the Government. So Franco wants him badly". Richard Aitken-Quack later denied being one of Franco's spies in his evidence.[2]

It is known, however, that he was in Gibraltar during the summer of 1937. In early 1940 Richard volunteered his services to Finland (the Finns were fighting a rear-guard battle against the might of the Soviet Union – see Chapter 14). He was one of the second draft of volunteers from the UK which left Middlesborough in early March. Commissioned as a Lieutenant in the Finnish Air Force Reserve (his flying record as submitted to the Finnish authorities is shown on p.214).

From October 1940 – Spring 1941 he worked for accountants Price Waterhouse in

Helsinki and also taught English for a while in early 1941. At this time he described himself as a hotel manager or accountant at home. Later Richard claimed to have courted a niece of Hermann Goering whilst in Finland (perhaps a relative of Count Gustav von Rosen).

The balding soldier-of-fortune left for Sweden around July 1941 where he remained until flying home in the diplomatic aircraft on 19 March 1942. Richard Aitken-Quack enlisted in the ranks of the RAF as an AC2 in May 1942 but soon became a Sergeant Pilot. Later in the year he joined No.609 Squadron but was shot down near Roubaix in France whilst flying from Lympne during 1943, in a Hawker Typhoon 1b(PR-S) and became a POW. Released at the end of the war he remained in the RAF until December 1946, when he left the service with the rank of Warrant Officer. His later years were spent in Papua, New Guinea, and Darwin, Australia. Richard Aitken-Quack died in Australia in the early 1960s.

Richard Aitken-Quack (third from right in back row) whilst with No. 609 Squadron, Manston, 1943.
(Courtesy Flt Lt S.H. Hanson)

BAMBOROUGH, William.

Mentioned as a British pilot with the Republican forces in an article by the famous chief foreign correspondent of the Hearst Newspapers and Universal Service, Karl von Wiegand, in the *Daily Express* on 19 September 1936. A "Bamboroug" is also included in a listing of members of the *Escadrille "España"*, dated 10 September 1936.

BRETFORD [sic][3]

Mentioned in a document appertaining to the Malraux/*España* Squadron, together with another Englishman called Totem [sic]. Said to have contacted Paris HQ of squadron and received a cheque for their engagement but later decided against going to Spain. Another man (English?) named Martin Trepp [sic] was rejected after approaching the centre in early September.

CARTWRIGHT.

According to Hugh Oloff de Wet, in his book *Cardboard Crucifix*, Cartwright "... only nineteen" was killed in action on 27 August 1936. De Wet admitted that he changed the names of several of the pilots and dates, if necessary, to fit his story. "Cartwright" was, in fact, Brian Griffin.

CLIFFORD.

According to de Wet, shot down and killed on 25 September 1936. "Clifford" was, in fact, Claude Warsow.

COLLINS.

According to de Wet, badly wounded in combat on 1 October 1936. "Collins" appears to be a combination of Eric Griffiths and Vincent Doherty.

CULLEN, Richard Nigel.[4]

Born in Australia, he raced motor-cycles at Brooklands in the mid thirties. It is said that he joined the International Brigades in Spain and was wounded in the stomach. Known as "The Ape" because of his size and strength, he became a fighter pilot in World War II with the RAF, claiming at least 16 victories before being missing on patrol in Greece in 1941.

ELSTOB, Peter Frederick Egerton.[5]

Born in London, 22 December 1915. His father was a chartered accountant and a former member of the RFC in World War I. Peter Elstob was educated at various schools in London, Paris, Calcutta, New York, New Jersey and the University of Michigan, USA. He threw up college in search of adventure and excitement and came to England where he obtained a Short Service Commission in the RAF in late June 1936. He was posted to No.5 Flying Training School, Sealand, Queen's Ferry, Chester, to learn to fly. However, his service in the RAF only lasted two months to late August because, in his own words, "... for low flying and inability to conform ..." He resigned his commission on request and being out of work and almost broke, and above all, "being twenty years old and loving flying ..." he offered his services as a pilot to the Spanish Republic and was interviewed at the British Communist Party Headquarters in Covent Garden. He claimed, tongue in cheek, that he had 430 flying hours but, as the interviewer was no expert, was accepted at the salary of £25 per week and £1,000 to his next-of-kin if he was killed.

Peter Elstob left London bound for Paris in mid-October 1936 where he joined up with other volunteers. The journey to Spain was by train to Perpignan and then by bus to the Spanish frontier. After a tiring journey they arrived at their destination, Figueras, and the large fort, El Castillo de San Fernando, where the group was to remain until the final destinations were known. Bored with waiting around he visited the town (which was out-of-bounds) and became under suspicion because he was wearing his RAF officer's field cap.

After several days he was arrested on suspicion of being an Insurgent spy – the fact that he had been writing down impressions of Spain during this period for articles when he returned to England had aroused the suspicion of the local militiamen.

After interrogation in Barcelona, Elstob was imprisoned in the ancient castle of Montjuich which dominated the harbour. There were over 500 military and political prisoners being held at Montjuich and he was to remain in the castle for a month until mid December. Finally released, Elstob reached France safely, arriving on the 22 December 1936 (his twenty-first birthday), without ever getting the chance to fly any aircraft in Spain. The full story of his experiences in Spain is told in his book, *Spanish Prisoner*. During World War II Peter Elstob served in the Royal Tank Regiment and subsequently has become a well known author and businessman. Secretary-General of International PEN (1974-81).

GALLIMORE, Marcel.

One of the most unlikely stories to come out of the Spanish Civil War was an article published in the Sunday newspaper, *The People,* on 3 January 1937. It was exclusively revealed that Marcel Gallimore, a young French pilot, who was said to have become the "Ace of Aces" of the Republican Air Force in Spain because of his feats of daring (he had brought down 24 Insurgent aircraft to date) was none other than a girl, a Miss Mercia Gilmore, who was the daughter of a Scots family who had settled in France. Her secret had come out when the "Dare-devil of the Air" had been wounded and taken into hospital.

GLOGAUER, Heinz Adolf.[6]

Although not a British national, Heinz Glogauer finds a place in this story because he learnt to fly in England and his name is included in the *Index to the Foreign Office Archives (1937)* in conjunction with Vincent Doherty, Pat Mertz and G. H. Porter (see below). He was born in Hanover, Germany, on 6 July 1911, where he lived until 1934. Glogauer had to leave his homeland, which he loved, after the Nazis came to power because one of his grandparents was Jewish. An aircraft apprentice, he lived at Witney in Oxfordshire and learnt to fly at the Witney & Oxford Aero Club, Witney, obtaining his 'A' licence in June 1935. After going on to get his 'B' licence (commercial pilot's) in 1936 he also went on to obtain his 'A' and 'C' Ground Engineer's licences. Despite all these qualifications he was unable to obtain employment in the UK because of his nationality. Sometime in 1936-37 he went to Spain to fly for the Republican Air Force but no details are known as the relevant documents are not now available. It is believed that Glogauer was killed in a flying accident in South Africa in 1939.

GRAND, Robert.

As per William Bamborough above.

HARRINGTON, William George.[7]

Said by one source to have been in the RAF, he served in the British Battalion of the XV
International Brigade before being wounded in the fighting that followed the crossing of
the River Ebro in July 1938. Brother of Henry Harrington (see p.138) he later joined
Wrightways Ltd of Croydon. During World War II he became a Merchant Navy Officer
and survived when the ammunition ship on which he was serving was sunk during one
of the convoys to Murmansk in North Russia. Later a cameraman with the Crown Film
Unit, he continued his photographic work after the war before going to live in Normandy
where he died c.1980. Claimed in later years to have been shot down into the sea whilst
flying a Dewoitine fighter during the Spanish Civil War.

HATTON, George Herbert Tillotson.

It was reported in the *Daily Worker* of 23 February 1937 that Hatton, a Corporal in the 1st
Battalion of the Rifle Brigade at Gosport, who had deserted in May 1936, had been arrested
on his return to England from Spain where he said that he had been serving in the
"bombing squadron of the International Column in Spain". No further information but
see, however, the story of Eric Griffiths (Chapter 8).

HUTCHINSON, Donald.

As per William Bamborough above. There is also a reference in the *Daily Mail* of 15
December 1936 to a Donald Hutchinson of London who was in hospital in Paris after
being wounded whilst fighting for the Republicans in Madrid.

JAFFE, Alfred Daniel.

Born at Godstone, Surrey, on 15 September 1907. He joined the RAF in March 1928, being
granted a Short Service Commission for five years. After training at No.1 Flying
Training School at Neatheravon he was posted to No.9 Squadron in 1929, flying Vickers
Virginia bombers. From May 1929 until the end of his service in 1933 Jaffe was at Gosport
and subsequently with Nos. 460 and 465 (Fleet Torpedo Bomber) Flights on the aircraft
carriers HMS *Eagle, Glorious* and *Furious*. He was transferred to the Reserve in March
1933. After leaving the RAF he obtained his 'B' licence and became a charter pilot with
various companies such as Aerofilms Ltd, Air Dispatch Ltd, Commercial Air Hire Ltd,
Birkett Air Service Ltd. On 15 August 1936 Jaffe flew a de Havilland D.H.84 Dragon (G-
ACKC) belonging to Commercial Air Hire from Croydon Airport non-stop to Prat de
Llobregat airfield at Barcelona, the aircraft's cabin being crammed with drums full of
fuel. He was paid £125 for the trip, one of many made by British pilots at this time. Jaffe
was offered £300 per month to fly for the Spanish Government but refused.

In 1937 he was involved in an affair in which he flew two Frenchmen illegally into

England in order to transact a deal to obtain some autogiros for the Basques – he was brought to court and subsequently fined. It is also believed that he was involved in other attempts to purchase aircraft for Spain in conjunction with other well-known "entrepreneurs" such as Leslie Charles Lewis, alias Stanynought, an associate of Edward Hillman.[8] Towards the end of September 1937 Jaffe was on his way back from Paris to Heston Airport with Lewis when the de Havilland D.H.85 Leopard Moth he was flying crashed at Chipstead in Surrey. He suffered a fractured skull in the accident which put an end to his flying for a while. In September 1939, however, Jaffe rejoined the RAF and served throughout the war before leaving the service in November 1945 with the rank of Squadron Leader. He died in Southwark on 31 July 1968.

KAARSBERE, A.

Reported in the Spanish Nationalist newspaper *El Norte de Castilla*, published in Pamplona, of 23 September 1936, to have offered his services as a pilot to the Spanish Embassy in London. Believed to have been the same man as Andrew Christian Anderson Kaarsberg, a shop assistant, born at Nisset on 21 October 1912, who received his 'A' flying licence at London Air Park Flying Club in May 1939.

LEAHY.

According to a Foreign Office document now at the Public Record Office,[9] he was recruited to fly in Spain by Captain "Browne" (see Chapter 11). Leahy, from Edgware in London, volunteered for service in Spain but his fiancée informed the police of his intention.

'MERE STRING' (Identity Unknown)

Author of an article in *The Aeroplane* of 17 November 1937. According to this story he was hired by the Spanish Government in Paris in March 1937 as a pilot and told to fly a Gourdou-Leseurre "fighter" from Paris to Bilbao but the aircraft crashed en-route. His flying career previously was "limited to Moths and sundry big flying-boats". Then he took ship from Marseilles to Barcelona but it was captured by the Nationalists and he was taken to Palma, Majorca, where entertained by Ramon Franco, whom he had met in 1929 when Franco had been rescued by the British aircraft carrier HMS *Eagle*, when the Dornier flying-boat he commanded in an attempt to fly the Atlantic had been forced down through lack of fuel. Released and returned to Paris. Later flew a Potez 560/1 transport aircraft to Bilbao. His aircraft reported to have been shot up and burned by own Basque troops at the airport. "Mere String" was later sent to Czechoslovakia on unsuccessful mission to purchase aircraft. Fact, fiction or a mixture? De Wet?

NOBLE, H.

Reported in the Spanish Nationalist newspaper *El Norte de Castilla*, of 23 September 1936, to have offered his services as a pilot to the Spanish Embassy in London. From Rushden in Northamptonshire. Possibly Harry Noble (born in Yorkshire 1898) who served in the RFC/RAF during 1918-19.

OLLERENSHAW, Arthur John.

Commissioned in RFC/RAF from November 1917 to April 1919. Later became a musician and was an early volunteer for the Loyalist cause in Spain where, because of his experience, he later became an instructor at a school for training officers and NCOs. Later was Second-in-Command of the British Battalion of the XV International Brigade in August 1937. Did not fly in Spain.

OVENDEN, Arthur (Bert).

From Folkestone, Ovenden had been a pilot in World War I with the RFC when only 17 years old. He travelled to Spain in August 1936 hoping to get into Spanish Republican Air Force but was unable to so joined militias. He later was part of an English group in Thaelmann Battalion of XII International Brigade and fought in battles around Madrid in the autumn of 1936. He was the only survivor (with Esmond Romilly, nephew of Winston Churchill, who died whilst serving with the RCAF with No.58 Squadron, RAF, in England in 1941) of action at Boadilla del Monte in late December. Returned to England with Romilly at the beginning of 1937 but later worked in Paris helping to organize further volunteers for the International Brigades. Died in Winchester in 1982.

PORTER, G.H.

The Index to the Foreign Office Archives (1937) refers to the above pilot in conjunction with Vincent Doherty, Pat Mertz and Heinz Glogauer as having flown in Spain. It has not been possible to identify with certainty this pilot although an airman of this name held a commission in the RAF from May 1937 after previous service in the ranks of the Reserve from August 1936.

RAYMOND, Richard/Marshall.

As per William Bamborough above. Karl von Wiegand also referred to "A young Scot from Renfrew" who told him that he was flying a Bristol Fighter, which turned out to be a two-seater built in France.

RAYNEAU . . . the mysterious Major.

The Liverpool Daily Post of 1 October 1936 carried the following item:

> With the departure (from Madrid) from Spain of Count Robert Raynei, an English airman who had been in the service of the Spanish Government as a pilot, comes the end of a tragic adventure. A week ago a fashionable bar in Madrid was enlivened by the presence of eight English airmen. Now there are none. Three are dead. The last has departed from Paris. (Reuters).

In November 1937 an article also appeared in the magazine *Popular Flying*, by a Major Rayneau, which told the strange story of his experiences as a pilot in Spain in the autumn of 1936. In this he told that he was one of 10 young Englishmen who had flown down to Burgos in August 1936 to volunteer their services to the Nationalists who asked them to form their own unit. Rayneau, because of his experience in both the French and British

Air Forces, was elected squadron commander. For the rest of August Rayneau and his friends flew fighter patrols (he states that they flew German Heinkel fighters) against the Dewoitine, Loire, Bloch 210, Potez 54 aeroplanes of the Republic. During this period four of his comrades were killed in air combat including "Tim", "Claude" and "David".

On 4 September 1936 Rayneau heard that the High Command were anxious to obtain inside information from Madrid so he volunteered to go. Rayneau left Spain and went to Paris where he volunteered to join the Loyalist Air Force and eventually arrived in Madrid where he was quartered at the Hotel Florida along with all the other foreign pilots including Hillman, Warsow, Downes-Martin, Griffiths and Wilson. Rayneau was sent to Barajas aerodrome and soon learnt all the information he had been asked to obtain. He also heard that his squadron was called the Richthofen Squadron by the Loyalists because of the German aircraft they flew. Rayneau then applied for leave to go to France and eventually made his way back to Burgos where he reported to Generals Mola and Cabanellas. The surviving English pilots were then ordered to join the Franco forces relieving the Alcázar at Toledo. Rayneau was subsequently promoted to Major and awarded the Order of Saint Ferdinand by General Franco. He later returned to Paris and stated in the article that he was going to Brazil to fly for a private company.

How much truth can there be in all this? It seems extremely unlikely that Rayneau could have been a fighter pilot for the Nationalists – they had no reason to recruit many foreign pilots in the same way as the Republic. Certainly there is no confirmation of all this from any other source. There was certainly no all-British squadron with the Nationalists. It does, however, seem he was in Loyalist Spain and is mentioned by Russian writer Koltsov[10] having destroyed five Nationalist aircraft. Until recently it was thought that Rayneau may have been a pseudonym for Charles Kennett or even Richard Aitken-Quack (note that it was also claimed that he too had been a spy for Franco). But Ministry of Defence records have shown that a Robert William Henry Rayneau, born at Aurignac in France on 30 August 1910, was commissioned in the RAF in October 1929. He learnt to fly at No.3 Flying Training School at Grantham; from January 1931 until he left the RAF in June 1932 he was with No.1 (Fighter) Squadron at Tangmere on Hawker Furys. The birthdate above is the same as that for Major Rayneau given in the article in *Popular Flying*.

ROSE, Reginald H.

From London. According to the *Evening Standard* of 20 November 1936, Rose had made his way to Madrid in mid-August and tried to join the Republican Air Force. Unable to do so he joined the militia and was assigned to the machine-gun company of the 5th Regiment. Wounded in October in a battle near Talavera and returned home in November 1936. No further details are known.

SIDEBOTHAM, C.E.R.

The *Index to the Foreign Office Archives (1938)* refers to a pilot of this name who was trying to enlist in the Spanish Republican Air Force. A Sergeant C.E.R. Sidebotham was killed-in-action on 28 December 1940 while on the strength of No.106 Squadron RAF. He enlisted in the Service in April 1937.

SMITH, Denis Norman Evelyn.

Born at Woodford in Essex on 10 June 1916. He learnt to fly whilst still a student and obtained his 'A' flying licence at the Northamptonshire Aero Club in November 1933. Smith subsequently obtained a second 'A' certificate at the Airwork School of Flying in September 1938 and also his 'B' commercial pilot's licence No.6124. When in June 1940 he was granted a commission in the Royal Air Force it was recorded that "prior to entry into RAF had carried out 2050 hours solo flying including, during 1937, 800 hours flying in the Spanish Air Force." No mention, however, of Denis Smith has been found in the *Index to the Foreign Office Archives* or in contemporary accounts. It is known that he flew as a pilot with British-American Air Services at Liverpool (Speke) Airport immediately prior to joining the RAF in 1940 and that he listed flying experience on de Havilland D.H.90, D.H.84, D.H.86, D.H.89 and Fokker F.XXII in his application for a commission in the RAF. Dennis Smith was posted to No.74 (Fighter) Squadron in the third week of July 1940 and was killed-in-action during an air battle off Clacton with Bf.110s of KG.26 on 11 August 1940. He was flying a Spitfire (R.6962) from Manston. Contemporaries with No.74 Squadron and the history of the Squadron affirm he was a pilot in the Spanish Republican Air Force during the Civil War.[11] Smith is buried at Ostend in Belgium.

Denis Smith, 1933. (Courtesy RAF Museum)

SMITH, Joseph Allan.[12]

From Nantwich, Cheshire (born 1909). He was a rigger and wood-worker with Airspeed Aviation Ltd of Portsmouth in 1936. When the Spanish Civil War broke out he decided to volunteer his services to the Spanish Government as an aircraft mechanic (he had previously served seven years as such in the RAF). Smith also had the bright idea of presenting the Republicans with an aeroplane at the same time knowing that the agents of both sides in the conflict were busy in England purchasing as many civil aircraft as they could get and paying exorbitant prices for them.

Although his flying experience was limited to a few hours as a passenger whilst in the RAF he decided that he would "acquire" an aeroplane from his employers and fly all the way to Spain. Of course, when he discussed this with his workmates at Airspeed Aviation they did not take him seriously, but he, somehow, managed to persuade a fellow wood-worker, Arthur C. Gargett (a twenty-two year old from Darlington) to accompany him.

Smith made plans to fly off early in the morning of 20 August 1936 in a brand-new Airspeed Courier (one of several awaiting delivery to customers at Portsmouth Airport). The evening before the flight they both went to Portsmouth Public Library and studied a map of Spain. They found that Spain lay due south, some 650 miles from Portsmouth, and decided to aim for San Sebastian. On the morning of the 20 August, Smith left home early after cutting himself "four beef sandwiches" and arrived at the Airport where he met Gargett. At about 8.00am a Courier (G-ACVE) taxied out for take-off – the two men had broken in to the flight test hangar and had managed to start the engine. The inevitable happened.

Airspeed Courier (G-ACVE) after crash at Portsmouth Airport, August 1936. (via R. T. Jackson)

Although the aircraft managed to wallow unsteadily into the air, it stalled and crashed into a moat near the northern boundary of the airfield. Both men were thrown through the cabin windows, the aircraft being completely wrecked. Smith sustained a broken leg and was badly cut. Gargett received severe injuries and subsequently died in hospital. Smith later told how they had hoped to teach themselves to fly once they were in the air – enough to get to Spain and manage to land. They had spent the previous few days trying to learn how to read a compass by studying one in the Airspeed stores. In the following month Smith was sentenced to four months in prison for stealing the aircraft but also later received a further term after the death of Gargett. Surely one of the strangest stories to come out of the Spanish Civil War.

SMITH-PIGGOT.

According to de Wet, shot down and killed on 27 September 1936. "Smith-Piggot" was, in fact, Downes-Martin.

SPRIGG, Christopher St. John.

Born in 1907, he was a well known pilot and author of detective stories and books on aviation. A Marxist and an idealist he insisted in going to Spain to fight for the Republic (he used the pseudonym of Christopher Caudwell). Killed in February 1937 whilst serving in the British Battalion of the XV International Brigade. No flying whilst in Spain.

THORNEYCROFT, Christopher.

A member of the well-known steam engineering family of Basingstoke. He learnt to fly whilst an engineering student at Oxford University in 1936. Thorneycroft left his studies to go to Spain in October 1936 where he tried, without success, to get into the Republican Air Force. He became armourer to the Thaelmann Battalion of the XII International Brigade in November 1936 because of his engineering skill. Later, in the summer of 1937, transferred his engineering skills to the medical services of the Republic.

TICKELL, Francis Oscar.

Born at Ilford on 16 October 1900. An aircraft inspector at Liverpool he is referred to in the *Index of Foreign Office Archives (1936)* in conjunction with Charles Kennett. The document in question has disappeared, but the AVIA/2/1976 files reveal the following information: "(1 September 1936). A man named F.O. Tickell called at the Warrington Labour Exchange last Friday morning to draw his unemployment benefit; he asked to be able to draw his money on the following morning instead of the asssigned time which was in the afternoon, as in the afternoon he had an appointment to meet someone with regards to piloting an aircraft to Spain. It was gathered that Tickell had either been a pilot or a mechanic in the RAF and held a pilot's licence." Tickell actually served in the ranks of the RAF from 1921-25 and obtained his 'A' flying licence at Liverpool & District Aero Club in December 1938.

VICKERS, Stanley George[13]

Born at Feltham in Middlesex on 17 June 1900. He learnt to fly in the twenties and was one of the five founder members of Singapore Flying Club in 1928. In 1930 he enlisted in the ranks of the RAF and was posted to No.601 Squadron, AAF, where he became an air-gunner on Hawker Harts (with the rank of LAC) until he left the service in 1934. In September 1936 he was surprised one day to receive a visit from a detective from Scotland Yard; a Spaniard had been stopped at Folkestone and on him had been found a list of pilots to be contacted, including Vickers. The police asked that he sign to the fact that he would not fly for either of the combatants in Spain. This Spaniard was none other than Antonio Ramos Oliveira and the scrap of paper found on him had said "Aviation pilot for Spain; to take a machine over and remain there – S.C. Bickers [sic], Licensed Pilot, Bombing Instructor . . ."[14] Stanley Vickers obtained a commission in the RAF in May 1938 and served throughout World War II until November 1945 when he left the Service with the rank of Squadron Leader. He died in the late 1970s.

WINTRINGHAM, Thomas Henry.

Born 15 May 1898. Educated at Gresham's School, Holt, Norfolk, and Balliol College, Oxford University, he served in the RFC/RAF in France from 1916-18. Later became a journalist and went to Spain early on in the Spanish Civil War. As mentioned previously became first leader of the British Battalion of the XV International Brigade before being wounded. After some time as an instructor he returned to the front. Wounded again in street fighting in Quinto in the late summer of 1937 he was invalided home to the UK in November 1937. In World War II advised on Home Guard training. Died in August 1949.

WISE.[15]

A Canadian, later reported to have served as a mercenary pilot in the Spanish Civil War. Served in No.149 (Bomber) Squadron RAF during World War II as an air-gunner as he was too old to fly as a pilot.

CHAPTER 12 – SOURCES/NOTES

Details regarding service careers of the pilots come from Ministry of Defence records and other details from their Royal Aero Club flying licences, now at the RAF Museum. Information regarding members of the International Brigades came from Bill Alexander and from his book (see Bibliography).

1. Many details regarding Richard Aitken-Quack come from his brother, Harold Aitken-Quack and Justin Brooke. Also Flt.Lt S.H. Hanson, MBE, Chairman of 609 Squadron Association.

2. *Evening Standard*, 14 July 1937, and *Isle of Thanet Gazette*, 31 July 1937.

3. Information from Angelo Emiliani and his book, *Nei Cieli di Spagna* (Milan 1986).

4. *Aces High: Fighter Aces of the British and Commonwealth Air Forces in World War II*, by Christopher Shores and Clive Williams; London 1966.

5. Information via Peter Elstob and from his books, *Spanish Prisoner* (London 1939), and, *Condor Legion* (New York 1973).

6. Much information regarding Heinz Glogauer was supplied by Mr R. J. B. Pearse.

7. Additional details of Bill Harrington were supplied by Mr Alec Lumsden.

8. F0371 File (1936) 20531.

9. F0371 File (1936) 20588,

10. *Diario de la guerra de España*, by Mikhail Kolstov; Paris 1963.

11. Information from Douglas Tidy and his book, *I Fear No Man: History of No. 74 Squadron*; London 1972.

12. *Airspeed: The Company and its Aeroplanes*, by D.H. Middleton; Lavenham 1982, and contemporary newspaper reports.

13. Information via Leslie Hunt, MBE, AE, FRGS and the late Sqd. Ldr Vickers.

14. F0371 File (1936) 20577.

15. Ibid 13.

CHAPTER 13

Flying for the Chinese Dragon

Another part of the world to take advantage of the advance in aviation caused by the pressures of World War I was China, then still a medieval country consisting of many semi-independent provinces ruled by warlords. These men exerted total domination over their territories and controlled private armies constantly at war with their neighbours. In 1919 the Peking Central Government was purchasing surplus military aircraft in Europe for training and commercial purposes. Group Captain F. V. Holt, CMG, DSO, considered to be one of the most promising officers in the RAF and then only 34 years old, was seconded by the Air Ministry in London to China as technical adviser. Group Capt Holt took charge in November 1920 and established a school for the training of Chinese commercial pilots at Nanyuan, near Peking. Other instructors were hired from France, Britain and the USA. Civil war, however, broke out in China in 1922 and Holt resigned and returned to Britain because many of his aircraft were taken away by the waring factions and converted to military use.

Chang Tso-lin, known as "The Old Tiger" and the most powerful warlord of North China, had various aircraft available to him including four Handley Page 0/400s but no one to fly them. After his defeat in the war of 1922 he purchased additional aircraft including 12 Breguet Br.14 light bombers from France. An Englishman named Talbot-Lehmann was hired as "Aeronautical Adviser", and a shrewd Australian or New Zealander (accounts vary) of Scots descent named McKenzie, who had flown with the RAF in World War I, taken on to instruct would-be Chinese pilots. McKenzie, although an experienced and capable pilot, did not have the patience necessary as an instructor. He also caused problems by constantly quarrelling with several French pilots who had arrived (a people for whom he had an abiding dislike after losing all his savings when the *Banque Industrielle de Chine* had abruptly closed). In 1923, ironically, McKenzie was replaced by two of the Frenchmen and disappeared from the scene.

In Canton, the veteran Chinese revolutionary, Sun Yat-sen, had established himself as President of the (Southern) Republic. He hired Morris "Two-Gun" Cohen (born in Stepney in 1889), who had served in the Canadian forces in France during World War I, as ADC and sent him to Canada to obtain pilots and aeronautical engineers. There he contacted Wilfred "Wop" May, DFC, a World War I "ace" with 13 victories to his credit, who had been involved in the air combat during which the famous German pilot Baron Manfred von Richtofen had been killed in 1918. May was willing and anxious to work for the Cantonese Government but could not obtain a passport and exit visa for China. Cohen then made his way to San Francisco where he recruited a young American pilot named

Abbott and several engineers. Charles Kennett (see Chapter 6), also claimed to have been an instructor for Sun Yat-sen's small air force at this time.

San Yat-sen died in 1925 and his lieutenant, Chiang Kai-shek, determined to unify the country, captured Hankow, Nanking and Peking from 1926-28. His Kuomintang forces were accompanied by two-seat biplane aircraft supplied by Russia (actually Soviet-built de Havilland D.H.9As) during the Northern Expedition in 1926. The Russian advisers had left the following year leaving the way open for others. One of these was Weston Bert Hall, famed soldier-of-fortune pilot and member of the American *Lafayette Escadrille* in France during World War I. Bert Hall went to China for the professed purpose of selling Douglas aeroplanes. Soon the newspapers in the USA carried the story that he was head of the Chinese Air Force. In fact he had become an adviser to one of the Chinese generals. His sense for business ended up with him serving a two-and-a-half year sentence in jail in the USA for selling to the Chinese 1,000 non-existent pistols and ammunition.

The pause in armed conflict in China after 1928 enabled commercial aviation to re-establish itself. In 1929 the China National Aviation Corporation was formed by a partnership, initally, between the Chinese Government and the American Curtiss-Wright Corporation with American pilots and aircraft. An ex-RAF officer, Raymond Vaughan-Fowler, also set up the Far-East Aviation Company in 1930 at Hong Kong and Shanghai. He had been at one time an instructor to the Imperial Japanese Air Service and held the Order of the Rising Sun of Japan – somewhat ironic in view of what was to follow in the next few years. Vaughan-Fowler set up a flying training school. He also sold many British military and civil aircraft to the Chinese including Avro Avians, Avro 621, 626, 637, Westland Wapitis, Armstrong-Whitworth Atlas IIs etc., with A.V. Harvey acting as his chief test pilot and demonstrator. Other Englishmen to teach Chinese pilots to fly were Flt. Lt (later Wing Commander) Frank Swoffer, a serving RAF officer and former instructor at the Hampshire Aeroplane Club, in Shanghai and Robert Scard, about whom little is known apart from the fact that he was employed for a time instructing Chinese Air Force pilots at Nanking, and Philip Holroyd Smith.[1]

When Japan seized Manchuria after the Mukden incident in the autumn of 1931 virtually no opposition was offered to them in the air. The Central Government of Chiang Kai-shek took no part in the Manchurian "Incident", but in January 1932 fighting broke out in the Shanghai area. Japanese naval aircraft bombed Shanghai. In late February 1932 a young American pilot who had gone to China as a civil pilot, Robert Short,[2] flying in a newly delivered Boeing 218 biplane fighter aircraft, was shot down and killed during an air battle with three Japanese fighters from the carrier *Kaga* over Soochow. Another American, Herbert "Bert" Gibson, later claimed to have shot down 38 [sic] Japanese aircraft in defence of Shanghai.[3]

By the time the fighting had died down in March 1932 the Chinese Government had realised the importance of building up a strong air force. It was reported in the Western press that China was to establish a foreign squadron and would be recruiting pilots for this in the near future. Applications had already been received from unemployed pilots in Canada and the USA and it was expected that the squadron would shortly be set up. It would be several years, however, before this unit was formed. In the meanwhile an "unofficial" American mission, led by Colonel John Jouett, arrived in China together with nine pilots and four mechanics. The Jouett mission trained over 300 Chinese pilots but refused to take part in aerial operations against internal rebels. This, combined with Japanese diplomatic pressure, caused the withdrawal of the mission in December 1934. An Italian Air Mission replaced the Americans and remained in China until October 1937.

In 1930 an Australian, Squadron Leader (later Group Captain) Garnet Francis Malley MC, AFC, arrived in China. He was to play a large part in Chinese aeronautical affairs in the late Thirties. Born in Mosman, New South Wales, on 2 November 1893, he served in Egypt as a gunner in the Royal Artillery before obtaining a commission in the Australian Flying Corps in 1917. Malley subsequently served as a fighter pilot in France, being credited with seven or eight victories over German aircraft before the end of World War I. A mechanic in civilian life, he set up his own business in Sydney before becoming technical adviser to Australian National Airways in 1928-29. In the following year he became organiser/aviation advisor to the regional Kwangtung Government in Canton, South China. In 1936, however, the Nationalist forces of Chiang Kai-shek moved against the Cantonese and the entire Cantonese Air Force of some 90 aircraft defected to Chiang. Resistance in Kwangtung crumbled and Marshall Chan Chi-tong, the Cantonese ruler, surrendered. Malley, however, remained in China as an aviation adviser to the Nationalist Air Force.

Flight Lieutenant Garnet Malley with Duke of York (later King George VI) in late 1920's.
(Courtesy Mrs Phyllis Garnet Malley)

The result of all the foreign advisers from the USA, Britain, Russia, Italy, Germany and France to China in the previous decade was that Chiang Kai-shek had obtained a vast array of aeroplanes from all around the world, many of which were now obsolete and of limited use. Besides, the maintenance of such a large number of different airframes and engines presented an almost impossible task. The quality of Chinese pilots also left much to be desired with the different standards expected by the various foreign training schools. Malley at once addressed himself to this problem and by early 1937 he advised that the number of squadrons be reduced in order to bring the remainder to a state of efficiency for war and maintain a supply of reserve aircraft. Many obsolete aircraft were to be written off. All this still left the Chinese having in its first-line air force Northrop 2EC attack aircraft, Douglas 02M biplanes, Curtiss A-12 Shrike fighter-bombers, Boeing 281 (export P-26) fighters, Curtiss Hawk II and III fighters, Vought O3U Corsair biplane reconnaissance aircraft (all from the USA); Savoia SM.72 bombers, Fiat BR.3 bombers, Fiat CR.32 fighters (from Italy) and several Heinkel He IIIA bombers (from Germany). A complete mixture of other types served as training and communications aircraft.[4]

In May 1937 a new American adviser arrived in China. His name was to become a legend and he was to have a vast impact on the equipment, personnel and efficiency of the Chinese Air Force. This was a recently retired US Army Air Corps Captain, Claire Lee Chennault. His first task was to fly around the country to inspect the air bases. What he found horrified him. Chennault was soon to get his chance to improve matters because, in early July 1937, the Japanese began their attack once more on China, a struggle that was to last until Japan was defeated in 1945 at the end of World War II. Chennault at once volunteered his services. Before long this blunt speaking American was given the job to reorganise the Chinese Air Force, which soon suffered heavy losses against the better equipped and trained Japanese pilots. The loss of trained pilots and the time taken to produce replacements led to the decision to once more recruit pilots from abroad to form an "International Squadron" to combat the rampant Japanese Air Forces.

The adventurous American, Hilaire du Berrier, had already made his way to China in the hope of obtaining lucrative employment for himself and others including Hugh Oloff de Wet and Robert Bannister Pickett. In the event only Vincent Minor Schmidt, recommended to Chennault by du Berrier, was to fly in the "International Squadron". Du Berrier himself flew as a transport pilot before falling out with Garnet Malley and returning to Hong Kong.

By August 1937 the Aeronautical Affairs Commission of the Chinese Government was attempting to attract foreign pilots to China to fight the Japanese. Vincent Schmidt advised the Commission in Paris that he was willing to bring out other pilots, all of whom were prepared to renounce their citizenship if necessary to fight in China. In America too approaches were made to likely candidates and soon flying men from many different countries and backgrounds were making their way surreptitiously to China. Garnet Malley, by now granted the rank of Wing Commander on the Reserve of the Royal Australian Air Force, was warned by the British Government that British subjects were precluded from engaging in war-like operations in China.[5]

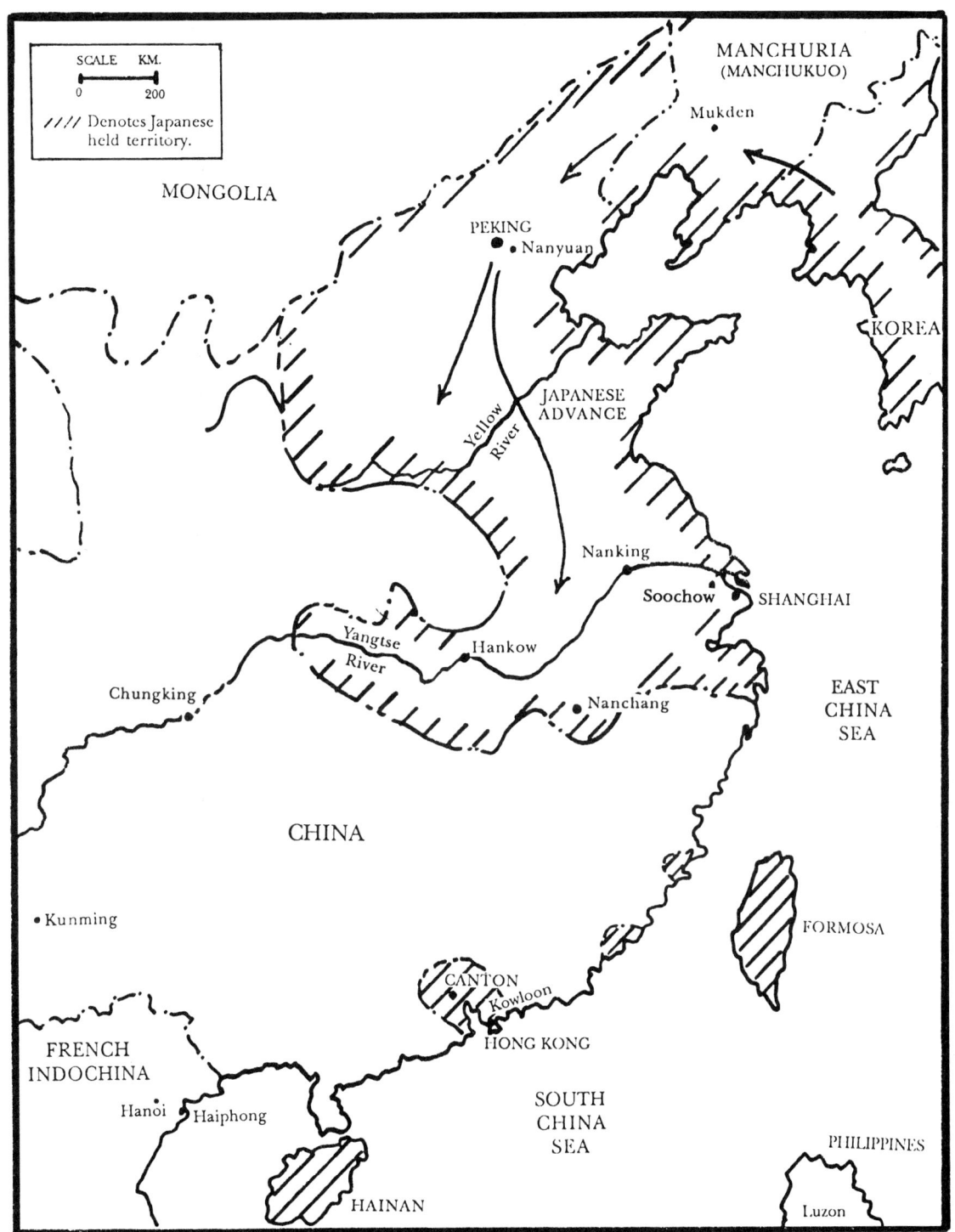

CHINA 1932-41

By now, Malley had already heard from a New Zealander, then flying in New Guinea, and other pilots with a view to serving in China. This New Zealander was yet another of the ilk of Eric Griffiths, Thomas Wewege-Smith or Vincent Doherty. Raymond Galbraith Whitehead was born in Wellington, New Zealand, on 29 October 1910. His father came from Lancashire in England and had emigrated whilst a young man to New Zealand where he set up a drapery business in Wellington with a friend and married a New Zealand girl of Scottish descent. Ron Whitehead, as Raymond was known to his family and friends, attended Wellington College from 1922-26 and showed ability in both academic studies and sporting activities. He then went to Victoria College, University of New Zealand, but in mid-1927 left to join the staff of the Wellington *Dominion* newspaper and over the next two years graduated from office-boy to inland telegram sub-editor. In late 1929 Ron resigned to travel to Europe with his parents and to try for a commission in the Royal Air Force. Devoted to flying Ron had already become a member of Wellington Aero Club. In London he was offered a job as a feature writer on the *Evening Standard* but turned this down after being granted a Short Service Commission in the RAF. He commenced his duties in late December 1930.

In January 1931 the youngster from New Zealand was sent to No.2 Flying Training School, Digby, Lincolnshire, where he spent nearly a year. One of his instructors at Digby was Flying Officer (later Air Vice-Marshall) Cyril Kay, who four years later was to beat Ron to be the first New Zealander to fly the Tasman Sea between Australia and New Zealand. Ron graduated from Digby with his pilot's wings at the end of 1931 and was posted to No.35 (Bomber) Squadron at Bircham Newton, near Sandringham, Norfolk, where he flew Fairey IIIF and Gordon biplane light bombers until the autumn of 1932. After a conversion course on single seater fighters at the Central Flying School, Ron was posted to the famous airfield at Biggin Hill where he joined No.32 (Fighter) Squadron to fly Bristol Bulldogs. He remained at Biggin Hill until the end of his service in March 1933 when he was transferred to the Reserve.

Ron Whitehead (second from the right in the front row) whilst in the R.A.F. c.1933. (Courtesy Mrs Sally Chao)

Returning to New Zealand, Ron worked for a time as advertising manager of his father's department store. But flying was now in his blood and he made his way to Australia, after obtaining his commercial pilot's 'B' Licence in September 1933. From there he hoped to go to China to deliver aircraft from the ports to various parts of the country. On this occasion he did not go East but became involved with Kingsford Smith Aviation Ltd and flew for the famous Australian world girdling pilot, Sir Charles Kingsford Smith, for some time before persuading his father to loan him enough money to puchase a second-hand de Havilland D.H.80A Puss Moth (VH-UON) in February 1934. With this aircraft, which cost £400, Ron began an air taxi business and also barnstormed around New South Wales and Victoria until the autumn of 1934.

During this period he became good friends with a young Australian pilot named Rex Nicholl and they made plans to fly the Tasman Sea, the shark infested stretch of water between Australia and New Zealand. This was truly a hazardous undertaking, for the single-engined aircraft was now nearly five years old and had flown nearly 1,000 miles. The two airmen removed two seats to make space for extra fuel tanks and planned to share the only remaining seat between them, changing places in mid-flight. Not surprisingly, perhaps, the Australian authorities cancelled the certificate of air-worthiness of the Puss Moth. The two men decided to go ahead with the flight and finally took off from a beach, about 60 miles south of Sydney, bound for New Plymouth, North Island, New Zealand. Only the most elementary navigational instruments were carried and the aircraft was without a radio. Nothing was heard of the airmen for 27 hours and an anxious watch for them was kept throughout New Zealand. They had, however, landed on a beach near the northernmost part of New Zealand after a fourteen-and-a-half hour flight. As soon as it was light they took off again for Mangere, near Auckland, where they received many congratulations for a remarkable flight. Both Ron Whitehead and Nicholl were later charged with a breach of the Air Navigation Act and had their licences suspended for a time. The Puss Moth was overhauled and given the New Zealand registration ZK-ADU in June 1935 and named "Faith in New Zealand".[6]

Whitehead's famous de Havilland D.H 80A Puss Moth (VH-UON) on New Zealand beach during barnstorming tour, 1935. (Courtesy Mrs Sally Chao)

Ron had spent most of the intervening period lecturing about the flight, but after his licence was restored barnstormed around New Zealand and flew joy-riders from many airstrips and beaches in the Puss Moth with Nicholl.

Ron made tentative plans to go to Ethiopia to fly against the Italian invaders and on one occasion his mother was horrified to find that he had cut up her fur coat to make a flying jacket "because it would be cold 20,000 feet up over Abyssinia". Nothing, however, came of this scheme and in early January 1936 Ron married a girl from Auckland and the young couple left Wellington immediately for Sydney in Australia where he hoped to obtain employment as a commercial pilot.

Shortly after arriving in Sydney Ron joined WASP (Western and Southern Provincial) Airlines but this company went out of business and he was left to chase after all sorts of jobs. Eventually he obtained a position as a pilot with North Queensland Airways, and the family (which now included a daughter born in August) moved to Cairns in the State of Queensland in November 1936. Their sojourn there was to be only very brief because Ron heard of the money to be made by bush pilots in New Guinea, so the following month they left Cairns for Wau in this huge island to the north of Australia where Ron joined E. J. Stephens Aviation Ltd.

The gold finds in New Guinea in the mid-twenties had brought many Australian bush pilots to get in on the action and excitement. They found a country with some of the worst flying conditions anywhere in the world. Its combination of razor-backed mountains, shrouding mists and sudden blinding tropical storms had to be combatted as well as its fever-breeding climate and all manner of lizards and insects on the ground. Ron flew dynamite, medicines, tools and rice into the gold fields, crossing the high mountain ranges and dense jungles. His companion during the Tasman Sea flight, Rex Nicholl, was also in New Guinea flying for a rival concern. In August 1937 Ron, who had heard of how the Chinese Government were trying to recruit pilots to fight the Japanese, cabled China and was told to report to Nanking as soon as possible for duty as a combat pilot, subject to flight checks. The salary payable would be £1,500 per annum, a considerable sum. Ron left New Guinea for China in September and his wife and daughter returned to New Zealand.

Ron sailed to Hong Kong. Shanghai was already nearly sealed off by the Japanese so he went to Canton. Here he teamed up with Bill Vyner-White (cousin of the Australian actress Margaret Vyner) who had left a farm in Kenya to offer his services to China. The high-spirited East African immediately became friends with Ron Whitehead, and they pooled resources whilst waiting to get to Nanking. Eventually they were collected by Garnet Malley who took them to the Chinese capital. White soon left because his log book only showed 30 hours flying time, together with two other pilots, Archie Randolph and Harry Stokes, who were rejected after flight tests.

In late October Ron arrived in Hankow where he met several other pilots waiting to be checked out at the airport by Madame Chiang Kai-shek's personal pilot, Ex-US Army Air Corps pilot, Julius Barr. These included two Frenchmen, Martial Laroche and Marcel Florein;[7] Jan Rouffaer and Heini Hendricks from the Netherlands;[8] Elwyn Gibbon,

Harold Welch and George Weigle from the USA. The flight checks were duly carried out on 9 November and Ron received the following evaluation from Barr:

> R.G. Whitehead passed all right. With him also I do not know his previous experience for which he was examined at Nanking, but he flew the Douglas OK and I'm sure that he will be all right for pursuit work. Perhaps with a few hours dual in multimotors he will be all right for a bomber.

Vincent Schmidt had also arrived in China with several other pilots and had been appointed Commanding Officer of the new squadron. Shanghai fell to the Japanese in early November and their forces raced on to Nanking, the capital. Ron had some flights in the newly arrived Vultee V-11 single-engined bombers but then with some French pilots was transferred to the 5th Pursuit Group at Nanchang flying Curtiss Hawk III fighters.

Curtis Hawk III fighters of Chinese Air Force at Hankow, 1938. (Gibbon Collection / San Diego Aero-Space Museum, via Richard S. Allen)

On 14 December 1937 Ron, together with his Chinese patrol leader and a Frenchman named Omer Poivre,[9] were ordered to intercept Japanese bombers reported to be on their way to bomb Nanchang. They found them at 12,000 feet over the city – there were 45 bombers and 15 fighters. In the ensuing dog-fight the Chinese patrol leader was immediately shot down and Ron and the Frenchman soon had the Japanese fighters on their tails. Despite all his frantic efforts the New Zealander soon found that the Japanese aircraft far outclassed his own and that it would be only a matter of time before he would be hit. Suddenly he received a terrific blow in his right shoulder. His right arm being out of action Ron grabbed the controls with his left hand and dived to get clear. As the Japanese dropped behind he took to his parachute and tried to pull the shrouds with his good arm to make it fall faster. By now the Japanese fighters were circling above him and firing at the descending parachute. Bullets ripped dozens of holes in the silk canopy. Finally Ron feigned death, hanging limply with his head slumped on his chest, and the Japanese aircraft departed convinced that he was dead.

He landed safely but found that he could not get to his feet. Some Chinese farmers found him and, having assured themselves that he was not a Jap, they made a litter and carried him to their village. After first-aid from the local schoolmaster, who spoke English, Ron was carried in relays to the aerodrome, an eight-hour journey. He was taken to the International Hospital in Hankow where the upper part of his body was put in plaster as his collarbone was broken. He was lucky because the Frenchman, Poivre, who had done his best to protect his colleague from attack after shooting down one of the Japanese bombers, was himself shot down and died later in hospital. Another pilot, a German named Kreuzberg, also later died fighting a lone battle against five Japanese fighters. Nanking had fallen to the Japanese on 13 December and the capital was shifted to Hankow, 300 miles to the west.

As Ron was unable to move during air raids his bed was transported to the basement. One day he was visited by Madame Chiang Kai-shek, then Secretary-General of the Aeronautical Affairs Commission, who saw that his only real hope of recovery was to get to Hong Kong for special treatment away from constant air raids. On 12 January 1938 Ron was flown there in one of her private aircraft. He was to remain there until the following March slowly recovering from his injuries.

In the meanwhile more foreign pilots arrived whilst China regrouped her forces and the Japanese rested. William Labussière, a Frenchman who had flown for the Republican Air Force as a fighter pilot during the Spanish Civil War, arrived together with another French pilot named André Boulingre, who had also been in Spain with the Malraux Squadron. Another pilot who had flown in Spain arrived in January 1938, Jim Allison from Texas, together with an ex-commercial pilot from the USA, Lyman Voelpel. Operations began in January for the 14th Squadron (as the International Squadron was officially known). Flying Vultee V-11 and Northrop 2EC attack aircraft some initial sorties were made. One of the Americans, Harold Welch, was killed in a crash at Hankow airport early in January. Already one of the problems associated with employing mercenary airmen was showing itself. Several of the pilots wrote to Schmidt expressing dissatisfaction with their pay and conditions in comparison with others. Such disputes, of course, did not aid morale within the squadron, especially as some of the pilots considered that Schmidt kept them uninformed as to decisions made and that the veteran soldier-of-fortune lacked the necessary tact when dealing with his Chinese superiors.

The first full squadron bombing mission took place in early February when six Vultees, led by Schmidt, successfully attacked Japanese troop concentrations to the north of Hankow. This raid set the pattern for the next month or so, and raids continued on Japanese positions north of the Yellow River and their airfields and strongholds. Many days, however, were spent simply in 'saving' bombing aircraft from Japanese attack by flying the aeroplanes away from Hankow Airport. The pilots with the 14th Squadron who had been in Spain, Allison, Labussière, Boulingre and Florein, once more had the chance to observe at close hand the Russian aircraft they had seen there, for also at Hankow were based Polikarpov I-15bis and I-16 fighters and Tupolev SB-2 bombers, with their Soviet pilots and groundcrew, part of a large contingent sent to aid China. As in Spain, the Russians kept to themselves and did not share facilities with the other foreigners.

One of the Frenchmen, Laroche, resigned in mid February after an accident when landing a Vultee at Hankow in which one of the Soviet groundcrew was killed. He felt responsible for the man's death. Florein also resigned and returned to France. The antics, however, of some of the other mercenary pilots also resulted in much animosity from the American service-trained instructors with the Chinese and many of the Chinese Air Force officers themselves. The fact that their Chinese mechanics, bombadiers and machine-gunners could not speak English also caused many problems and misunderstandings.

In late February whilst the 14th Squadron raided a Japanese rail centre near the Yellow River, the Russians bombed Formosa. In the evening several of the Americans were drinking at a bar when they were approached by a journalist who asked them about the bombing of Formosa. Tongue in cheek, they led him to believe that it was the 14th Squadron who had carried out this raid. Soon the story was being carried by the press all over the USA. As this attack was considered the outstanding performance to date by the Chinese all the publicity being given to the mercenary airmen again caused much resentment.

During early March new aircraft arrived for use by the 14th Squadron – Martin 139 twin-engined bombers, which were assembled at Henyang and flown to Hankow. With the arrival of these aircraft the squadron turned over its remaining Vultees to the Chinese. Further discussions on pay for the pilots were held with Chennault and Madame Chiang Kai-shek, but events in mid-March brought about the end of the squadron. Firstly, several of the Martins were damaged in an evening raid on Hankow airfield by Japanese bombers. Various writers since, including Chennault himself, blamed the pilots of the 14th for revealing the presence of the fully bombed-up aircraft on the airfield whilst under the influence of alcohol in Hankow. The ever vigilant Japanese intelligence network did the rest. And secondly, there were several unpleasant incidents between some of the Americans and Captain Hsu, a Chinese who was to take over as commander of the squadron from Schmidt. Finally on 20 March, the pilots were called together and told that the squadron was being disbanded. The news was officially released two days later – the reason given was "lack of homogeneity".

Some of the soldiers-of-fortune left immediately for home: Allison and Voepel later flew as ferry pilots during World War II. Voepel was still living in Southern California in the early 1980s. Gibbon also left in early April for the USA but was arrested by the Japanese for being a member of China's flying foreign legion when his boat called at Yokohama. He was released some days later after diplomatic pressures were brought to bear. During World War II he became a test pilot in Karachi, India, on Vultee P-66 Vanguards destined for China. Gibbon was killed in a crash in one of these fighter aircraft during August 1942.

Vincent Schmidt returned to Paris but other pilots in the 14th Squadron remained in China and were given other assignments, including George Weigle, who became a test pilot with the Central Aircraft Manufacturing Company at Chungking (he too was killed whilst testing an aeroplane in May 1939).

By now another British pilot had arrived in Hankow, former RAF officer Harris who had previously served in No.9 Squadron (court-martialled in 1920). His arrival in China from Australia was reported to the Foreign Office in London by the British Air Attaché at Shanghai on 7 March 1938.[10] Unfortunately no further information is available.

Ron Whitehead returned to Hankow in March 1938 to find that the 14th Squadron had been disbanded. By May he was fit again for active duty and was ordered south to Yunnan (Kunming) to pick up some new French Dewoitine D.510C cannon-armed fighters. The first two of these aircraft, which had been shipped to Haiphong, were assembled at Hanoi and test-flown there, but the French administration in Indo-China forbade the assembly of the remaining D.510s on French territory and the crates containing the aircraft were shipped from Haiphong to Yanan-fui. Ron was left to wait until all these aircraft were ready for combat. This took several months. He was then attached to a newly formed squadron at Kunming in August 1938 which included two of the French pilots who had previously been in the 14th Squadron, Labussière and Boulingre. This group broke up after a few months due to internal bickerings in the command, and Ron returned to fly with the Chinese Defence Group on Curtiss Hawk IIIs based at Kunming (Hankow had fallen to the Japanese in October 1938 and the Chinese Government had moved to Chungking). By now practically all combat flying had ceased by the Chinese Air Force as Chennault had pulled back the remaining aircraft and aircrews to the interior of the country for large-scale training operations, the results of which would be seen during World War II. Most of the combat flying from the end of 1938 to 1941 against the invaders was by the Russians who operated under the orders of Moscow.

Hilaire du Berrier and Eric Griffiths, soldiers-of-fortune supreme, returned to the Chinese scene in 1939, obstensively to join the embryo air force of one of China's rebel generals. Two sources state that Griffiths was accompanied by another New Zealander named L.A. Willicombe, "a tall, strong, silent guy".

In February 1939 the Chinese discovered that one of the French pilots still retained was reporting to the *Deuxième Bureau,* the French Intelligence agency, so cancelled the contracts of the Frenchmen and Ron Whitehead although these were "for the duration". Ron was later told to reapply but, by this time, he had negotiated a contract with Texaco to carry fuel for the Chinese Army from Indo-China to Chungking. He operated ten trucks for a year and a half making a small fortune for himself, but lost it all when the Japanese forced the French to close the frontier. At that moment all the vehicles were on the wrong side. Ron just managed to get out of Indo-China before the Japanese arrived in 1940 by taking a taxi 65 miles through back country, and then walking another 30 miles to the Chinese border. Three of his former colleagues in the 14th Squadron, Labussière, Boulingre and Laroche, had joined the French forces in Indo-China at the outbreak of World War II and flew against the Thai Air Force during the fighting that erupted between the French Colonial Forces and Thailand in 1940-41, Labussière claiming at least one "victory" over Thai aircraft.

Back in Kunming, Ron's troubles continued and he nearly succumbed to smallpox, but lived to join the newly formed American Volunteer Group (the famous Flying Tigers) under Claire Chennault in mid-1941, first as Group Transportation Officer and then as Assistant Operations Officer, being responsible for the air defence of Yunnan. Labussière was also offered a contract by Chennault to fly with the AVG but he was arrested and imprisoned by the Vichy authorities before he could leave Hanoi. The story of the Flying Tigers is well known. Their heroic defence of Burma and China during those dark days in early 1942 showed that the Japanese Air Forces were not unbeatable.

In March 1942 a medical examination of Ron by Dr Gentry of the AVG showed that he was unfit for flying "by reason of faulty depth perception and hyperphoria of an excessive degree".[11] Like many of the original American volunteers Ron refused an offer to join the regular USAAF and was discharged at the end of May 1942. He still hoped, despite the medical report, to join the RAF as a pilot but, in the end, resumed his civilian engineering and transport business. His adventures were not yet over, however, for Ron was approached by British Intelligence to work for them. From late 1942 until the end of the war in 1945 he was involved in many operations on their behalf. The story of these is worth a book in themselves. Perhaps the biggest job of all was when the leader of the China based Tonkinese, later to become famous as Vietnam's Defence Minister, Vo Nguyen Giap, arranged the theft of the entire Japanese Order of Battle for Southeast Asia from its safe in the Japanese HQ in Hanoi. It was replaced, without the Japs ever knowing it had been taken to China by relays of runners, copied in three days and then returned.

In 1945 Ron set up an export-import business in Hong Kong which thrived until the spreading Nationalist-Communist conflict disrupted foreign trade. After a year spent working as a confidential investigator for the Hong Kong Government, he returned to his first love – journalism. He became Chief Editor of *Agence France-Presse*, then Editor of the *South China Morning Post*, and correspondent for NBC Radio and NBC – TV.

Sadly his first marriage ended in divorce in 1948 as his family in New Zealand had not heard from him for years. Ron's later years were spent mostly in his adopted home of Hong Kong on radio, television and journalism. He also had a long spell teaching senior classes in language and business studies. During these years he was visited by his daughter who had last seen him in New Guinea in 1937 and father and daughter built up a good relationship with each other. Ron worked as a free-lance journalist until the end. He died on 15 May 1980 in Kowloon Hospital, one of the last of the adventurers from those great days of flying.

William Labussière escaped from Indo-China in 1944 and served as Liaison Officer of the French Military Mission in China until the end of the Pacific war. He then set up an air freight company in Indo-China with Boulingre (who had also been jailed by the Vichy Government there for Free French activities) which operated until 1953 when they returned to France. Labassière also took time off during this period to serve as an aeronautical advisor to the Syrian Air Force until a revolution necessitated his escape. He later rejoined the French Air Force, serving in Algeria and France, before his retirement. He now lives in Paris. Boulingre also lives in France, but Laroche died in Nice in 1976.

Claire Chennault died in America in July 1958. Ron Whitehead's former chief in China, Garnet Malley, remained there until 1940 when he was recalled to Australia by the Royal Australian Air Force and sent on a special intelligence mission to Singapore, returning to Australia before the capitulation. Made Director of Combined Operational Intelligence, the now Group-Captain Malley was attached to General Douglas MacArthur's staff at Army Headquarters, South West Pacific Area, but was later called to Canberra to take charge of the Chinese section of security. With his health seriously affected by his strenuous war activities, Group-Captain Malley retired and went to live on his coconut plantation in Lau, Fiji, where he died in May 1961. His significant contribution towards the build-up of the Chinese Air Force in the 1930s has largely been ignored by historians who have generally concentrated on the American involvement during these years.

All writers, however, are only as good as their sources and many of the accounts that have appeared both in the USA and France over the years about the foreign 'volunteer' airmen in China during the thirties have been, to say the least, somewhat inaccurate. One example will suffice; René Drouillet (who had been in Ethiopia in 1936) later told how he had gone to the Far East and shot down five Japanese aircraft over Canton whilst flying a light two-seater training aircraft fitted with a 'borrowed' machine-gun. Similar tales have also appeared regarding American airmen in the 14th Squadron. Of such are legends made.

CHAPTER 13 – SOURCES/NOTES

Much of the information concerning Ron Whitehead came from his daughter, Mrs Sally Chao. Other details regarding his flying career come from Ministry of Defence records and contemporary newspaper reports etc. Mrs Phyllis Garnet Malley kindly supplied much information on her late husband's career and the Ministry of Defence (Australia) also added other details. For the story of the American involvement in China and the 14th Squadron, I am greatly indebted to Ed Leiser of the San-Diego Aero-Space Museum, Bob Miller and Richard Sanders Allen in the USA. Gerry Beauchamp in Canada supplied much additional information on the French pilots involved and William Labussiére also added many details and corrected information given previously regarding the 14th Squadron.

1. Information regarding China during the Twenties has come from many sources including the article 'The Chinese Air Force during the Warlord Era 1916-1928'. by Anthony B. Chan; *The Army Quarterly, Vol. 113, No.1.* January 1983.

2. 'Robert Short, the Making of a Hero', by Martin Cole; *American Aviation Historical Society Journal. Vol. 15, No.1*, Spring 1970.

3. Royal Canadian Air Force/*Public Relations Release No. 580*, 1942. Courtesy Allan Levine.

4. F0371 File (1937) 20968.

5. F0371 File (1937) 20969.

6. *Wings Across the Tasman 1928-1953*, by John W.L. Jillett; Wellington 1953, etc.

7. Florein had served with the Malraux Squadron in Spain in 1936-37.

8. Rouffaer and Hendricks were in the USA. when they decided to go to China. Rouffaer later became a commercial pilot with KLM and died in Mexico in 1973.

9. Poivre was a former French Air Force pilot and test pilot with the Farman company.

10. F0371 File (1938) 22139.

11. Chennault Collection, Stanford University, USA. *Report* dated 5 March 1942 & *Special Order No. 119* of 31 May 1942. Courtesy Bob Miller.

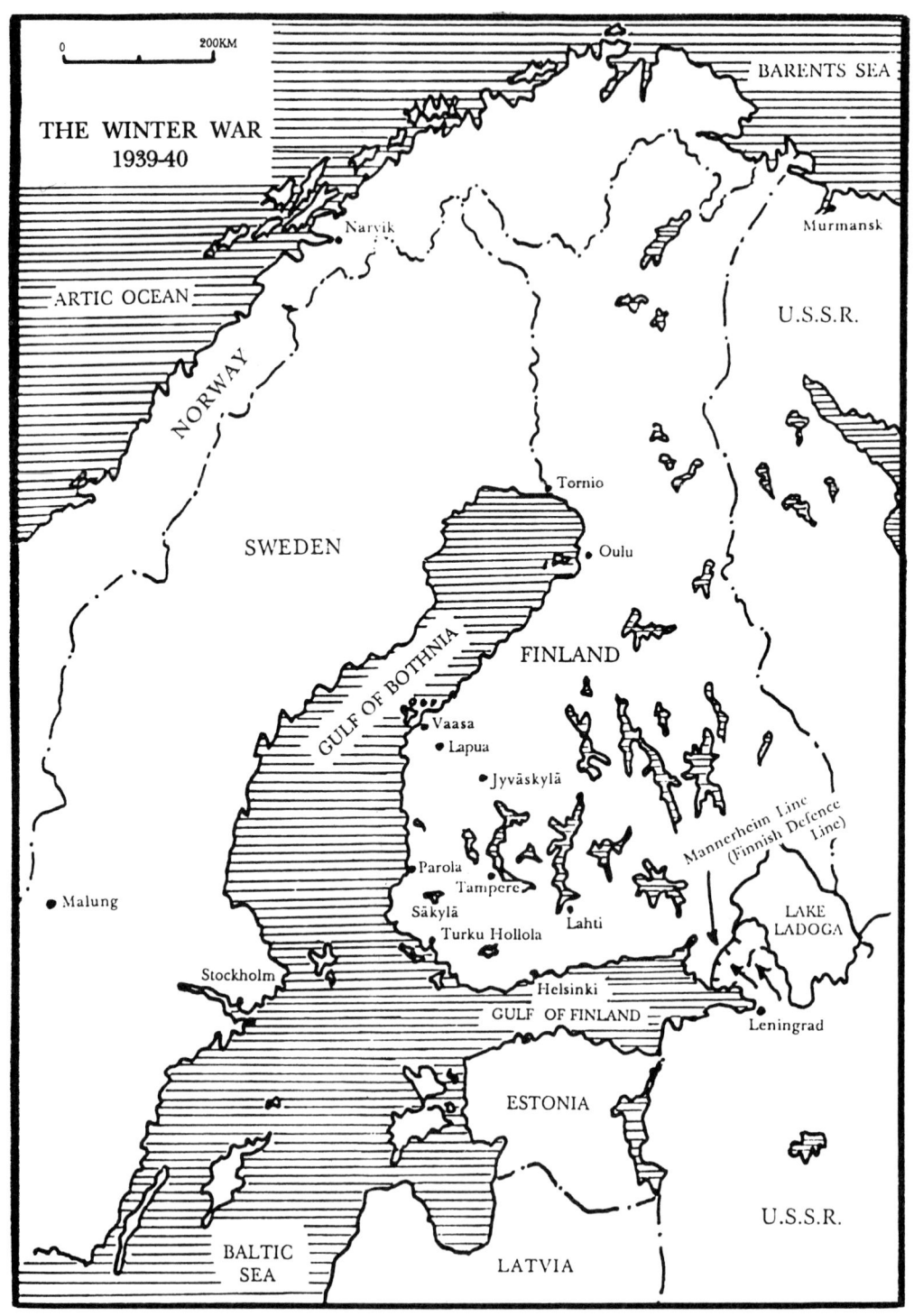

THE WINTER WAR
1939-40

0   200KM

BARENTS SEA

Narvik

Murmansk

ARTIC OCEAN

NORWAY

U.S.S.R.

Tornio

SWEDEN

Oulu

GULF OF BOTHNIA

FINLAND

Vaasa

Lapua

Jyväskylä

Mannerheim Line
(Finnish Defence
Line)

Malung

Parola

Tampere

LAKE
LADOGA

Säkylä

Lahti

Turku Hollola

Stockholm

Helsinki

GULF OF FINLAND

Leningrad

ESTONIA

BALTIC
SEA

U.S.S.R.

LATVIA

CHAPTER 14

Volunteers with Frozen Feet

When World War II broke out in September 1939 many of the British and Comonwealth flyers-of-fortune volunteered to fight in the regular armed services of their countries, whereas others found that there were no vacancies immediately available or that they were now considered too old. Towards the end of the year, however, a new conflict that flared up in northern Europe gave them one further chance to offer their services as combat pilots.

In October 1939 the Soviet Premier, Josef Stalin, having recently digested the Baltic states of Latvia, Lithuania and Estonia, turned his eyes to the north. He summoned a delegation of diplomats from Finland to Moscow and presented them with various territorial demands including the cession of nearly 750 square miles of land in the Karelian Isthmus, the thin strip of territory between the Gulf of Finland and Lake Ladoga, to Russia. The Finnish Government were under no illusions about what could soon take place and attempted to negotiate with Russia over the next few weeks, meeting offer with counter offer again and again. It was all in vain as Stalin was determined to get what he wanted by force if he could not get it by diplomacy. In early November he broke off negotiations. It seemed as though it would be an easy matter for the gigantic Soviet war machine to overrun the tiny armed forces of Finland. On 30 November 1939, Stalin's troops invaded Finland, which appealed to the League of Nations for assistance. This crumbling organisation expelled Russia from membership and called for members to send assistance to Finland.

Although the Finns were outnumbered 50 to one, their gallant resistance to the invading Russians during the next few weeks was to win the admiration of the world. It was a war of ambush fought against the background of the frozen terrain of woods and swamps which the Finnish troops, clad in white winter gear, knew intimately. The Russians lost thousands of men in these dense forests. Newspapers carried stories of Finnish victories daily, which stirred adventurous men to come to her aid from all over Europe and America, many of whom were flyers who wished to serve in the Finnish Air Force. Representatives of the Finnish Government in countries throughout the western world began to receive a steady stream of enquiries from volunteers. Others made their own way to Finland to offer their services.

At the outbreak of war the small, but efficient, Finnish Air Force had only 120 first-line aircraft, including 36 Fokker D.XXI, 10 Bristol Bulldog IVA fighters, 16 Blenheim I bombers, seven Fokker C.VE, 29 Fokker C.X biplane general purpose aircraft, 15 Blackburn Ripon and seven Junkers K 43 seaplanes. Against these the Russians had over 900 aircraft immediately available. By early January 1940 the courageous Finns had already inflicted such large losses on the Red Air Force that the Russians were forced to bring up more aircraft. By now a number of Danish volunteers had arrived and had been posted to the fighter squadrons. A complete Swedish volunteer unit also arrived in January equipped with J8As (Gloster Gladiator II fighters) and Hawker Swedish-Hart light bombers, and began to fly operations from the frozen Lake Kemi. Another arrival from Sweden in January was Count Carl Gustav von Rosen (see Chapter 4). Von Rosen flew to Finland in a Douglas DC-2 transport aircraft which had been presented to the Finnish Air Force by the Swedish airline ABA *Aerotransport*. Re-christened *Hanssin Jukka* by the Finns, this aircraft subsequently was used as a bomber during the Winter War, piloted by von Rosen.[1]

The British War Cabinet gave their approval for the formation of a Committee to Aid Finland in late January 1940. At the end of the month the Finnish Aid Bureau was set up, with Harold Gibson MC as its Director. Volunteers were then directed by the Finnish Legation to the Bureau's headquarters at Thorney House, Smith Square, London SW1. A special Royal licence was granted to the Bureau in early February to legalise the recruitment of personnel for foreign armed services — it being against British law under the Foreign Enlistment Act of 1870. Applicants wishing to offer their services to the Finnish Air Force had to enlist as infantry privates on the understanding that they would be able to transfer later on in Finland.

The first draft of volunteers left London on 29 February 1940, travelling to Finland by ship from Middlesborough to Narvik in Norway, then by train to Tornio. A second draft, including Richard Aitken-Quack (see Chapter 12), left a few days later. Also with this group was Hugh James Shaw-Kennedy, born in London on 4 February 1902, an Old Etonian and pilot who had held a flying licence since 1924. A third, and largest draft, followed shortly afterwards.

TO BE COMPLETED BY INTERVIEWER IN THE CASE OF MEN WITH FLYING EXPERIENCE ONLY

Name....AITKEN-QUACK, Richard Welford.

Details of Military Service.......
        Royal Air Force, 1935-36

        Spanish Air Force 1936-37

Types Flown......FURY, HARTS, AUDAY, BOEING. [sic]

Total number of hours solo......
        700 Hours.

Courses taken......

When did you last fly?.......September, 1939

Number of hours on twin-engined aircraft.......50 hours

Richard Aitken-Quack's "Curriculum Vitae", 1940. (Courtesy Institute of Military Science, Office of War History, Helsinki)

Many other would-be flyers from Britain also arrived in Finland about this time. Alfred Clucas Lace, born in Ramsgate on 4 April 1897, who had been commissioned in the

RFC/RAF from 1917-19 and an eminent motor-racing driver; Albert Henry Waugh, born in Wolverhampton on 23 September 1883 (other sources give 1886 and 1890), also ex-RFC/RAF 1918-19; Denis Neale Dalton, born in Southport on 4 July 1918; Raymond Dixon, born in Monkseaton on 17 October 1914, who claimed 180 flying hours.

The most famous pilot to arrive from Britain was Reginald Watson Kenworthy, born in Wakefield on 13 September 1896, former chief test pilot for Blackburn Aircraft at Brough. He had flown the Blackburn "Pellet" seaplane that was to have competed in the 1923 Schneider Trophy Race off Cowes, IOW. The aircraft had crashed during trials at Cowes prior to the race leaving Kenworthy with his hearing permanently impaired which had prevented him being accepted into the RAF at the outbreak of war. He was thought to have been the first British aviator to be accepted as a volunteer for Finland.

From the Commonwealth came Edward Bloomfield Waller, born in Toronto, Canada, on 17 July 1896, another ex-officer in the RFC/RAF from 1915-19. Another pilot was Eric Heywood Brown from Melbourne, Australia, born on 13 April 1916, who had served in the Australian armed forces in the mid-thirties before obtaining a commission in the RAF in January 1939 – he had left the service, however, by the outbreak of World War II as his commission was terminated in July 1939.

Before long all these men were joined by several American flyers who had made their way to Finland from Paris, including Vincent Schmidt (late leader of the 14th Squadron in China), Frederic Ottesen, Marcus J. Clark, George Folds and Charles Stehlin.[2]

The Finns were at a loss to know what to do with such a large influx of pilots with widely differing flying ability and set about checking their credentials. Many were sent to Air Training Regiment 2 at Parola, others were used later as ferry pilots, collecting new aircraft from Sweden, whilst a few joined the bomber squadrons. A few received commissions in the Finnish Air Force.

In late January the British Government had sold 30 Gloster Gladiator II fighters to the Finns together with 10 Bristol Blenheim IV bombers and another 12 Blenheim Is. Thirty Morane-Saulnier MS.406s from France also entered the battle in February.

All through March more volunteers were arriving almost daily in Finland. These included further Danish and Swedish pilots, Polish and even Italian and Spanish flyers. From Britain came Kenneth Armstrong, born in Hull on 1 March 1915, a laundry manager who had been an officer in the RAF for the short period of two months at the beginning of 1939; Eric George Maund, born at Caerphilly in Wales on 21 November 1912, whose flying licence gained in September 1938 states he was a chauffeur by profession (!) but is believed to have been a motor engineer; David Vere Stead, born in Melbourne, Australia on 21 May 1906, who had gained his flying licence in 1934 at Heston in England.

From Canada came Harry Stuart Taylor, born in Regina, Saskatshewan, on 16 May 1918, who had been commissioned in the RAF from May 1937 until late January 1940 with some 400 hours solo to his credit by the time he reached Finland. He later told another volunteer that he had been discharged from the RAF in England after taking part, as pilot of a Wellington bomber, in a daylight raid upon one of the well-defended German naval bases which had resulted in some very heavy losses to the RAF aircraft taking part. Also from Canada came John Cameron McMaster and John W. Jenkins.

More pilots arrived from the USA, Donald K. Willis, David S. Bondurant (who had flown for several years for the Ontario Forestry Air Service in Canada), Eero M. Davidson, Frank Clevenger, Frans McEachen and Charles Doran.[3] Of those listed above Davidson became a ferry pilot, Bondurant was commissioned as a Captain in the Finnish Air Force, and subsequently flew Blenheim bombers. Taylor also was commissioned as a 2nd Lieutenant in the Finnish Air Force, flying Blenheim bombers with LeR4 based at Luonetjärvi. Two more Britons were in Finland at this time, one named Windton, in LeR3 (Flight Regiment 3), who ferried aircraft from Sweden to Finland, and another named Barrington, who was in LeR2 (the fighter regiment) in February 1940.

Despite all the efforts of the Finns and the foreign volunteers, the tide of war was beginning to turn against them. Russian strength in the air increased to about 2,000 aircraft during February. To combat this huge increase in enemy airpower the Finns only received the first examples of 44 Brewster 239 Buffalo fighters, part of a contract declared surplus by the US Navy, and 14 Fiat G.50 fighters from Italy.

The initial batch of Brewsters were issued to a new squadron, HLeLv 22, late in February at Hollola. Commanded by Captain Erkki Heinilä, the personnel of this unit were mostly foreign volunteers including the now commissioned Lieut McMaster and Sergeant Jenkins; two Danes, Thorup and Wittrup; two Spaniards, Alfonso Reyes (alias Nikolai Beres) and Maginera.

Many of the foreign pilots found that the Brewster fighter was difficult to handle. When McMaster took his first flight in one on 9 March he ran off the airstrip on landing and the aircraft nosed over. He was initially awarded the Finnish decoration, the Cross of Freedom (Class 4), because it was thought that he had been wounded in action. This was later taken away in June 1940 when the true facts came to light. The displeased Finns had in the meanwhile sent McMaster back to the Training Wing. According to one source in Finland,[4] the Spaniard, Reyes, refused to fly the Brewster even though he claimed to have flown 3,000 hours before going to Finland. The Brewster Company had sent out their test pilot, Robert Winston, to Finland with the aircraft and he subsequently trained Finnish fighter pilots on the aeroplane which proved very successful in this arena during the Continuation War against the Soviet Union which broke out in 1941.

Other foreign pilots joined HLeLv 26, which received the Italian Fiat G.50 fighter (although they were not ready to take part in the Winter War). These included a Hungarian, Wilhelm Bekassy, who lost his life when ferrying one of these aircraft from Sweden, and an Italian, Diego Manzocchi, also killed when force landing one of the Fiats on ice in early March. The Fiat test pilot, Carlo Cugnasca, flew in some of the Italian fighters from Sweden.

During this period many of the foreign aircrew were with the training units or assigned to the reserve. According to Hilaire du Berrier, all Vincent Schmidt did in Finland was to get frozen feet. Other volunteer airmen continued to arrive, amongst these were reported to be Americans, Herbert R. Winter, William H. Wallace, Harry Schell and Emil S. Toussaint. The famous Norwegian pioneer airman, Bernt Balchen, served as an adviser to the Finns during the war, although he did no flying. Two other Canadians named Kent and Newhouse are also reported to have gone there.

Early in March, Soviet troops began advancing over the frozen Gulf of Finland. All available aircraft were used by the Finns to attack the Red Army with strafing attacks. This time, however, the overwhelming forces available to the Russians beat down the gallant defence and Finland, was forced to accept an armistice on 13 March 1940, ceding a large part of the country to the Soviet Union. The end of the war put an end to plans by the British Government to send several RAF units (including No. 604 Squadron)[5] to Finland. The large contingent of volunteers that had been recruited in London were placed by the Finns in a military camp at Lapua to await a decision about what was to be done with them.

Some of the would-be flyers, however, including Dalton, continued their journey southwards to Parola to join Air Training Regiment 2. Dalton soon decided to make his own way home and arrived back in London before the end of March. Others followed his example during the next week or so including two others, Montague Philip Everson Harrison (born in Belfast on 15 July 1898) and Malcolm Harry Wellmon (born in Southsea on 1 November 1911).

The Air Force volunteers remaining at Lapua were under the command of Alfred Lace, who was commissioned as a Captain in the Finnish Air Force. Some of the volunteers at Lapua also elected to return home, including Dixon and Peter Macalister Farragut (born in Cork, Eire, on 6 March 1913). On reaching Norway, however, they met the invading German forces and had to escape back to Sweden where they remained for over a year until flown back to the UK. On 1 April 1940 the main body of Air Force volunteers left Lapua to join various flying units. Sixteen would-be pilots went to Parola whilst some 18 aspiring air-gunners were sent to Air Training Regiment 1 at Karvia. Many of the older pilots were found not to be up to the Finn's physical standards and were returned to Lapua. While at Parola, Eric Brown and another British pilot, named Leonard George Bowhay-Saunders (born in Broadstairs on 3 September 1913), planned to steal a Finnish Blenheim bomber and fly it home, but on breaking into the hangar they found that it had insufficient fuel in its tanks.

Also at Parola in April 1940 was a pilot from Britain who used the name "Edward Manuel Graham" whilst in Finland. His real name was, in fact, Prince Emanuel Galitzine. Born in the Caucasus region of the USSR on 28 May 1918, he changed his birthplace to St Petersberg and date to 1914 on "Graham's" passport.[6] Educated at Lancing College in Sussex and a naturalised British subject, he was appointed a sub-lieutenant in the Finnish Air Force reserve. He showed much ability as a fighter pilot and was selected for training on the Fokker D.XXI with the Canadian, Harry Taylor. "Graham" then joined HLeLv 32 on Fokker D.XXIs, together with Armstrong, who had previously served in LeR4 at Luonetjärvi with Lace and Maund.

'Edward Manuel Graham' (Prince Emanuel Galitzine) in cockpit of his Fokker D.XXI fighter at Siikakangas, Finland, 1940. (Eino Ritaranta Collection)

One of the most renowned soldiers-of-fortune did not reach Finland until nearly a month after the armistice was signed. This was none other than Hubert Fauntleroy Julian, the "Black Eagle" (see Chapter 4). He had been recommended to General Lundqvist, Commander of the Finnish Air Force, by their Military Attaché in the USA. Accepted as a Captain on 11 April and posted to HLeLv 28, he made one flight in a Morane-Saulnier MS.406. He soon left the squadron and the Air Force, being repatriated shortly afterwards to the USA.[7]

Although no "official" British air forces reached Finland, 16 volunteer ground crew from Nos. 56 and 151 squadrons had reached Finland by early March 1940. The British War Cabinet had approved the sale of 12 Hawker Hurricane I fighters to Finland in late January and agreed to send experienced ground staff to maintain them. These men were discharged from the RAF and became employees of Gloster Aircraft Company (the aircraft being collected by Finnish Air Force pilots from the Gloster Aircraft Co.'s airfield at Hucclecote). These men spent five weeks in Finland, showing the Finns how to service the Hurricanes at the frozen-lake airfields at Säkylä and Hollola, before returning home by various devious routes due to the German invasion of Norway. Some did not reach home until early 1941 after a journey via the USSR, Turkey, Syria, Palestine, Egypt and South Africa.[8]

During the Winter War in Finland there were some 190 volunteers, including ground crew, in the Air Force from 17 countries. Of these, some 80 were pilots. Many came too late to participate in the War or were still in training units at the time of the armistice. The Institute of Military Science (Office of War History) in Helsinki recently informed a researcher, with regard to the foreign volunteer pilots in Finland during the Winter War, that although there was no doubt of their sympathy towards Finland, they lacked the necessary professional skill in flying. If they did know how to fly, they did not have any training on such aircraft like the Fokker D.XXI, Gloster Gladiator and Bristol Blenheim, not to mention the Brewster. Only some Danish and Swedish pilots, together with a Hungarian and an Italian, actually took part in combat. The way of living of some of the pilots whilst in Finland also left "quite a heap of problems of a social kind to solve" after they left the country.

Of the airmen remaining in Finland, Waller had been stationed at Joroinen, in south-east Finland together with Kenworthy. They were demobilised in August 1940 and joined Lace, Armstrong, Taylor and Maund at Jyväskylä where the volunteers awaiting repatriation were concentrated. Also there were two future RAF pilots who had not managed to get into flying units in Finland – Harold Watkins (born in Rochdale on 1 February 1915), a dental mechanic in civilian life, and Montague Frank Baxter (born in Wandsworth on 2 May 1915). Watkins and Baxter went to Helskini in September to find work, "borrowed" a yacht to try to get back to Britain but were captured by Russian coastguards. Taken to Leningrad and then Moscow, they were held in prison by the Russians and interrogated continually. Finally they were sentenced to five years' detention in a labour camp for violating territorial waters and transferred to a camp over 600 miles east of Gorkiy, Luckily for them word had reached the Foreign Office in London that they were being held by the Soviets (who were now allies of Britain) and they were brought back to Moscow and released in mid-October 1941. The British Embassy there sent them to Persia where they joined the RAF. After flight training in Rhodesia they returned home in early 1943. Flying Officer Baxter was killed on a bombing raid in November 1943 whilst with No. 10 Squadron. Watkins was commissioned in early 1944 and served in Nos. 9, 61 and 617 Squadrons on Lancasters, including taking part in the sinking of the German battleship, *Tirpitz*. Squadron Leader Watkins DFC left the RAF in January 1947 and joined BEA. He later went into air charter and flew all around the world. In the 1960s he was chief pilot for British Eagle Aviation. Harold Watkins died in Surrey in January 1986.[9]

Other members of the British contingent in Finland took various jobs whilst waiting for repatriation to the UK. Kenworthy, Taylor and Maund worked for the British Council teaching English. Stead was working for the British Legation, Helsinki, early in 1941 and is thought to have returned home from there in the autumn of 1941. Taylor returned home with Stead via Sweden, Germany, France, Spain and Portugal in September 1941. The others, with Armstrong, Lace, Waller, etc, left for Sweden in July/August 1941 and were housed in a camp at Malung where they remained whilst attempts were made to get them home. Maund went to Arvselen in August to do forestry work but disappeared with another volunteer in early September. It is thought that they went to Norway to steal a boat to cross the North Sea. They were never seen again.

Jyväskylä, Finland, summer 1940. Left to right; Kenneth Armstrong, Dr Herford (Army), Richard Aitken-Quack, Eric Maund. (Von der Pahlen archives, via Justin Brooke)

Others were luckier – "Graham" was back in London by June 1941, Armstrong and Dixon were flown home from Stockholm in the autumn, but others had to wait in Sweden until 1942, including Kenworthy and Aitken-Quack. Trying to return by sea, Lace was captured by the Germans on a Norwegian tanker which left Gothenberg on All Fool's Day 1942 and spent the rest of the war in an internment camp for seamen. Waugh too was captured by the Germans trying to reach home and was held in Germany until 1945.

Back in the UK, Taylor, McMaster and Aitken-Quack all later served in the non-commissioned ranks of the RAF as pilots. Taylor was killed on a routine flight between bases later in the war. Prince Emanuel Galitzine (Graham) was commissioned in the RAF and later flew no fewer than 11 different marks of Spitfire fighters. Whilst with the Special Service Flight at Northolt in September 1942 he took part in the highest aerial battle of World War II, attacking a Junkers Ju 86R in his Spitfire IX at over 40,000 feet.[10] Prince Galitzine also served in Nos. 504, 611, 124, 72 Squadrons in Britain, France, Italy and Corsica; later also serving in Nos. 52 and 147 Squadrons in Transport Command. He left the Service in 1946 and became an airline pilot in India before joining the flying staff of BEA. In later years he went into management in the aircraft industry with A. V. Roe & Co Ltd and Hawker Siddeley Aviation Ltd before going to live in South America. Shaw-Kennedy was also commissioned in the RAF and died in September 1969.

Armstrong later became a publican in Buxton, Derbyshire.

Of the American pilots, both Schmidt and Julian later joined the United States armed forces in World War II. Willis flew with No. 121 "Eagle" Squadron RAF before flying Lockheed P-38 fighters in the USAAF. After the war Schmidt returned to live once more in Paris where he died peacefully in 1962. Julian continued his colourful career in Latin America and in Africa after World War II (he died in the early 1980s).

Only Count Carl Gustav von Rosen was left to carry on the traditions of his calling. After leaving Finland he flew for the Swedish national airline for the rest of the war including the courier service between Stockholm and Berlin. For ten years after the war von Rosen was again in Ethiopia, where he became commander of the air force, but then returned to airline flying in Sweden. By 1960 he was in his 50s but his adventures were not yet over. War broke out in the Congo, and von Rosen flew in supplies for the United Nation troops.

In 1968 he flew as relief pilot and was co-ordinator for the Scandinavian Churches airlift of supplies to the starving people of Biafra during the bloody civil war with Nigeria, often braving the jet fighters of the Nigerians in DC-7 cargo aircraft. Not content with just breaking the blockade, the idealistic Swede thought up a fantastic plan to destroy Nigeria's jet fighters. Five Swedish light sports aircraft, the MFI-9B, were purchased and secretly transported to Libreville in Gabon. Here they were fitted out with rockets under the wings and their Swedish markings painted out. Then, in May 1969, von Rosen, with two other Swedish pilots and two Biafrans, raided Port Harcourt airfield in Nigeria destroying several aircraft on the ground. Raids followed on other airfields at Benin and Enugu causing considerable damage to both aircraft and installations. The "will-of-the-wisp" Minicoin aircraft were in and away before the surprised Nigerians could react. These actions and later raids caused much controversy throughout the world but von Rosen (by now 60 years old) maintained that his sole aim was to help the suffering people of Biafra. He had only put off the inevitable, for Nigeria defeated Biafra early the following year.

For three years in the 1970s von Rosen flew in food and medicine to the drought areas of Ethiopia before being killed in a guerrilla attack against a settlement in southern Ethiopia in July 1977. He was 68 years of age. He died as he had lived most of his years — actively helping suffering people.[11]

A new generation of aerial soldiers-of-fortune appeared after 1945 but theirs is another story.

CHAPTER 14 – SOURCES/NOTES

The story of the pilots in Finland could not have been told without the help of former volunteers Prince Emanuel Galitzine and Justin Brooke. Mr Brooke allowed me sight of his detailed records of all the British volunteers of 1940 – his book about these men, *The Winter War Canaries* (published in Finland in 1984 under the title *Talvisodan kanarialinnut*) gives a full record of all the military volunteers who went to Finland's aid from Britain. Other information was also supplied by the Institute of Military Science (Office of War History) in Helsinki and Finnish air historian, Eino Ritaranta. Information about the men from the USA and Canada came from Richard Sanders Allen and Allan Levine. Other details about the service careers of some of the airmen came from Ministry of Defence Records. Air Ministry documents which refer to British aid for Finland now at the Public Record Office are AIR 16/18: AIR 14/1162; AIR 14/1109.

1.   *Air Pictorial*, May 1965 and June 1968.

2.   *Time* Magazine, 22 January 1940, and *New York Times*, 27 January 1940.

3.   The Institute of Military Science (Office of War History), Helsinki.

4.   Eino Ritaranta.

5.   The Finnish Air Force insignia (a blue swastika) had been applied to the Blenheim aircraft of No. 604 and No. 23 Squadrons ready for the expedition and squadron vehicles hurriedly fitted with chains and tracks.

6.   Prince Emanuel Galitzine.

7.   Ibid 3.

8.   'RAF Men in the Winter War', by Humphrey Wynn, Air Historical Branch MOD; *RAF Quarterly*, Summer 1975. Courtesy Ministry of Defence, Air Historical Branch.

9.   *The Sky Tramps: The Story of Air Charter*, by Peter Jackson; London 1965.

10.   *Spitfire: A Documentary History*, by Alfred Price; London 1977.

11.   *Soldiers of Fortune*, by Sterling Seagrave; Alexandria, Virginia 1981. *The Nigerian Civil War*, by John de St Jorre; London 1972. *The New Mercenaries*, by Anthony Mockler; London 1985.

BIBLIOGRAPHY

BOOKS

Alexander, Bill *British Volunteers for Liberty: Spain 1936-1939*; Lawrence & Wishart 1982.

Alcofar Nassaes, José Luis *"Spansky": Los Extranjeros que lucharon en la Guerra Cívil Española*; Edition Dopesa, Barcelona 1973.

Alvarez Albert, Abdón *Con Llamas en el Aire*; Imprenta Militar, Asunción, Paraguay (Date ?).

Ansaldo, Juan Antonio *Memoires d'un Monarchiste Espagnol 1931-1952*; Éditions du Rocher, Monaco 1953.

Baker, Carlos *Ernest Hemingway: A Life Story*; Collins 1969.

Balchen, Bernt *Come North With Me: Autobiography*; Hodder & Stoughton 1959.

Barker, Ralph *The Schneider Trophy Races*; Airlife 1981.

Boca, Angelo del *The Ethiopian War 1935-1941*; University of Chicago Press 1969.

Bolin, Luis *Spain: The Vital Years*; Cassell 1967.

Boule, Pierre *The Source of the River Kwai*; Secker & Warburg 1967.

Brooke, Justin *Talvisodan kanarialinnut (The Winter War Canaries)*; Werner Söderström, Helsinki 1984.

Bruce, Michael *Tramp Royal*; Elek Books 1954.

Buckley, Henry *Life and Death of the Spanish Republic*; Hamish Hamilton 1940.

Caidin, Martin *The Ragged, Rugged Warriors*; Elsevier-Dutton, New York 1966.

Castells, Andreu *Brigades Internacionales de la Guerra de España*; Editorial Ariel, Barcelona 1974.

Cathcart-Jones, Owen *Aviation Memoirs: Including Australia and Back and Other Record Flights*; Hutchinson 1934.

Cheesman, E.C. *Brief Glory: The Story of A.T.A.*; Harborough 1946.

Chennault, Anna *Chennault and the Flying Tigers*; Paul S. Erickson, New York 1963.

Chennault, Claire Lee *Way of a Tiger: The Memoirs of Claire Lee Chennault* (edited by Robert Hotz); G.P. Putnam's Sons, New York 1949.

Cluett, Douglas (with Joanna Nash and Bob Learmonth) *Croydon Airport: The Great Days 1928-39*; London Borough of Sutton Libraries & Arts Services 1980.

Coffey, Thomas M. *Lion by the Tail*; Hamish Hamilton 1974.

Coules, Virginia *Looking for Trouble*; Hamish Hamilton 1941.

Cox, Geoffrey *Defence of Madrid*; Victor Gollancz 1937.

Cunningham, G.H. *Mac's Memoirs: The Flying Life of Squadron Leader McGregor*; A.H. & A.W. Reed, Wellington, New Zealand 1937.

Cunningham, Valentine (Ed) *Penguin Book of Spanish Civil War Verse*; Penguin 1980.

Curtis, Lettice *The Forgotten Pilots: A Story of the Air Transport Auxiliary 1939-45*; G.T. Foulis 1971.

Cutlack, F.M. *History of Australia in the War of 1914-1918, Vol VIII, Australian Flying Corps*; Angus & Robertson, Sydney (Date ?)

Davis, Burke *Get Yamamoto*; Arthur Barker 1971.

Delmer, Sefton *Trail Sinister: An Autobiography*; Secker & Warburg 1961.

Drage, Charles *Two-Gun Cohen*; Jonathan Cape 1954.

-ibid- *General of Fortune: The Fabulous Story of One-Arm Sutton*; Heinneman 1963.

Editors of Time-Life Books *The Bush Pilots*; Time-Life Books, Virginia 1983.

Elstob, Peter *Spanish Prisoner*; Macmillan 1939.

-ibid- *Condor Legion*; Ballantine Books, New York 1973.

Emiliani, Angelo (and Guiseppe F. Ghergo) *Nei Cieli Di Spagna 1936-1939: Immagini e Documenti Della Forze Aeree in Guerra*; Giorgio Apostolo Editore, Milan 1986.

Ethiopian Airways (compiled by) *From Mules to Jets: A Short History of Aviation in Ethiopia*; Addis Ababa 1981.

Everard, Conrad *Luftkampf über Spanien: Kriegserlebnisse eines freiwilligen Englischen Kampffliegers bei der Nationalen Armee*; Scherl Verlag, Berlin 1937.

Ewing, Ross (and Ross MacPherson) *The History of New Zealand Aviation*; Heinneman (N.Z.) 1986.

Farmer, Rhodes *Shanghai Harvest: A Diary of Three Years in the China War*; Museum Press 1945.

Freeman, Roger A. *The Mighty Eighth*; Macdonald 1970.

García Lacalle, André *Mitos y Verdades: La Aviación de Caza en la Guerra Española*; Ediciones Oasis, Mexico 1973.

García Morato, Joaquín *Guerra en el Aire*; Editoria Nacional, Madrid 1940.

Gisclon, Jean *Des Avions et des Hommes*; Éditions France-Empire, Paris 1969.

-ibid- *La désillusion: Espagne 1936*; Éditions France-Empire 1986.

Gwynn-Jones, *Terry The Air Racers*; Pelham Books 1984.

Haugland, Vern *The Eagle Squadrons*; David & Charles 1980.

Hemingway, Mary Welsh *How it Was*; Weidenfeld & Nicholson 1977.

Herrera Alonso, Emilio *Entre el anil y el colbalto: Los Hidroaviones en la Guerra de España*; Instituto de História y Cultura Aeronáutica, Madrid 1987.

Herrmans, Ralph *Carl Gustav von Rosen*; Wahlström & Widstrand, Sweden 1975.

Hotz, Robert *With General Chennault: The Story of the Flying Tigers*; Coward-McCann, New York 1943.

Hunt, Leslie *Twenty-One Squadrons: History of Royal Auxiliary Air Force 1925-1957*; Garnstone Press 1972.

Ingram, Kevin *Rebel: The Short Life of Esmond Romilly*; Weidenfeld & Nicholson 1985.

Jackson, A.J. *British Civil Aircraft Since 1919 (3 Vols)*; Putnam 1973-74.

Jackson, Peter *The Sky Tramps: The Story of Air Charter*; Souvenir Press 1965.

Jillett, John W.L. *Wings Across the Tasman 1928-1953*; A.H. & A.W. Reed, Wellington, New Zealand 1953.

Jorre, John de St. *The Nigerian Civil War*; Hodder & Stoughton 1972.

Julian, Hubert (as told to John Bulloch) *Black Eagle*; Jarrolds 1964.

Kemp, Peter *Mine Were of Trouble*; Cassell 1957.

Kennerly, Byron (as told to Graham Berry) *The Eagles Roar*; Harper & Row, New York 1942.

Kennett, Charles *Stormy Petrel*; Hurst & Blackett 1936.

Knickerbocker, H.R. *The Siege of the Alcázar: A Warlog of the Spanish Revolution*; Hutchinson 1937.

Knoblaugh, H. Edward *Correspondent in Spain*; Sheed & Ward 1937.

Kolstov, Mikhail *Diario de la guerra de España*; Ruedo Ibérico, Paris 1963.

Lamb, Dean Ivan *The Incurable Filibuster: Adventures of Colonel D.I. Lamb*; Hutchinson 1934.

Laureau, Patrick *L'Aviation Républicaine Espagnole 1936-39*; Docavia No.8/Éditions Larivière, Paris 1978.

-ibid- *La Aviación Republicana Española 1936-1939* (2 Vols); Pamiers, France 1980 & 1982 (Privately printed).

Leary, William M. Jr. *The Dragon's Wings*; University of Georgia Press 1976.

Leonard, Royal *I Flew for China*; Doubleday, New York 1942.

Liron, Jean *Les Avions – Farman*; Docavia No.21/Éditions Larivière, Paris 1985.

Lloyd, Alan *The Gliders*; Leo Cooper 1982.

Malraux, André *Days of Hope*; G. Routledge 1938.

McCormick, Donald *One Man's Wars: The Story of Charles Sweeny, Soldier of Fortune*; Arthur Barker 1972.

MacGovern, Terence (as told to E.C. Trelawney-Ansell) *It Paid to be Tough: The Life of a Modern Mercenary & Vagabond*; John Long 1939.

McIntosh, R.H. (in collaboration with Jeffrey Spry-Leverton) *All-Weather Mac: Autobiography of Wing Commander R.H. McIntosh DFC AFC*; Macdonald 1963.

Middleton, D.H. *Airspeed: The Company and its Aeroplanes*; Terence Dalton 1982.

Mockler, Anthony *The New Mercenaries*; Sidgwick & Jackson 1985.

Moulson, Tom *The Flying Sword: The Story of No. 601 Squadron Royal Auxiliary Air Force*; Macdonald 1964.

Nally, Bernard C. *Tigers over Asia*; Elsevier-Dutton, New York 1978.

Nugent, John Peer *The Black Eagle*; Steen & Day, New York 1971.

Price, Alfred *Spitfire: A Documentary History*; Jane's 1977.

Richards, Denis *Royal Air Force 1939-1945, Vol I, The Fight at Odds*; HMSO 1953.

Ries, Karl (and Hans Ring) *Legion Condor 1936-1939*; Verlag Dieter Hoffman, Maintz 1980.

Romilly, Esmond *Boadilla*; Hamish Hamilton 1937.

Rosholt, Malcolm *Flight in the China Airspace 1910-1950*; Rosholt House, Winconsin, USA 1984.

Ryan, Frank (editor) *Book of the XV Brigade*; Frank Graham, Newcastle 1976.

Salas Larrazabal, Jesús *La Guerra de España desde el Aire*; Ediciones Ariel, Barcelona 1969.

-ibid- (English version) *Air War Over Spain*; Ian Allan 1974.

-ibid- *Intervencion Extranjera en la Guerra de España*; Editoria Nacional, Madrid 1974.

Salvador, Tomas *La Guerra de España en sus Fotos*; Ediciones Martes, Barcelona 1966.

Sanchís, Miguel *Alas Rojas Sobre España*; Publicaciones Españolas, Madrid 1956.

Seagrave, Sterling *Soldiers of Fortune*; Time-Life Books, Virginia 1981.

Shores, Christopher F. *Spanish Civil War Air Forces*; Osprey 1977.

-ibid- (and Clive Williams) *Aces High: Fighter Aces of the British and Commonwealth Air Forces in World War II*; Neville Spearman 1966.

Simmons, Thomas E. *The Brown Condor: The True Adventures of John C. Robinson*; Bartleby Press, Silver Spring, Maryland 1988.

Stenton, Michael (and Stephen Lees) *Who's Who of British Members of Parliament Vol III, 1919-1945*; Harvester Press 1979.

Swinson, Arthur *The Great Air Race*; Cassell 1968.

Thomas, Hugh *The Spanish Civil War*; Hamish Hamilton 1977 & 1986.

Thornberry, Robert S. *André Malraux et l'Espagne*; Librarie Droz, Geneva 1977.

-ibid- (editor) *Revue André Malraux Review, Vol 19 Nos. 1/2, Vol 20 No.1*, Spring/Fall 1987, Spring 1988; University of Alberta, Canada 1988.

Tidy, Douglas *I Fear No Man: The Story of No.74 (Fighter) Squadron Royal Flying Corps and Royal Air Force*; Macdonald 1972.

Tinker, Frank *Some Still Live: Experiences of a Fighting-plane Pilot in the Spanish

War; Funk & Wagnalls/Lovat Dickson 1938.

Toynbee, Philip (editor) *The Distant Drum: Reflections on the Spanish Civil War*; Sidgwick & Jackson 1976.

Villa de Tapiá, TCnel Aviador Amalia *Alas de Bolivia (Tomo II)*; Bolivian Air Force, Cochabamba, Bolivia (Date ?)

Watson, Keith Scott *Single to Spain*; Arthur Barker 1937.

Waugh, Evelyn *Waugh in Abyssinia*; Longman 1936.

-ibid- *When the Going was Good*; Duckworth 1946.

Wet, H. Oloff de *Cardboard Crucifix*; Wm Blackwood & Sons 1938.

-ibid- *Valley of the Shadow*; Wm Blackwood & Sons 1949.

Wewege-Smith, Thomas *Gran Chaco Adventure: The Thrilling and Amazing Adventures of a Bolivian Air Caballero*; Hutchinson 1937.

Whelan, Russell *The Flying Tigers*; Macdonald 1943.

Winston, Robert *Aces Wild: An American Test Pilot in Wartime Europe*; Holiday House, New York 1941.

Wintringham, Tom *English Captain*; Faber & Faber 1939.

Wright, Lawrence *The Wooden Sword*; Elek Books 1967.

Yerex, David *Yerex of TACA; A Kiwi Conquistador;* Ampersand Publishing, Carterton, New Zealand 1985.

Zichy, Count *That was No Gentleman – That was Zichy*; Polybooks 1974.

Ziegler, Frank *Under the White Rose: History of No. 609 Squadron Royal Auxiliary Air Force*; Macdonald 1971.

Also

Foreign Relations of the United States: Diplomatic Papers 1936, Vol II; Washington DC, 1954.

Partes Oficiales de Nacionales Guerra 1936-1939; Servicio Histórico Militar, Madrid 1977.

Partes Oficiales de Guerra (Republicano) 1936-1939; Servicio História Militar, Madrid 1978.

Solidarity with the Spanish Republic 1936-1939; Soviet War Veterans Committee, Moscow 1975.

Soviet Volunteers in China 1925-1945; Progress Publishers, Moscow (Date ?)

Who's Who & Who Was Who; A & C Black (various issues).

Who's Who in British Aviation; Bunhill Publications/Temple Press (various editions).

The Aeroplane Directory/Flight Directory of British Aviation/Royal Air Force Lists, (various editions).

PERIODICALS

UNITED KINGDOM
Aeropilot
Aeroplane Monthly
Aeroplane, The
Air Britain Digest
Air Enthusiast (Quarterly)
Air International
Air Pictorial
Blackwoods Magazine
Cross & Cocade Journal
Flight
Flying
Flying Review International
Guide & Ideas for Competitors
Popular Flying
Profile Publications (various)
RAF Flying Review
RAF Quarterly

FRANCE
Fanatique de L'Aviation, L'Album du
Icare, revue de l'aviation français
IPMS Journal (France)
Gens De La Lune, Les
Revue de Paris

USA
1919-1939 Air Wars
Air Classics
American Aviation Historical Society
  Journal
Army Quarterly
Flying Aces
Historical Aviation Album
New American
Popular Aviation
Readers Digest
Shipmate
Soldier of Fortune
Southern Flight
Time
True
Wings

SPAIN
Alas Gloriosas
Alas Plegadas
Avion
Revista de Aeronáutica y Astronautica

NEW ZEALAND
Aviation Historical Society of New
Zealand Journal
New Zealand Wings

NEWSPAPERS

UNITED KINGDOM
Belfast Irish News
Bournemouth Daily Echo
Bournemouth Weekly Post & Graphic
Catholic Herald
Cheshire Observer
Daily Express
Daily Herald
Daily Mail
Daily Mirror
Daily Sketch
Daily Telegraph
Daily Worker
Evening News (Portsmouth)
Evening Standard
Guardian, The
Isle of Wight Times
Isle of Thanet Gazette
Liverpool Daily Post
Liverpool Evening Express
London Gazette
Manchester Guardian
Middlesex Chronicle
News of the World
News Chronicle
Northwich Guardian
Oxford Mail
People, The
Romford Recorder
Southern Daily Echo (So'ton)
Southend Times
Star, The
Sunday Dispatch
Sunday Graphic & Sunday News
Sunday Mirror
Sunday Referee
Times, The
West Essex Gazette
Wiltshire Times

USA
New York Times

CANADA
Toronto Daily Star

AUSTRALIA/NEW ZEALAND
Dominion
Evening Post (Wellington)
Launceston Examiner (Tasmania)
New Zealand Herald
Southland Times
Sydney Sun

Fiji Times

South China Morning Post (Hong Kong)

SOUTH AFRICA
Cape Argus

FRANCE
Journal, Le (Paris)
Petit Parisien

ITALY
Corriere Della Sera, Il (Milan)

SPAIN
Commercío, El (Gijon)
Norte de Castilla, El (Pamplona)

Index

This index does not include, generally, sources covered in Appendices to each chapter. Some notes of importance, however, are covered. Reference to illustrations and maps are shown in **Bold** characters.

British-American Air Services Limited, 191
Brenner, Sam (US airman), 162, 164, 170
Bretford (British airman), 185
Brewster aircraft (USA), 216, 219
Bristol aircraft,
    Blenheim I: 213, 215-216, 219, 222
    Blenheim IV: 25, 215
    Bulldog: 202, 213
    F.2B Fighter: 13, 87, 134, 136, 159, 160, 174-175, 189
British Airways Limited, 31-32, 41, 116
Brondello, Nino (Italian pilot), 140-141
Brooke, Justin, 222
Brooks, William C. (US pilot), 14, 15
Brophil, Captain Maurice R.N., 61
Brown, Eric H., 215, 217
'Brown Condor', see Robinson, John C.,
Browne, Arthur Russell, 158, 160, 164, 166
'Browne', T.K. or F.K., 175, 188
Broxbourne Aerodrome, 63
    Advertisement: **63**
Bryers, George (?), 28, 30
Buckeridge, Jack (NZ pilot), 133
Buenos Aires (Argentina), 13, 16, 87
Burgos (Spain), 30-32, 34-36, 38-39, 47-49, 189, 190
Byrd, Commander Richard E. (US explorer), 93, 134, 136

Cáceres (Spain), 48, 120
Camacho Benitez, Colonel Antonio (Spanish Air Minister), 67
Campbell Black, Thomas, see Black, T. Campbell,
Campbell, Roy (poet), 82
Canarias (Spanish warship), 178
Canary Islands, 27-29, 90
Canning, Douglas (US pilot), 142
Cant aircraft (Italy): Z-501, 48
Canton (China), 102, 199, 204, 210
Cape Palos (Spain), 69
Cardozo, Harold G. (British journalist), 97
Carías Andino, General Tiburcio, 15-16
Cartagena (Spain), 48, 71, 106, 108
Carter, Charles K.U-., see Kennett, Charles,
'Cartwright', 120, 185
Casablanca (Morocco), 28, 30, 76
Cascón Briega, Manuel (Spanish pilot), 94-95

Rosen, Carl Gustav von, Count (Swedish pilot), 58-59, 61, 184, 214, 221
    Photograph, **59**
Ross, William, 39, 48
Rouffaer, Jan (Dutch pilot), 204, 211
Rougy, Captain (French soldier), 140
'Rouse, Captain', 154
Royal Air Force: Flying Training Schools,
    No 1 FTS: 187
    No 2 FTS: 117, 202
    No 3 FTS: 53, 157, 190
    No 4 FTS: 65
    No 5 FTS: 185
    No 7 FTS: 49, 115, 183
    No 11 FTS: 117
Royal Air Force (also Royal Flying Corps) Squadrons,
    No 1: 190
    No 2: 157
    No 4: 13
    No 6: 159
    No 9: 87, 187, 208, 219
    No 10: 53, 219
    No 11: 160
    No 13: 159
    No 14: 115, 157, 174
    No 23: 22
    No 26: 160
    No 27: 115
    No 30: 159
    No 32: 202
    No 35: 202
    No 36: 117
    No 45: 65, 115
    Group photo: **66**
    No 52: 220
    No 56: 218
    No 58: 189
    No 61: 219
    No 72: 220
    No 74: 191
    No 79: 92, 97
    No 84: 159-160
    No 100: 117

ACKNOWLEDGEMENTS

The research for this book has taken many years and involved much detective work. Many blind alleys have been followed and, without the help of many correspondents and friends, the book could not have been written. Apart from all those mentioned in the Introduction and in the Sources/Notes, I would like to thank the following for their assistance during the research on this book. In the UK: Mr W.A. Bishop, Mr B.A. Bolland, Air Vice-Marshall Sir Ivor Broom DCB CBE DSO DFC AFC, Sir Geoffrey Cox, Cmdr Charles Drage, Ronald Gillman, Mr L. O. Harrison DFM, Air Vice-Marshall C.E. Kay, Lachie McDonald. In South Africa; Mike Schoeman. In New Zealand; Mr D.B. Annesley, Arch Blyth, Air Commodore R.J. Cohen, Geoff Danvers, Mr D.D. Lynch, Gordon Milne, Joe Sweeney, Mr R.J. Todd, Captain H.C. Walker. In Hong Kong; Miss Lili Whitehead.In Australia; Ian Primmer.

Also the Aerospace Studies Institute, Maxwell AFB, Alabama, USA; the Musée de l'Air (Paris) and the New Zealand National Archives.

While every effort hs been made to secure permissions, it has not always been found possible to trace or contact the present copyright holders of some material or illustrations used. The author and publisher would be pleased to hear from these and apologize for any offence caused.

Grateful acknowledgement is made to the following for permission to reprint copyright material;

Mr Anthony Cathcart-Jones

Blackwood, Pillans & Wilson Limited for permission to reprint excerpts from *Blackwoods Magazine* of February and June 1938 (articles by the late Hugh Oloff de Wet).

Sheed & Ward Limited (1937) for permission to reprint excerpts from *Correspondent in Spain*, by H. Edward Knoblaugh.

Crown-copyright material in the Public Record Office is reproduced by permission of the Controller of Her Majesty's Stationery Office with respect to the following documents:

FO 371/19176 No J2664/5/1

FO 371/20547 No W15491/62/41

FO 371/21284 Nos W2902/1/41 & W2999/1/41.

Also to the Public Record Office to reproduce extract from FO 371/22687, W7611/7512/41.

Aeroplane Monthly for permission to reprint extracts from *The Aeroplane* magazine.

Flight International for permission to reproduce information from *Who's Who in British Aviation* and *Flight Directory of British Aviation*.

A & C Black (Publishers) Limited for permission to reproduce information from *Who's Who* and *Who Was Who*.

A.D. Peters & Co Ltd for permission to reproduce extract from *Waugh in Abyssinia*, by Evelyn Waugh (Longman & Co Ltd., an imprint of Century Hutchinson, 1936).

Macmillan, London and Basingstoke, for permission to use material from *Spanish Prisoner*, by Peter Elstob (Macmillan & Co Ltd., London 1939).